Karl Polanyi and the Contemporary Political Crisis

Also Available from Bloomsbury

Politics in the Times of Indignation: The Crisis of Representative Democracy, Daniel Innerarity

The Bloomsbury Companion to Marx, ed. Andrew Pendakis, Imre Szeman and Jeff Diamanti

From Marx to Hegel and Back: Capitalism, Critique, and Utopia, ed. Victoria Fareld and Hannes Kuch

Right-Wing Culture in Contemporary Capitalism: Regression and Hope in a Time without Future, Mathias Nilges

Karl Polanyi and the Contemporary Political Crisis

Transforming Market Society in the Era of Climate Change

Peadar Kirby

BLOOMSBURY ACADEMIC

LONDON • NEW YORK • OXFORD • NEW DELHI • SYDNEY

BLOOMSBURY ACADEMIC
Bloomsbury Publishing Plc
50 Bedford Square, London, WC1B 3DP, UK
1385 Broadway, New York, NY 10018, USA
29 Earlsfort Terrace, Dublin 2, Ireland

BLOOMSBURY, BLOOMSBURY ACADEMIC and the Diana logo
are trademarks of Bloomsbury Publishing Plc

First published in Great Britain 2021
This paperback edition published in 2022

Copyright © Peadar Kirby, 2021

Peadar Kirby has asserted his right under the Copyright,
Designs and Patents Act, 1988, to be identified as Author of this work.

Cover design by Charlotte Daniels

All rights reserved. No part of this publication may be reproduced or transmitted in
any form or by any means, electronic or mechanical, including photocopying,
recording, or any information storage or retrieval system, without prior
permission in writing from the publishers.

Bloomsbury Publishing Plc does not have any control over, or responsibility for,
any third-party websites referred to or in this book. All internet addresses given
in this book were correct at the time of going to press. The author and publisher
regret any inconvenience caused if addresses have changed or sites have
ceased to exist, but can accept no responsibility for any such changes.

A catalogue record for this book is available from the British Library.

Library of Congress Cataloging-in-Publication Data
Names: Kirby, Peadar, author.
Title: Karl Polanyi and the contemporary political crisis : transforming
market society in the era of climate change / Peadar Kirby.
Description: New York, NY : Bloomsbury Academic, 2021. | Includes
bibliographical references and index.
Identifiers: LCCN 2020032046 (print) | LCCN 2020032047 (ebook) | ISBN
9781350117822 (hardback) | ISBN 9781350195394 (paperback) | ISBN
9781350117839 (ePDF) | ISBN 9781350117846 (eBook)
Subjects: LCSH: Capitalism–Environmental aspects. | Socialism–Environmental
aspects. | World politics–21st century. | Polanyi, Karl, 1886–1964.
Classification: LCC HD75.6 .K564 2021 (print) | LCC HD75.6 (ebook) |
DDC 335–dc23
LC record available at https://lccn.loc.gov/2020032046
LC ebook record available at https://lccn.loc.gov/2020032047

ISBN:	HB:	978-1-3501-1782-2
	PB:	978-1-3501-9539-4
	ePDF:	978-1-3501-1783-9
	eBook:	978-1-3501-1784-6

Typeset by Integra Software Services Pvt. Ltd.

To find out more about our authors and books visit www.bloomsbury.com
and sign up for our newsletters.

Do chomhluadar éiceaphobail Chloch Shiurdáin: is uathusan a d'fhoghlaim mé go leor atá sa leabhar seo agus gan iad ní bheadh leabhar mar seo scríofa agam

To the community of Cloughjordan ecovillage: from them I have learnt a lot of what is in this book and without them I could not have written it

Contents

List of figures and tables	viii
Foreword by President Michael D. Higgins	ix

Part 1 Loss of hope

1	A world in transition	3
2	Understanding the crisis	21

Part 2 An alternative future?

3	Beyond capitalism	41
4	Mapping an eco-social future	59

Part 3 From commodification to decommodification

Introduction to Part Three		77
5	Fictitious commodities: Land	87
6	Fictitious commodities: Labour	103
7	Fictitious commodities: Money	121
Conclusion to Part Three		137

Part 4 Whither and how?

8	Towards a new public philosophy	143
9	Beyond market society	161

Appendix	178
Notes	183
Bibliography	218
Index	235

Figures and tables

Figures

6.1	Declining taxes, 1970–2012	113
6.2	Inequality and carbon emissions	115

Tables

1.1	Share of global growth captured by income groups, 1980–2016	7
2.1	Strength of ultra-right parties in Europe, 2019	24
6.1	Decommodification index	108

Foreword by President Michael D. Higgins

Economic sociologist Karl Polanyi is perhaps best known for what has been regarded as his masterpiece, *The Great Transformation*, in which he argued that the emergence of market-based societies in modern Europe was not inevitable but historically contingent. Polanyi was in every sense a migrant thinker. Beyond physical migration, his intellectual work moved through different movements and models but always in pursuit of a life that could be experienced with dignity for all through a shared collective will.

This new book, drawing on Polanyi, is a highly timely contribution by Professor Peadar Kirby, employing many of Polanyi's key ideas – in particular the 'new public philosophy' concept that emphasizes the need to overcome the current economistic prejudice which so obscures our social vision. Professor Kirby offers an alternative understanding of the economy, while elaborating on the key challenges we face as global citizens standing as we are on an existential precipice. As a survey of current discussion of responses and alternatives to our current interacting crises, this book will appeal to a much wider readership than those of us who advocate for a new eco-social paradigm of embedded social economy served by seeing the economy as instrument rather than hegemonic determinant.

Peadar Kirby's new work proposes a paradigm 'beyond market society', one based on human dignity, one in which the public space is recovered. It examines evidence of where paradigm change is already happening today, or envisaged – in the Green New Deal, in harnessing automation, in the new politics of mitigating gaps (e.g. gender). It offers an alternative future – a postcapitalist, eco-social future in which 'decommodification', 'degrowth' and 'deglobalization' all form key elements. Professor Kirby's book will chime in harmony, too, with other substantive work by contemporary economists, such as Ian Gough and Mariana Mazzucato, and is a valuable contribution to an emerging and much-needed discourse on the interacting global crises that we face and the emancipatory possibilities of achieving a radical break with a failing and destructive paradigm.

Polanyi's idea of the market society was based on the belief that the Industrial Revolution in Britain had resulted in a society forced to obey the self-governing mechanisms of the market, a market without interference, a society run 'according to the needs of the economy, rather than an economy serving the needs of society'. He quite prophetically identified that such a model would have catastrophic consequences for society, especially workers, and their relationship to nature.

Polanyi's view ran counter to the orthodox economics of his time. It still does today in a period of a prevailing neoliberal economic discourse, a model which advocates markets without regulation, has led to distorted global trade and an unrestricted globalization in so many aspects of life, the priority of the price mechanism in defining value, the practice of commodification, speculative investment, all of which result in rampant consumption and yawning inequality facilitated by the destructive extraction of natural resources.

Such a model is, of course, unsustainable from economic, environmental and social standpoints. It is a model that privileges the insatiable accumulation of the few at the cost of the many and their children's future, the very future of the planet itself in terms of lost biodiversity.

Polanyi provides hope for the emancipatory power of humanistic social science. What a great failure it is that these powerful, liberating ideas, so eloquently articulated in *The Great Transformation*, were not given space, failed to influence the dominant narrative that emerged – the second coming of the beliefs of free-market theorists and the influence they would have, not only on theory, but on the public policies that would be privileged in the United Kingdom, the United States and elsewhere in the 1980s and 1990s.

These policies were not chosen among competing options, but were drawn from a single hegemonic version of a connection between markets, economy and society itself that attributed an unquestioned logic to a market evolution which should decide the role of the economy as instrument of the market, and society as a residual human context, source of labour and reservoir of consumption for ever-expanding market forces.

Over the last forty years, decades of Keynesianism have given way to decades influenced by the theories of those such as Friedrich Von Hayek and Milton Friedman, to unrestrained, unregulated market dominance, and a communications order with a discourse that 'privileges' aggressive individualism. It is not just that interventionist social policy has been brushed aside, but even in the academy, the pluralism of scholarship itself has been forced or induced to give way.

The prevailing, largely uncontested paradigm of connection between economy, society and the natural world has consequences for us all, our institutions and indeed our democracies. It is a paradigm that, in its assumptions, dominates and distorts the connection between scholarship, politics, economy and society – indeed the peaceful, inter-relationship of societies. It has lost social cohesion in so many societies and has been the source of alienation that has been exploited.

This failing paradigm, which has gained strength in recent decades, has encouraged an individualism without social responsibility, within and beyond borders. It not only asserts a rationality for markets but also, in policy terms, has, even for the most conservative of commentators, delivered *laissez-faire* markets with clearly inadequate regulation.

Its colonization of language itself, distortion of concepts, even emancipatory ones, has assisted, for example, in the concept of 'freedom' being re-defined in a reductionist manner to 'market freedom'.

As we live through this period, a period where the concept of society itself has been questioned and redefined narrowly and pejoratively, when the public space in so many countries has been commodified, we must come together to co-operate and encourage the merging of the consciousnesses of ecology, human need, dignity, respect for sources of truth and consolation, reasoned and revealed, so that we may achieve an exit from extreme individualism.

Professor Kirby's new book will be of invaluable assistance in a discourse we urgently need to develop, encourage and disseminate. The recovery of Karl Polanyi as a resource for our times seems very appropriate, and Peadar Kirby has served this task well.

Michael D. Higgins
President of Ireland
February 2020

Part One

Loss of hope

1

A world in transition

Writing in the early 1950s, Austro-Hungarian intellectual, educator and socialist Karl Polanyi (1886–1964) described the period as 'an age of unprecedented transition' requiring 'all the orientation that history can provide if we are to find our bearings'.[1] These words describe even more accurately our contemporary period than they did the period in which they were written. For, to borrow Gareth Dale's pithy summation of where we find ourselves as 'liberal-civilisational disintegration',[2] today's world is displaying ever more severe strains of multiple and reinforcing dislocations that are, indeed, unprecedented. The 2020 coronavirus pandemic highlighted this for many people, shattering a belief in society's stability and progress. While some speak of the contemporary period at the beginning of the twenty-first century as an 'interregnum',[3] arguably we have far less sense of where we may be transitioning than had those reading Polanyi's words when they were written. Or, to put it more accurately, the world of the early 1950s was settling into a contested landscape of East versus West that was to shape the following forty years. This was unsettling, and it grew particularly scary as nuclear weapons added a terrifying potential to the standoff shaping the world at that time. But, as it settled down, it offered categories that made sense to most of the forces shaping and contesting the world order.

Our times are very different. Some see similarities with the breakdown of the liberal order in the last decade of the nineteenth century and the first decades of the twentieth. However, as filmmaker David Attenborough put it so starkly when addressing the UN climate summit in Katowice, Poland, in December 2018: 'Right now, we are facing a man-made disaster of global scale, our greatest threat in thousands of years. If we don't take action the collapse of our civilisations and the extinction of much of the natural world is on the horizon.'

This is the enormous threat that distinguishes our era from any previous one and adds hugely to an acute sense of disorientation and uncertainty about the future. But, while it is the most grave, it is far from being the only source of disorientation and uncertainty. The two chapters that form Part One examine the loss of hope that characterizes our period of human history. This chapter identifies the multiple and overlapping dislocations that contribute to making it, in the words of Yuval Noah Harari, 'an age of bewilderment'. The following chapter examines how the crisis is being interpreted with a central focus on the threats to our liberal order and the rise of the 'new populism'. For, a major part of our disorientation lies, as Harari puts it, in the fact that 'the old stories have collapsed, and no new story has emerged so far to replace them'.[4] Constructing a new story, adequate to the multiple dislocations we face and offering an orientation about how to lay the foundations of a new society adequate to overcoming the system breakdown that currently dominates, is the objective of this book.

As well as outlining the plan of this book, this chapter undertakes two tasks. Firstly, it seeks to identify the nature, scale and interrelationship of the many dislocations that are shaking up our world and disorienting our worldview. The core of the argument here is that we are facing a multifaceted breakdown of our society beyond anything humanity has faced before. This can be seen as constituting the 'unprecedented transition' mentioned in the chapter's opening. The chapter then goes on to examine where we can discover the orientation from history to help us find our bearings. We need to remember that the social democratic era that followed the Second World War took its orientation from the works of John Maynard Keynes since he provided the theoretical understanding of how the state should correct market failures to ensure full employment. The neoliberal era that replaced it found its orientation in the very different theoretical claims of Friedrich Hayek who feared state involvement as an infringement of individual liberties and saw state interference in the functioning of the economy as harmful to society. As neoliberalism collapses, no clear orientation has yet emerged to offer a broad theoretical grounding in a new understanding of the roles of the state, the private market and civil society, and how they interrelate. The central argument of this book is that the *oeuvre* of Karl Polanyi offers the essential elements of the theoretical grounding so badly needed. 'Polanyi invites us to step outside the box of formal models of market transactions to explore the real needs of real people and the variety of institutional arrangements that can satisfy them, writes his daughter, Kari Polanyi Levitt.[5] This opening chapter offers a brief introduction before drawing extensively on his work in subsequent chapters.

System breakdown

Writing about the 2019 Davos get together of the world's powerful, *Guardian* columnist Aditya Chakrabortty reports on a survey of a thousand bosses, money men and 'Davos decision-makers' in which the majority confess to mounting anxieties about 'populist and nativist agendas' and 'public anger against elites', identifying two shifting tectonic plates, climate change and 'increasing polarization of societies'.[6] In contrast to these anxieties, Dutch author Rutger Bregman in his bestselling *Utopia for Realists*? sees a 'world of plenty'. He reports how technologies are transforming our healthcare, how billions are being lifted out of poverty, how malnutrition, child mortality and maternal deaths have been hugely reduced, how common diseases are being eradicated, how levels of education and average IQ are constantly improving, and how crime rates are falling in the developed world. Even Bregman, who believes we've never had it so good, acknowledges that most people in developed countries believe their children will be worse off than their parents.[7] There is therefore a techno-optimism that gives some people grounds for a more positive view of the future though this cannot avoid the widespread subjective sense of malaise. The discussion here is structured around six key features of our contemporary global situation to marshal evidence about what sort of future we face. These are the unravelling of our social model, the erosion of political representation, the migration crisis, the dark side of technology, climate change and biodiversity loss, and a widespread sense of personal impotence.[8] For many, the loss of hope is very real.

Social model unravelling: it was largely social issues that, at the advent of industrial society in the nineteenth century, mobilized the discontented and exploited to organize and demand better conditions. This they did both through reforms within the dominant system and through revolutionary change to transform that system. These included conditions of employment, levels of pay, housing, health and education, and inequalities of power and wealth. These struggles in the nineteenth century laid the foundations for a socialist movement that, in different forms, won major advances on all these social issues throughout much of the twentieth century. This laid the foundations for decades of progress that underpinned a secure sense that each generation would enjoy better material conditions than their parents. However, the period since the late 1970s has seen this model progressively unravel to the point that a growing sense of vulnerability in people's material conditions fuels a sense of insecurity about the future,[9] a sense greatly enhanced by the Covid-19 crisis. In the 1980s it became common to speak of the end of the Third World as neoliberal recipes for economic and social development spread thereby integrating developing countries in global flows of trade and finance.[10] The end of the Second World (the communist world) is dated from the collapse of the Berlin Wall in 1989 and the subsequent demise of the Soviet Union. Can we now speak of the collapse of what used to be called the First World, the world's bloc of developed countries? A common characteristic is that the gains of growth go disproportionately to the very top of the class structure as shown in Table 1.1. The symptoms of this collapse constitute a long list: secular stagnation in many Western economies as economic growth falters, the surge in inequality, the systematic reduction of the protections offered by the welfare state, a growing housing crisis as prices and rents become unaffordable for many, post-industrialization leaving many regions of heavy industry devastated, and the decline in the value of academic qualifications to access secure and well-paid employment.[11] While these processes happen in different ways and at different rhythms in different countries and regions, it is now clear that they constitute deep-rooted tendencies in contemporary societies. As Edward Luce has written:

> Since the late 1970s, Western governments of right and left have been privatising risk. To one degree or another – most sharply in the US and the UK – societies are creeping back to the days before social insurance. What was once underwritten by government and employers has been shifted to the individual. When people hit the buffers, they knew there were funds to ride them over. Those guarantees have been relentlessly whittled down.[12]

Table 1.1 Share of global growth captured by income groups, 1980–2016

Income group	China	Europe	India	Russia	US-Canada	World
Total population	100%	100%	100%	100%	100%	100%
Bottom 50%	13%	14%	11%	-24%	2%	12%
Middle 40%	43%	38%	23%	7%	32%	31%
Top 10%	43%	48%	66%	117%	57%	67%
Top 1%	15%	18%	28%	69%	35%	27%
Top 0.1%	7%	7%	12%	41%	18%	13%

Data sourced from: World Inequality Report 2018, Table 2.1.2

Erosion of political representation: in being the main agents identified with these tendencies, Western governments are themselves largely responsible for a backlash against liberal politics that has emerged over decades. It has now reached a point that threatens the very foundations of the liberal order. This is a second great system breakdown, linked to but distinctive from the first. The process has long been analysed, though the implications of the attrition of parties as they retreated from the mobilization of citizens to become more technocratic machines to administer states seemed to have little impact on how politics and politicians functioned.[13] As the centre-right and the centre-left moved to a politics of implementing neoliberalism[14] through privatization, marketization and the liberalization of controls on financial, commercial and labour flows, it resulted in 'a demobilization along the broadest possible front of the entire post-war machinery of democratic participation and redistribution. It all took place slowly but steadily, developing into a new normal state of affairs.'[15] Even as new-right parties entered government in a number of European countries, the gravity of the threat to the liberal order did not seem to register with many. Yet, as Jan Zielonka recognizes, the 'counter-revolutionary insurgents', as he calls the new-right movements, want to replace the elites who have presided over the post-1989 liberal order in Europe, and he acknowledges their appeal: 'They set the tone of the political discourse and establish which issues are debated; they give voice to people's anxieties and expose liberal flaws; they arouse the politics of fear, acrimony, and vengeance.'[16] And he fears that 'the counter-revolution will not just stop at correcting liberals' mistakes; it will go further by destroying many institutions without which democracy cannot function and capitalism becomes predatory.'[17] And, as evidence from beyond Europe shows – the United States, Turkey, the Philippines, India and Brazil – the phenomenon is global.

Blaming the outsider: the third great system breakdown relates to immigration. It is clear from the discourse of Donald Trump, Victor Orban, Marine Le Pen, Matteo Salvini, Geert Wilders and some proponents of Brexit that fears about immigration are consolidating a base of support for the new-right and endangering social values of tolerance and diversity that underpin a liberal order. The dramatic images in 2015 of waves of immigrants fleeing violence in countries like Syria, Iraq and Afghanistan and seeking out safety, particularly in Germany, seemed to mark a watershed in public consciousness and played a role in the emergence of the Alternativ fur Deutschland as German's main opposition party. However, framing immigration in the language of crisis creates very misleading impressions since it both exaggerates the scale of migration and reduces the complexities involved, thereby making it difficult to find humanitarian solutions. Furthermore, it focuses public attention on abstract numbers rather than on the human tragedies of those involved.[18] Instead of solutions, more and more countries are reducing their national quotas for the resettlement of refugees and asylum seekers, delivering their fate into the hands of people traffickers or forcing them into overcrowded and insanitary camps. In an essay written just before he died, the sociologist Zygmunt Bauman drew attention to the consequences of the climate of mutual mistrust, suspicion and competition that is emerging in this context: 'In such a climate the germs of communal spirit and mutual help suffocate, wilt and fade (if their buds have not already been forcibly nipped out)' and the possibilities for concerted actions of solidarity in the common interest lose their value and grow dimmer,[19] vividly illustrated by the difficulties of coordinating international responses during the coronavirus pandemic. In this context, promoting a culture of dialogue will require nothing short of 'another cultural revolution', he writes.[20] Debates about racial difference are nothing new in Europe. Indeed, in parts of medieval and early modern Europe, rulers welcomed refugees and saw them as an asset.[21] By the nineteenth century, however, spurious scientific theories justified a hierarchical ordering of peoples on racial grounds; these were discredited and after the Second World War gave way to debates based more on cultural and religious differences, often with sharply racist overtones.

These issues, therefore, have never been easy ones but they are clearly becoming much more divisive. The system breakdown being threatened by the emerging standoff is highlighted by Harari: 'If Greeks and Germans cannot agree on a common destiny, and if 500 million affluent Europeans cannot absorb a few million impoverished refugees, what chances do humans have of overcoming the far deeper conflicts that beset our global civilization?'[22]

Technology's dark sides: identifying technology as a symptom of system breakdown runs counter to the techno-optimism that characterizes our technological civilization. After all, people widely credit technology with making our lives easier, better and longer. Our governments invest large sums of money in technological research as a means of solving many of the great problems that beset us, not least climate change. Yet, while technologies are presented to us as inherently emancipatory, James Bridle reminds us that our lives are utterly enmeshed in technological systems that shape how we act and think:

> Our technologies are complicit in the greatest challenges we face today: an out-of-control economic system that immiserates many and continues to widen the gap between rich and poor; the collapse of political and societal consensus across the globe resulting in increasing nationalisms, social divisions, ethnic conflicts and shadow wars; and a warming climate, which existentially threatens us all.[23]

In case this seems an exaggeration, let's take the example of two contemporary sources of major anxiety, directly linked to technological developments. The first is the threat of mass unemployment with the rise of the robot. As robotics and advanced self-service technologies are increasingly deployed across nearly every sector of the economy, they are predicted to threaten lower-paid jobs in the first instance with 'dire, cumulative consequences for employment over the long run'. Furthermore, 'the machines are coming for the high-wage, high-skill jobs as well'.[24] Some foresee that robots will eventually 'invade virtually every workplace and swallow up nearly any white-collar job that involves sitting in front of a computer manipulating information'.[25] A second major anxiety relates to the impact of two major scientific breakthroughs – bioengineering and artificial intelligence (AI). The first is understanding and manipulating the human brain and human feelings, while AI is using sophisticated algorithms to influence our decision-making. Hariri is probably exaggerating the consequences, but he draws attention to their far-reaching potential: 'When the biotech revolution merges with the infotech revolution, it will produce Big Data algorithms that can monitor and understand my feelings much better than I can, and then authority will probably shift from humans to computers.'[26] While no one can foretell the impact of these technological revolutions on our social and personal lives, we cannot underestimate their potential. At least one leading US sociologist, Randall Collins, envisions a future, perhaps less than fifty years from now, 'when almost all work is done by computers and robots, with a few human technicians and repair personnel'. He concludes:

> The bottom line remains: technological displacement of the middle class will bring the downfall of capitalism, in places where it is now dominant, before the 21st century is over. Whether these transitions will be peaceful or horrific remains to be seen.[27]

Climate change and biodiversity loss: undoubtedly, the greatest system breakdown relates to how society's development model systematically destroys the natural ecosystems on which humans depend for resources. This erodes the conditions that allow us to live comfortably on this planet and threatens our very survival as a species. For long focused on environmental destruction, on a warming climate and on biodiversity loss, only recently is a wider awareness dawning that we are facing a threat to our very existence, to our social and economic systems, and to our wellbeing (see Box 1.1 on environmental breakdown and human systems). As the 2018 Intergovernmental Panel on Climate Change report put it, 'Climate-related risks to health, livelihoods, food security, water supply, human security, and economic growth are expected to increase with global warming of 1.5°C and increase further with 2°C.'[28] And, as UN Secretary General António Guterres told the 2019 Davos Forum, 'Climate risk is the most important systemic risk for the future. I believe we are losing the race. Climate change is running faster than we are. And we have this paradox: the reality is proving to be worse than scientists had foreseen.'[29] A related but distinct problem is the alarming loss of biodiversity being uncovered in recent research. Some of this is summarized in the 2018 *Living Planet Report* from the World Wildlife Fund (WWF). This reveals a 60 per cent decline between 1970 and 2014 in the population size of thousands of vertebrate species around the world with declines being especially pronounced in the tropics. Marine and freshwater ecosystems are also facing huge pressures, says the report. Again, it is the implications of these changes for human society that are often overlooked. The WWF report highlights that 'our health, food and security depend on biodiversity' as 'all our economic activity ultimately depends on nature'. It concludes:

> Stable planetary systems have enabled modern human society to develop. Without healthy natural systems researchers are asking whether continuing human development is possible.[30]

Box 1.1 'The age of environmental breakdown'

In assessing the social and economic impacts of environmental breakdown, the UK think tank, the Institute for Public Policy Research (IPPR), states that such breakdown 'acts as a "threat multiplier", driving and amplifying social and economic disruption, with far-ranging consequences for stability' which are 'unprecedented in their scale, speed, severity and complexity'. Furthermore, the actions required to mitigate breakdown are 'structural, involving deep and rapid economic, social and political change across all of society and every nation on Earth', on a scale that is 'unprecedented in human history'. Yet, these challenges are being faced 'at a time of growing socio-economic instability, including a changing international order, the development of new technologies, shifting consumer habits and the rise of nativist and nationalist politics'.[31]

The report identifies the consequences of environmental breakdown for human systems in three key areas:

1. Localized impacts: this puts the focus on the impacts of extreme weather events on disrupting infrastructure and affecting people's health and wellbeing; this is the dominant focus of much climate change discourse.
2. Systemic consequences: this looks at how globalized economic systems transmit the impacts of local events, for example, in the ways that damages to agricultural systems will affect supply chains, causing shortages and raising prices.
3. Interaction with socio-economic context: this brings into the picture wider social and economic trends such as those outlined in this chapter, showing how environmental breakdown will worsen them; an example are the ways climate breakdown is hitting the poor and exacerbating inequalities.

These impacts are creating a 'domain of risk' unlike anything seen in recent history, says the IPPR.[32]

Personal impotence: 'What clear social change marks out our era from those that precede it?' asked journalist George Monbiot. The answer he gives would not be the first to occur to many: ours' is the Age of Loneliness. He cites evidence that loneliness has become an epidemic among young people and is linked to dementia, high blood pressure, alcoholism and accidents, as well as depression, paranoia, anxiety and suicide.[33] A team of twenty-eight global mental health experts assembled by the *Lancet* medical journal reported in 2018 that the world faces a mental health crisis with epidemics of anxiety and depression resulting in monumental loss of human capabilities and avoidable suffering. Yet, while the burden of mental ill-health is rising everywhere, states the Lancet Commission, the quality of mental health services is routinely worse than those for physical health.[34] There is evidence therefore that links the breakdown of our social systems and their relationship with living ecosystems, with a crisis in human wellbeing. Philosopher Marina Garcés makes the link explicit: 'Our actual impotence has a name: informed illiteracy. We know everything but we're able to do nothing. With all of humanity's knowledge at our disposition, all we can do is slow down or accelerate our fall into the abyss.'[35] She argues that a growing awareness of the unsustainable nature of our society – not just environmental unsustainability but the unsustainability of capitalism itself and its constituent elements of economic growth, mass consumerism and productivism – has moved us from a postmodern condition to one she calls posthumous. In this condition, the question changes from 'where are we going?' to 'for how long?': how long will I have a job, how long will I live with my partner, how long will pensions last, how long will Europe remain white, secular and rich, how long will we have drinking water, how long will we believe in democracy? As a result, we are condemned to live in an eternal and anxious present, surrounded by a cultural credulity ('the collective imaginary of our time is full of zombies, draculas and skulls'[36]) and with a severe weakening of critical rationality, a situation characterized by anxiety, disorientation and depression. Faced with the lack of a viable future, all we are offered are technical solutions. 'The forms of oppression that follow on from this credulity are diverse: from new forms of material inequality and cultural extremes, to forms of degraded life in all its aspects, physical and mental.'[37]

As is well illustrated by the anger of the youth generation now taking to the streets in millions around the world, a sense of foreboding about the future fills many. At its heart is an unravelling of the systems that have given structure and stability to our social lives – our social, economic and political systems and the ecosystem in which they are embedded, an unravelling greatly intensified by the coronavirus pandemic. This unravelling is impacting on the psychological processes that gave a sense of psychic predictability and security to people's individual lives. Psychologist Steven Taylor, who studies the psychological effects of pandemics, predicts that 'this pandemic will have profound psychological effects on the people living through it'.[38] History furnishes many examples of societies breaking down in this way – through foreign invasion, dictatorships of different types, and natural disasters like earthquakes, pandemics or volcanic eruptions. But what is different today is that the breakdown is global, though impacting societies and social groups in different ways, and touches on our very survival as organized societies. For novelist Barbara Kingsolver, 'This looks like the end of the world as we know it. … We are trying to hold on so tightly to a world that is clearly gone':

> There are many ways in which the crisis of this moment is far beyond anything humans have had to figure out before: we've wrecked the planet good and well. This is not the fall of the Roman empire, this is a larger scale.[39]

Towards 'the great collapse'?

When historians of science and technology, Naomi Oreskes and Erik M. Conway, were asked to write an article about why scientists' attempts at communicating the realities of climate change were proving so ineffective, they turned instead to fiction. Their short novel, entitled *The Collapse of Western Civilization: A View from the Future*, looks back from 2393 to mark the tercentenary of the end of Western culture (1540–2093) and recounts the events that led to that end. The conclusion was that 'a second Dark Age had fallen on Western civilization, in which denial and self-deception, rooted in an ideological fixation on "free" markets, disabled the world's powerful nations in the face of tragedy.[40] In a subsequent interview contained in the same book they make clear that the writings of neoliberal economists Milton Friedman and Friedrich Hayek play a starring role in their account of the collapse. This is because of the close links they forged between economic freedom and political freedom with the result that government intervention in the market was seen as bad. 'Can a neoliberal regime act with long-term caution?', they ask. 'No, because the neoliberal worship of deregulation leads directly to the poisoning of ourselves and the rest of the world.'[41]

While they acknowledge that their account of the collapse of Western civilization is speculative, they stress that the book 'is extremely fact-based. All the technical projections are based on current science.'[42] Nor is the idea of putting a date on Western collapse relegated only to the realms of fiction. French economics professor Serge Latouche offers a number of possible dates based on his reading of the celebrated *Limits to Growth* book first published in 1972 and updated thirty years later.[43] Based on this comprehensive marshalling of scientific evidence which has proven a very accurate prediction of trends over the period since first produced and depending on what countervailing measures are taken, he offers three dates: 2030, 2040 or 2070. The first date is based on the crisis of non-renewable resources (including petrol, gas, coal, uranium, other materials and water); 2040 due to pollution, lack of climate regulation and the death of the oceans; 2070 due to the food crisis, desertification and deforestation. Latouche predicts that collapse won't come in one gigantic cataclysm but rather as a series of innumerable catastrophes.[44] A more rigorous attempt to estimate the projected timing of abrupt ecological disruptions from climate change estimated these would begin before 2030 under a high emissions scenario.[45]

Paul Raskin undertakes a more detailed look back from 2084, charting possible stages of the great transition to a more sustainable future. He begins in our 'turbulent time' identifying the systemic risks of climate change, economic instability, population displacement and global terrorism. One cardinal defect in trying to address these major twenty-first-century challenges, he writes, is our twentieth-century ideas: territorial chauvinism, unbridled consumerism and the illusion of endless growth. 'Coherent responses ... lie beyond the grasp of a myopic and disputatious political order.'[46] He traces two possible scenarios between now and 2100: Great Transition (GT) and Market Forces (MF) under the headings of Population, Gross World Product, Work Time, Poverty, Energy, Climate, Food, Habitat and Freshwater. The MF trajectory traces likely outcomes under present assumptions while the GT involves major system changes. So, for example, the much lower Gross World Product predicted for GT is achieved through eliminating immense non-productive expenditures on military armaments, advertising and other wasteful activities. Consumption and work time reduce along with more equitable income and wealth distributions. Under energy and climate, the MF scenario sees a big increase in nuclear and renewables sources but economic growth relentlessly drives greenhouse emissions higher, whereas the GT scenario manages to reduce energy demand as the economy shrinks and less energy-intensive service sectors come to dominate. On food, GT manages a shift to ecological and biodiverse farming, whereas MF meets increasing demand through an intensification of the industrial agriculture model. As a result, the MF scenario leads to a further decline in natural habitats and ecosystems, whereas the GT scenario slows the loss of species and leads to nature restoration. The final part of the exercise is to imagine the stages of change that happen if the GT scenario is to become the dominant one. This happens over five stages:

- Takeoff of the Planetary Phase (1980–2001): a unitary social-ecological global system emerges based on the globalization of production and consumption;
- Rolling Crisis (2001–23): a freewheeling turbo-capitalism leads to more unrest, violence, displacement, pandemics, recession and environmental disruption;
- General Emergency (2023–8): multipronged crises gather into a mighty chain reaction of systemic distress; massive public reaction finally galvanizes deep reform;
- Reform Era (2028–48): a new generation of leaders ushers in enlightened international governance pushing for resilience economies constraining markets to function within more compassionate social norms and firm environmental limits;
- Commonwealth of Earthland (2048–84): a world constitution creates the Commonwealth of Earthland; masses of citizens mobilize to defeat sectoral interests and nativist bases that oppose the new order.

The value of these imaginative exercises is to highlight that the road we are currently on is leading us to breakdown and collapse. Indeed, the Rolling Crisis period, during which this book is written, is proving frighteningly accurate. While it can be argued whether some of the symptoms identified in this chapter – such as the new populism, growing inequality, robotization and AI – would result in collapse, it is the issue of climate change that makes collapse inevitable if continued. Devastating forest fires, droughts, melting ice and rising sea levels, soil erosion, and biodiversity loss all add up to a system breaching its limits. A radical change of direction is required to ensure a better future for humanity. Raskin ends his scenario study by writing that 'Earthland stumbles into the future as a complex admixture of competing tendencies': corporate-led development and cultural homogenization, efforts to civilize globalization and push towards policy reform, social antagonism and environmental degradation, cultural experimentation and popular struggles, all compete to be the decisive shapers of the future.[47] But behind these lie deeper shapers, namely the dominant theoretical orientation that provides the 'common sense' of the era. Oreskes and Conway make clear that a neoliberal orientation shapes their story of collapse. Although this is on the wane, it still exercises a strong sway over public values and consciousness as well as over policy paradigms and assumptions. To guide humanity towards a Great Transformation that avoids destructive collapse a new orientation is needed that offers different values and a narrative of different possibilities. Just as the neoliberal narrative resulted in new types of political leadership with new policies and new public values, so too such a new narrative can provide the basis for the transformations now required at all levels, from individual practices to global leadership.

Orientation

'The present situation offers significant analogies with the political polarization, institutional instability and collective hatred that Polanyi experienced first-hand,' writes César Rendueles.[48] This is why his writings have been re-discovered over recent decades as his insights into the social destruction wrought by free markets resonated with the experiences of the age. From the beginning of the twenty-first century, the anti-globalization movement and some influential economists critiquing neoliberalism, notably Joseph Stiglitz, were drawing on Polanyi's ideas to inform their struggles and analyses.[49] Central to what Polanyi offered, as Block and Somers put it, was the insight that, while markets are necessary, they 'are also fundamentally threatening to human freedom and the collective good', thus challenging the prevailing neoliberal orthodoxy driving globalization and the liberalization of markets. Furthermore, Polanyi's writings drew attention to the fact that the so-called free market cannot ever exist and what is claimed to be a free market is actually a set of political, legal and cultural arrangements 'that mostly disadvantage the poor and the middle class and advantage wealth and corporate interests'. In essence, then, free market ideology sidelines politics and reduces the agency of social struggle to shape society.[50] The major themes being derived from Polanyi's thought can be summarized as follows:

1. Market society: a central argument of Polanyi's classic work *The Great Transformation* is that the British Industrial Revolution introduced a novel system whereby society was made to obey the self-governing mechanisms of the market. What was created therefore was a market system which 'must be allowed to function without outside interference' and which was a catastrophe for society, especially for workers and for nature. This 'produced the typical strains and stresses which ultimately destroyed that society', he argued.[51] He gave the term 'market society' to the system that resulted, namely a society run according to the needs of the economy, rather than an economy that serves social needs.
2. Social destruction: this entirely new relationship between economy and society that emerged meant that 'instead of economy being embedded in social relations, social relations are embedded in the economic system',[52] which 'required that the individual respect economic law even if it happened to destroy him'.[53]
3. Fictitious commodities: central to the creation of this market society was the treatment of land, labour and money as if they were commodities allocated a price to be bought and sold in the marketplace. But this 'commodity fiction disregarded the fact that leaving the fate of soil and people to the market would be tantamount to annihilating them'.[54]
4. Double movement: Polanyi identified a spontaneous counter-movement to check the inroads of market forces which emerged from both the left and the right from the end of the nineteenth century as regulations around public health and factory conditions were introduced, social insurance established, and public utilities and trade associations set up.

18   *Karl Polanyi and the Contemporary Political Crisis*

This pragmatic self-protective response Polanyi saw as 'the principle of self-protection aiming at the conservation of man and nature as well as productive organization'.[55]

5. Social integration: in his research into the economy-society relationship in societies prior to the British Industrial Revolution, Polanyi identified three mechanisms whereby the economy was embedded to serve social needs: reciprocity (free exchange within communities), redistribution (a central power redistributing goods) and exchange (within locally based markets).

With the anti-globalization struggles to protect nature, decent working conditions and social protections against the inroads of market mechanisms, these ideas of Polanyi took on a new resonance and began to be widely referenced. Many could identify with the counter-movement, seeking the regulation of the market by state actions. However, particularly since the economic and financial collapse of 2008, the ability of the new populist right to capture swathes of public opinion and become major political forces in many stable Western democracies challenges this picture of a progressive path towards overcoming market society. Indeed, as Polanyi recognized, the double movement during the inter-war period also resulted in the rise of fascism which seemed to offer stability and protection to those whose livelihoods were destroyed. This undermines any easy conclusion that, what Polanyi sought, was simply taming capitalism's excesses, as social democrats tend to read him. Instead, it forces a deeper consideration of Polanyi's core commitment to an alternative future beyond capitalism consistent with the trajectory of a GT.[56]

Polanyi therefore turns out to be both a more demanding guide and one that forces us to look more radically and deeply at many assumptions that have underpinned the dominant liberal order of the past fifty or so years. His understanding of the place of community in society, the essence of freedom in a rich social web of interdependencies, his great fears of how to maintain human freedom in the age of the machine and his firm belief in the possibility for a truly democratic order in which human agency can construct new social conditions that help transform the culture and quality of people's lives are all profoundly important. They make a unique contribution to us finding a way beyond the system breakdown of the present and transforming market society in the unique conditions of the era of climate change. These will help guide the rest of this book as we seek to map out a future beyond breakdown.

Chapter 2 'Understanding the Crisis' examines the narratives that dominate analyses of today's global political crisis as a threat to the liberal order from illiberal forces, the rise of the 'new populism' and the emergence of identity politics. Drawing political economy into the discussion allows a focus on the relationship of economy to society, informed by Polanyi's understanding of the importance of social embeddedness and the destructive consequences of the commodification of land, labour and money. Part Two of the book interrogates the possibility of an alternative future. Chapter 3 examines the disconnect between analyses of the new 'populist' turn in politics and structural analyses of the crises of capitalism. It identifies the failure of the socialist tradition to offer a creative way of identifying the root causes of the present system breakdown, particularly in the demise of social democracy. The need to transition to a post-carbon society makes a return to a sustainable capitalist future virtually impossible to imagine, raising the question of what might replace it. Chapter 4 maps an alternative understanding of socialism, examining the reasons why a robust socialist response to today's system breakdown is lacking. It draws on Polanyi's understanding of what he called 'guild socialism' to elaborate an alternative bottom-up, participatory form of socialism and ends by identifying the alternative for our times as an eco-social paradigm.

The three chapters of Part Three look in turn at the decommodification of land, labour and money, Polanyi's three 'fictitious commodities'. It begins with an introduction to explain what he meant by commodification and how it could be reversed by re-embedding the market to serve society. Chapter 5 on land opens by tracing the consequences of its commodification and goes on to examine its impact in various areas – cities, energy, the human person – before looking at processes of decommodification. Chapter 6 traces the cycles of the decommodification and recommodification of labour over recent decades, examining issues of poverty, inequality and automation while showing that the fightback against marketization has begun. Chapter 7 outlines the financial system that emerged based on treating money as a commodity, the contemporary form this has taken in the financialization of capitalism, and alternatives being created. A brief conclusion closes Part Three.

Part Four is 'Whither and how?' At the heart of Polanyi's contribution is what Block and Somers call his 'new public philosophy' and this is the subject of Chapter 8. It emphasizes, with Polanyi, the need to overcome the 'economistic prejudice' that so obscures our social vision, outlining Polanyi's alternative understanding of the economy and elaborating four key challenges if the market is to be embedded in society. It ends by looking at the politics of this new story. The final chapter 'Beyond Market Society' examines evidence of where paradigm change may be happening today – in the new politics of the gaps, in the potential of the Green New Deal and in harnessing automation. The chapter ends by drawing the strands of the book together to focus on transforming market society.

2

Understanding the crisis

As commentators point out again and again, the major stresses and strains to the global order, which Karl Polanyi sought to understand in his life's work, echo key issues that are convulsing today's world.[1] Some see history repeating itself and view the rise of the new right as a major threat to Western liberalism, ushering in a new authoritarian era and the end of democracy as we have known it throughout the post-war period.[2] Others disagree, arguing that the institutions and practices of democracy have put down much deeper roots and that comparison to the 1930s fails to appreciate these differences.[3] These disagreements draw attention to the different ways in which historical epochs are analysed and understood. The previous chapter offered one narrative presenting the breakdown of key components of our civilization, what was described as system breakdown. Of the six dimensions presented there, the threat to our liberal order is the one receiving most attention in mainstream analyses, while immigration looms large in far-right narratives. Climate change and species extinction are receiving growing attention amid mounting evidence of their gravity and threat to our way of life, but this tends to take place in a separate domain of discourse and is rarely linked to the threats to our liberal order. Recognizing therefore that the ways we frame and order our diagnoses can be crucial for the prescriptions we offer, this chapter devotes attention to dominant narratives about our present malaise.

These narratives encompass not only the threats that predominate because they are identified as the most urgent and immediate, but also what is seen to be causing them. The purpose is to map some dominant understandings, to see both what is being emphasized in analysing a system under strain and what is not being given sufficient understanding, thereby identifying some of the limits to the dominant worldview, its assumptions and its blindspots. Polanyi was able to offer an original diagnosis and a radical prescription for the social

22 — *Karl Polanyi and the Contemporary Political Crisis*

strains of his era, drawing attention in a way few did to fundamental causes and keeping a sharp focus on what needed to be done to address these. The same is urgently needed as we face system breakdown and possible civilizational collapse. The chapter is organized around three interlocking themes, selected as dominant ones in the mainstream diagnoses of the crises of our times.[4] These are the threats to our liberal order, the rise of the 'new populism' and identity politics. The chapter ends by returning to Polanyi's core insights, to help uncover the deeper causes of today's widespread malaise.

Western liberalism on the defensive

Influential journalist and commentator Edward Luce, in a wide-ranging account, focuses on what he calls 'the retreat of Western liberalism'. He draws a conclusion that is almost shocking in its clarity: 'Western liberal democracy is not yet dead, but it is far closer to collapse than we may wish to believe. It is facing its gravest challenge since the Second World War.'[5] His analysis recognizes the impact that the integration of the global economy is having on the living standards in the West (growing inequality, vanishing mobility and pushing the poor out of sight) and on the rise of Asia, particularly China, threatening the 500-year dominance of the West. Technology also has a starring role, squeezing jobs and earnings at an ever-accelerating rate. These are the structural reasons that created the conditions which give the message of the new right a mass appeal. Therefore, he warns:

> Can the West regain its optimism? If the answer is no – and most of the portents are skewing the wrong way – liberal democracy will follow. If the next few years resemble the last, it is questionable whether Western democracy can take the strain. People have lost faith that their systems can deliver. More and more are looking backwards to a golden age that can never be regained.[6]

Luce's focus is on the liberal economic and political order that emerged in the nineteenth century in Europe and North America rather than on liberalism itself as a set of ideas and fundamental principles. Severely tested in the first half of the twentieth century, it emerged strengthened firstly in western Europe by mid-century and, for a brief period towards the end of that century, seemed to put down roots in eastern Europe, throughout much of Latin America and in parts of Asia and Africa. However, the tide has truly turned as influential books with titles like *How Democracies Die*[7] (2018) and *The Strange Death of Europe*[8] (2017) attest to a serious concern that this liberal order is now struggling to survive. The coronavirus pandemic adds another existential challenge: will authoritarian regimes like China or will Western liberal democracies prove more effective in overcoming it? The answer hinges on the use of coercive power; as Runciman puts it, 'The contest in the exercise of that power between democratic adaptability and autocratic ruthlessness will shape all of our futures.'[9]

Turning to liberal thought, Zielonka reminds us that there are different varieties but that key principles do underpin a liberal political order. Up to recently, these principles were widely accepted, certainly by the vast majority of Europeans and North Americans. They include individual liberty, the rule of law, a fair, tolerant, inclusive and impartial political system, and personal security. These values were associated in the past with a social market economy that saw the need to intervene on behalf of less privileged social groups. However, in recent times, liberal values have come to be associated more and more with neoliberalism, the retreat from efforts to modify the inequalities and elitism of capitalism and, in fact, the imposition of a technocratic, deeply divisive and socially corrosive system. Liberalism has therefore come to be seen by many as the new ideology of an elitist state:

> By privatizing and deregulating the economic sector liberals have effectively prevented the electorate from changing the course of economic policies. Liberals have also spread, some would say 'imposed', their atomistic model of society, their interpretation of history, their favourite films, even their dietary habits.[10]

Zielonka acknowledges that liberals themselves, both politicians and intellectuals, intentionally present oversimplified accounts of complex economic and social issues and spread fears to undermine opponents' claims. But he goes further in asking whether the liberal vision can 'sufficiently account for people's fears and passions, collective bonds and traditions, trust, love and bigotries.'[11] He contrasts the liberal's rational, detached, abstract and universal conception of society with the illiberal, demagogic claims of the right, often based on myths and emotion rather than on evidence and rationality. He calls for a more self-critical, compassionate liberalism, willing to struggle against the vested interests that support neoliberalism. In this, he identifies well the fundamentally different worldviews that antagonistically divide the defenders from the attackers of the liberal order.

There is much evidence to support this way of framing the threat to the dominant socio-economic order. However, there are also major limitations both to the diagnosis and, even more so, to the prescriptions offered. It is relatively easy to dismiss the worldview and discourse of those new-right forces attacking the liberal order as being conspiratorial, lacking nuance or clarity, playing on emotions rather than on rational examination of issues, and on offering simplistic solutions in place of solid and credible ones. Yet in many ways this is a self-defeating stance as it fails to appreciate that the discourse so easily dismissed is, in fact, having a very significant appeal among growing numbers of electors in a wide range of countries in Europe, North America and beyond (see Table 2.1). Instead of dismissing it and offering a staunch and determined defence of the liberal order as the way forward, a greater effort needs to be made both to recognize the limitations of liberalism and to offer responses that can address the reasons why people are attracted by the proponents of what is sometimes called 'illiberal democracy', now a very widespread if varied group of political movements and leaders.

Table 2.1 Strength of ultra-right parties in Europe, 2019

Hungary	Fidesz: 49% Jobbik: 19%	Spain	Vox: 15%
Poland	Law and Justice: 43.6% Confederation: 6.8%	France	National Rally: 13%
Switzerland	Swiss People's Party: 25.8%	Netherlands	Freedom Party: 13%
Denmark	Danish People's Party: 21%	Germany	Alternative for Germany: 12.6%
Belgium	New Flemish Alliance: 20.4%	Czech Republic	Freedom and Direct Democracy: 11%
Estonia	Conservative People's Party: 17.8%	Bulgaria	United Patriots: 9%
Finland	The Finns: 17.7%	Slovakia	Our Slovakia: 8%
Sweden	Sweden Democrats: 17.6%	Greece	Greek Solution: 3.7%
Italy	Liga: 17.4%	Cyprus	ELAM: 3.7%
Austria	Freedom Party: 16%		

Data sourced from: 'Europe and Right-Wing Nationalism: A Country by Country Guide', BBC News, 13 November 2019

Box 2.1 Global values versus local virtues

On the centenary of philanthropist Andrew Carnegie's 1913 bequest of $2 million to the Church Peace Union in New York to avert global conflict through promoting dialogue among the world's religions, academic and writer Michael Ignatieff teamed up with the Carnegie Council for Ethics in International Affairs to undertake a global study of ethics in action. Just as a century ago, Carnegie's hope was that economic progress would help foster an ethical convergence among peoples the world over, so the project was to find out how far this has actually happened in our time. Identifying human rights discourse as one candidate for a new global ethic, answers were to be found to the questions of how far and deeply this has spread, how much it has displaced local moral codes, and how the battle between the local and the universal, the contextual and the global, plays out in the lives and communities of ordinary people.

The project team visited local communities in societies struggling to reinforce communal values and institutions in unjust, dangerous and divided societies in the United States, South Africa, Bosnia, Brazil and Myanmar. It hoped to understand 'how the ordinary virtues give us common cause with the human beings with whom we share this fragile planet'.[12] The findings of the study give a rare insight into the disconnect between the spread of a global ethic of equality, which the project team encountered wherever they went, and the gap 'between what the norm prescribes and what social life allows'.[13] Some of the findings were to be expected: the voices of the rich and propertied, the voice of money, have far greater weight than those of the poor, and the purpose of the moral life is less and less about obedience to established authorities and more and more about affirming the self and one's moral community. But they also found that the abstract discourse of rights has little purchase. What matters are not moral prescriptions that can be generalized but the virtues that make sense of life's harsh struggles and bind people to their communities: national pride, local tradition, religious vernacular. These are their defence against the globalizing forces of money and power that can destroy communities.[14]

Ignatieff's inspired examination of 'the ordinary virtues' around the world offers a unique window on the challenge to liberalism today. For it identifies that even though we live in a globalized world in which moral values are converging, there are competing moral systems in operation, global and local. His conclusion is of immense importance:

> We were struck, everywhere we went, by the primacy of the local. Even in a globalized world, local sources of moral life – our parents and siblings, our home, our place of worship, the local school, if there is one – are bound to be the primary shaping forces of our ordinary virtues.

> And Ignatieff recognizes that 'democratic sovereignty and the moral universalism of human rights are on a collision course everywhere' as universalist claims such as the right to asylum or nationality are rejected in the name of a democratic defence of local values.[15]

For most people the world over, it is the experiences and relationships of the local that most fundamentally shape their values and outlook, as Ignatieff finds (see Box 2.1). This, then, shifts the focus from defending liberalism to examining the ethical bonds that hold communities together at local level, the vital importance of which became powerfully evident during the Covid-19 pandemic. It raises major questions about how 'liberal freedom' supports and enhances or, alternatively, undermines and weakens, local virtue. The crucial variable is institutions. These make all the difference. If they treat people with a basic decency, an evident equality, a tolerable efficiency, then they will tend to reinforce sociability and the bonds of community. However, ordinary virtues cannot flourish if honest, non-collusive and responsive institutions are lacking, and liberal democracy is no guarantee against elite capture, corruption and inequality.[16] But Ignatieff's conclusions go further than simply seeking to ensure that liberal institutions act according to the liberal universalist values that they purport to live by. For, perhaps more than he realizes, Ignatieff's project shifts the focus away from the need to defend universalist, abstract value systems and on to the conditions for the flourishing of the ordinary virtues that bind communities together and underpin the decencies of daily life. This doesn't necessarily invalidate the claim that liberal democracies are usually a better guarantee of upholding such value systems than are autocratic or illiberal systems, but it does raise the question of why they are failing so badly and so widely to do that. And, when we reach the point where those who attack and flout basic liberal freedoms gain mass following, do we not need to understand more deeply and address more effectively the reasons for this over and above simply defending liberal values in the face of those attacking them? Let us therefore examine more closely the new wave of illiberal democrats that seems to be having so much appeal.

The 'new populism'

The UK vote to leave the European Union and the election of Donald Trump, in June and November 2016 respectively, heightened concern about 'the rise of the new populism'.[17] Yet the steady growth of new-right parties in Europe has been an emerging phenomenon over more than two decades and it is estimated that populist parties have tripled their vote in the region over that period, entering government in at least eleven countries. In some of these, populist leaders like Le Pen, father and daughter, in France, Geert Wilders in the Netherlands, and Jorg Haider in Austria forced the mainstream liberal parties of left and right to act in concert to try to keep the populists out of power (though in Austria the conservative People's Party finally succumbed and went into coalition with the ultra-right Freedom Party), with very mixed results. Neither is populism only associated with the right: in Latin America it was the emergence of a wave of left-wing populist leaders since the late 1990s, particularly Hugo Chavez in Venezuela, Evo Morales in Bolivia and Rafael Correa in Ecuador who defined the populist turn in that region. In Europe, such left-wing parties as Syriza in Greece and Podemos in Spain have been included in the embrace of populism. Since it is viewed as the main threat to liberal democracy, it is important to ask what is meant by 'the populist explosion'.[18]

What characterizes the term 'populist' above anything else is its use as a term of dismissal by its critics. 'Populism is routinely portrayed as a home for extreme nationalists, often a dangerous step on the slippery slope to fascism,' write Eatwell and Goodwin.[19] Arguably, this says more about the inability of liberal critics to understand and respond to the factors driving extensive popular support for populists. Identifying common features of different populist expressions is a more fruitful way of understanding the phenomenon. For what characterizes populists is the claim to speak for the people, distinguishing them from the elites who dominate power (political, economic but also cultural) who in their eyes fail to address adequately the needs of the people. A classic expression of this is the use by leaders of the Spanish Podemos party of the term *la casta*, the cast, to dismiss the political elites who have dominated Spanish democracy. In siding with the people against the elites, populists therefore present themselves as being anti-establishment, and even when in power use claims of obstruction by elites to excuse their own failures.[20] However, as used by populists, the term 'the people' lacks clear sociological content and is much more used as a kind of moral term embracing 'the common people' whose interests identify both with those of the common good and with the good of the nation. As British parliamentarians struggled to define how to leave the EU in 2019, it was notable that advocates of a hard Brexit often resorted to this 'pure' view of respecting the people's vote against all attempts to water it down. This invested the term 'the people' with a mystique – they were supreme and had to be obeyed. Linked to this are the undertones of xenophobia that often characterize populist discourse, the outsider seen as a threat. Former Italian Interior Minister Matteo Salvini instituted a policy of turning away from Italian ports ships laden with terrified North African refugees while Donald Trump insists on building his wall against the invading hordes of Central Americans he portrays as threatening the United States. Muller therefore sums up the logic of populism as 'a particular *moralistic imagination of politics*, a way of perceiving the political world that sets a morally pure and fully unified – but ultimately fictional – people against elites who are deemed corrupt or in some other way, morally inferior' (emphasis in original).[21] So populism is much more a *style* of politics rather than a coherent political ideology with clear policies and objectives. But why does it emerge with such strength at this time?

Much has been made of the educational and class background of those groups identified as key supporters of this political shift to the right, resulting in stereotypes of the angry white male, more often than not elderly, and with lower levels of education. Yet while there is evidence that Trump and Brexit were widely supported by a working class feeling under threat and those without degree-level education, Eatwell and Goodwin caution against a tendency to therefore dismiss them as did Hilary Clinton with her lamentable phrase describing half of Trump's supporters as 'a basket of deplorables'. Instead they break down the appeal of the new populism to the four Ds: *distrust* of established political and economic elites, a sense of *deprivation* based on falling behind other social groups, a potent fear of the *destruction* of their way of life (linked to perceptions of immigrant groups being favoured by elites), and a process of *de-alignment* as the old bonds between the people and traditional parties have begun to break down. Instead of some of the 'misleading myths that have become entrenched in wider debates', they identify common threads that unite the appeal of the new populists:

They have won over support from a fairly broad alliance of people without degrees and social conservatives who share traditional values and a cluster of core concerns about their lack of voice, the position of their group relative to others, and in particular immigration and ethnic change.[22]

It is for this reason that Runciman writes that 'conspiracy theory is the logic of populism' and that 'populism promotes paranoia on all sides'.[23] Conspiracy theories are nothing new in politics and tend to flourish among the losers who feel the benefits are not reaching them and the rules of the game are stacked against them. The danger arises, says Runciman, when the permanent losers outnumber the occasional winners, 'when conspiracy theory moves from being a minority pastime to a majority pursuit. We may be in the middle of just such a shift.'[24] Recognizing the central role that conspiracy theories play in populist politics is essential to addressing the challenge it poses. Firstly, conspiracies not just are seen by those who feel left behind, but also are fuelled by populist rulers. A good illustration is Trump's constant re-iteration that both the impeachment proceedings against him in late 2019 and the Mueller investigation into possible collusion with Russia in the 2016 election were witchhunts against him, thereby turning a potential threat into further fuelling the anger of his core support base. Secondly, and perhaps more importantly, the mobilizing force of conspiracy theories negates what for decades has been seen as the winning formula in democratic politics – summed up by the famous slogan associated with Bill Clinton's election campaigns: 'It's the economy stupid.' Those partial to conspiracy theories easily dismiss as 'fake news' the warnings of economic and financial experts about the economic consequences of certain populist policies. Identity, a sense of righteous indignation, is proving much stronger than economic self-interest.

Disembedded identities

Much is made of the centrality of identity politics in the challenge to today's liberal order. The Spanish sociologist Manuel Castells captures well the processes that have brought this to the fore. Adding to a crisis in the representation of interests within our democratic systems is an identity crisis, he writes:

The less control people have over the market and over their state the more do they fall back on a core identity that cannot be dissolved in the vertigo of global flows. They find refuge in nation, territory, God. While the triumphal elites of globalisation proclaim themselves world citizens, broad sections of society entrench themselves in the cultural spaces where they find recognition and in which their value depends on their community and not on their bank account. A cultural fracture is therefore added to the social fracture.[25]

The social fracture that drives support for today's 'illiberal democrats' has been charted in detail. For example, David Goodhart, writing about Britain, provides a wealth of evidence to identify 'the central divide in British society' and to profile the two 'tribes' that inhabit both sides of this divide: the Anywheres and the Somewheres.[26] These groupings cannot easily be mapped onto conventional social categories, being looser alignments of sentiment and worldview. The Somewheres are not only those who feel 'left behind', economically, educationally and culturally, but also those who feel more ambivalent about wider social trends, being more linked to community and their place of belonging. Goodhart estimates that they constitute about half the British population. By contrast, the Anywheres are those who can feel at home anywhere, due to their higher levels of education, their cultural mobility, and their sense of attachment to and entitlement in the dominant society. Their ideology is that of a 'progressive individualism'. Based on opinion surveys, Goodhart estimates that these constitute between 20 per cent and 25 per cent of the British population. This leaves quite a significant group of what he calls 'Inbetweeners'. He emphasizes that few people belong completely to either group; however, the range of data he assembles about education, mobility, class and value clusters to describe these two 'tribes' does identify a fundamental divide in society that goes a long way to explaining the attraction of new populist forces for a large section of the population.

Luce sums up what lies at the heart of the divide, identifying the cultural fracture that results: 'I would suggest the craving for dignity is universal. When people lose trust that society is treating them fairly, they drift into a deeper culture of mistrust. It should be little surprise that they come to view what the winners tell them with a toxic suspicion.'[27]

It is important to avoid jumping to the conclusion that this culture of mistrust is very new. Runciman likens our current condition not to the 1930s and the rise of fascism but to the 1890s, a period marked by a breakdown of trust in democratic institutions and the proliferation of conspiracy theories, both in the United States and in Europe. Yet that populist challenge gave an 'enormous injection of energy' to early twentieth-century democracy, he writes, and 'elected politicians were forced to confront public anger and find ways to assimilate it back in the mainstream'. This age of populism was followed 'by a great age of reform'.[28] Pankaj Mishra also calls our era an 'age of anger' and finds many similarities with the nineteenth century when anarchists and nationalists planted bombs in public places in various European cities. But he is less sanguine as he finds our predicament, 'in the global age of frantic individualism, is unique and deeper, its dangers more diffuse and less predictable'.[29] This is due to the contradictions between the 'shocks of modernity' – bursts of technological innovation and growth – and the weakening structures of family and community, and the state's welfare system, which in the past helped absorb these shocks. By contrast, today's individuals are directly exposed to them 'where it is easy to feel that there is no such thing as either society or state'. Today's multiple shocks of deep-rooted inequality, political dysfunction, economic stagnation and climate change are leading to 'an intense mix of envy and sense of humiliation and powerlessness, *ressentiment*, as it lingers and deepens, and is presently making for a global turn to authoritarianism and toxic forms of chauvinism'.[30]

Box 2.2 Aligning identity and interests

There is a tendency in the literature on today's political crisis to juxtapose the identity politics of today with the politics of an earlier era based on economic interests. This politics formed the basis for centre-left (largely social democratic) and centre-right (largely Christian democratic) parties throughout Europe, providing predictability and stability over decades. However, Peter Mair makes clear that the difference lies not in a politics of interests over identities, but rather in the way political parties functioned to align social identities and economic interests.

In this 'golden age', writes Mair, voters had a sense of belonging to their parties and the act of voting was seen, not as a calculated choice based on economic self-interest, but rather 'as an expression of identity and commitment'. Parties were built on a foundation of social communities 'in which large collectivities of citizens shared distinct social experiences, whether these were defined in terms of occupation, working and living conditions, [or] religious practices'. Crucially, however, such social collectivities were 'in their turn cemented by the existence of vibrant and effective social institutions, including trade unions, churches, social clubs and so on'. In this way, the success of parties lay in their ability to channel a cohesive social identity in a way that strengthened the bonds of belonging.

It is important to remember that none of this happened automatically and required the conscious intervention of parties 'actively mobilizing citizens into a set of collective political identities'. Their success rested on cementing 'the loyalties of their voters by building strong organizational networks on the basis of shared social experiences'. Loyalties were reinforced through distinct policy programmes to reflect the interests of their constituency, and priority was given to representational integrity (single-party government) to implement their programme. As a result, voters felt represented by their party in government, government *by* the people and *for* the people.

This model of representative politics, of aligning identity and interests, has been undermined for two main reasons. One is the fragmentation of the cohesive social networks on which such parties were based, as workplace practices grow more and more segmented, trade unions, social and church networks contract and weaken, and an ethic of individual self-realization becomes more predominant. However, the other side of the equation is the 'inexorable withdrawal of the parties from the realm of civil society towards the realm of government and the state', thereby weakening their links to society and their representative functions.[31]

But our era is not simply a replay of times past, whether the 1890s or the 1930s. As Runciman puts it, 'Ours are not the first democracies in history to get stuck in a rut of conspiracy theories and fake news. But ours are the first with no obvious way out.' In the past, war was the way to recovery but that is hardly a prescription to cure our ills. Reforms are possible but may be insufficient. However, perhaps many commentators' hostility to the evident incoherence, rhetorical sleight of hand, fomenting of division and violence, and phobias against foreigners, women and many minority groups that characterize today's populists may blind them to the fact that they are succeeding in doing at least some of what Mair (see Box 2.2) identified as the bases for the successes of the 'golden age' of politics. Some populists' success in galvanizing significant bases of support, in some cases virtually overnight, gives the lie to Runciman's claim that 'common cause is much harder to find than it once was'.[32] Furthermore, at least some of this base of support rests on forging links with civil society groups, hosting street festivals and promising a return to a strong welfare state, though usually directed at 'insider' groups and deliberately excluding 'outsider' groups.[33] However, this does foster a sense of belonging to a political family. Evidence has even been uncovered that populist governments are doing better at reducing inequalities than are liberal ones.[34] For example, one of the reasons given for the success of Poland's Law and Justice party in the October 2019 elections, in which they saw their share of the vote increase from 38 per cent to just under 44 per cent, was their generous welfare policies.[35] Yet these efforts to align identity and interests rest on fomenting deep divisions within society, between insiders and outsiders at a national level and, in many cases, between humanity and the ecosystem so precariously poised on the edge of catastrophic tipping points. We need better ways of addressing the breakdowns we face. Yet these are far from clear and, as Runciman puts it so pithily, 'we may be stuck'.[36]

Polanyi: Diagnosing our 'social calamity'

The analysis so far has taken us beyond two frames that dominate discussions about the rise of the new populism. The first is a defence of the values of the liberal order against attacks from demagogues who fool the people with simplistic solutions to complex problems, turning them against elites and experts on the one hand and against outsiders on the other. The second is a recognition that our contemporary politics is proving unable to respond to the needs of those sectors that feel left behind, abandoned and forgotten. These then respond to the appeal of a strong anti-establishment discourse (though many of the new populist leaders come from the heart of the economic establishment). The response of those who hold the first view is in essence a staunch defence of the status quo even if some of them are critical of its defects; those who hold the second view tend to see no obvious way out. Yet examining developments in the 1930s that saw fascist leaders coming to power as they seemed to offer firm answers to social breakdown, Polanyi did see ways out through penetrating to the deeper causes. As Dale summarized it, referring to Polanyi: 'Although sharing Schumpeter's belief that the rising bourgeoisie had contributed to the peaceful nineteenth century, he introduced a novel thesis: that its crusading drive to universalize capitalist institutions at the global level spawned contradictions that ultimately brought the system crashing down.'[37]

This gets to the heart of Polanyi's diagnosis: what he identified were the contradictions that resulted when the practices and values of the free market were imposed on society resulting finally in the collapse of the social system in war and revolution. We too are coming out of a period when, particularly since the early 1980s, market practices and values have been imposed on society through the liberalization and privatization drives associated with Thatcherism in the United Kingdom and Reaganism in the United States. What was called the 'Washington Consensus', based on the primacy of the market as a response to economic and social challenges, then became the dominant policy prescription for much of the world.[38] Just as happened in the 1930s, this again spawned the contradictions that result when communities and individuals see their livelihoods disappear as jobs are outsourced to distant places, and who are stripped of the social protections that provided a support in hard times. The loss of a sense of control and of trust in the future is palpable. Central to these are the tensions that are reshaping politics: between the local and the universal, between the heart and the head, between human bonds and technical fixes. As Dale states, 'Few other texts come close to such a powerful and evocative account of the disintegration of a society's normative and customary fabric under the impact of marketisation as *The Great Transformation*.'[39]

Polanyi is not the only voice recognizing the destructive impacts of global market forces on local communities. Former director of the Reserve Bank of India and chief economist of the International Monetary Fund (IMF) Raghuram Rajan charts accurately the steady breakdown of local community cohesion and capacity due to technological innovations, state neglect and economic shocks 'transmitted through manufacturing and finance across the increasingly integrated world economy'.[40] And he recognizes that having lost trust in the system 'the aggrieved masses are fertile ground for the radicals no matter what the configuration of the mainstream'.[41] Many of today's problems, including the rise of the new populism, he traces to 'the diminution of the community' and the solutions lie 'in bringing dysfunctional communities back to health'.[42] Polanyi would not disagree. But where they part company is that Rajan thinks markets have the ability to reform themselves so that they improve community wellbeing. 'Within markets, powerful participants must be trusted to do the right thing by society,' he writes.[43] Finding an equilibrium between the three pillars of market, state and community is now required, he believes: 'It is better to improve the functioning of the market, even while also refocusing the state and strengthening the community,' he concludes.[44]

Polanyi focused on the market as a mechanism beyond the control of individuals. It was the imposition of this mechanism that was the cause of the dislocation of society as he described so powerfully. He outlines in detail how the central mechanism of the market, requiring treating land (nature), labour (human beings) and money as commodities – what he calls 'the commodity fiction' since they can never be reduced to items bought and sold in a marketplace – supplied 'a vital organizing principle in regard to the whole of society' (see Part Three on commodification and decommodification). Allowing this market mechanism 'to be the sole director of the fate of human beings and their natural environment indeed, even of the amount and use of purchasing power, would result in the demolition of society'. Polanyi eloquently describes the destruction that results:

> In disposing of man's labour power the system would, incidentally, dispose of the physical, psychological, and moral entity 'man' attached to that tag. Robbed of the protective covering of cultural institutions, human beings would perish from the effects of social exposure; they would die as the victims of acute social dislocation through vice, perversion, crime, and starvation. Nature would be reduced to its elements, neighbourhoods and landscapes defiled, rivers polluted, military safety jeopardized, the power to produce food and raw materials destroyed. Finally, the market administration of purchasing power would periodically liquidate business enterprise, for shortages and surfeits of money would prove as disastrous to business as floods and droughts in primitive society.[45]

In this passage, Polanyi focuses on the destruction wrought to human beings, to nature and to the productive economy by the imposition of the market mechanism. But he goes further in identifying the cultural dislocations that also result. This takes us beyond the categories of poverty reduction and social exclusion that are more commonly used today when discussing how markets fail to serve society. Instead, Polanyi recognizes that the destruction wrought by the market mechanism is not fully captured by economic deprivation alone but rather it is cultural disintegration that is the cause of the 'social calamity':

> Not economic exploitation, as often assumed, but the disintegration of the cultural environment of the victim is then the cause of the degradation. The economic process may, naturally, supply the vehicle of the destruction, and almost invariably economic inferiority will make the weaker yield, but the immediate cause of his undoing is not for that reason economic; it lies in the lethal injury to the institutions in which his social existence is embodied. The result is loss of self-respect and standards, whether the unit is a people or a class, whether the process springs from a so-called culture conflict or from a change in the position of a class within the confines of a society.[46]

Polanyi's novelty was his identification of the self-regulating market system, colonizing ever greater parts of the social and natural world, as the cause of the stresses and strains of the political order. While, as seen, there are echoes of this in some of today's analyses and prescriptions, Polanyi's core insight lies in his identification of the self-governing market as a mechanism imposed on society with very destructive results. Unless politics can address this, it will remain dysfunctional. One illustration, which a Polanyian lens helps to uncover, is the difference between 2008 and 2016 (see Box 2.3).

Box 2.3 From 2008 to 2016, a Polanyian reading

Holmes uses Polanyi's diagnosis to powerful effect in understanding the difference between events in 2008 and 2016. Although the financial crash discredited mainstream economics, 'without any new paradigm to take its place, neoclassical economics lived on, if only in "zombie" form'.[47] Despite being under challenge from Keynesian proposals and from a strong mobilization behind introducing a Universal Basic Income (see Box 6.2), neoliberal prescriptions still dominated, focused at all costs on a return to growth while imposing severe austerity on those least able to bear it.

Using one of the ways Polanyi presents the tensions of market society, namely that between improvement (understood as growth and efficiency) and habitation (namely a sense of secure belonging), Holmes sees that the events of 2008 did not result in any decisive rebalancing in favour of habitation since they failed to modify the obsession with improvement. With the vote for Brexit and the election of Donald Trump in 2016, all changed however. Holmes sees these victories as resulting from the principle of habitation because they promised direct action to defend livelihoods in non-technical language understood by those who felt forgotten by state and market (remember Trump's promise to defend 'beautiful coal'):

> The very fact that the campaigns appealed to voters in terms of livelihood and habitation meant that they could not be disproved by opposed appeals rooted in the language of improvement. The battle was over competing visions of the nature of the economy, not empirical knowledge which could be verified as 'non-fake'. The appeal of these ideologies lay in the promise to defend people's livelihoods directly, rather than in promising a better life indirectly through generalised processes of economic improvement. … However right or wrong the economics of Brexit or Trumpism may have been, it is that direct discursive orientation to questions of habitation that underlined a big part of their electoral appeal.[48]

In other words, it took the votes in 2016 to throw into crisis the dominant commitment to growth and improvement at all costs, and to open the way for a 'value-laden, normatively driven political economic debate in which choices and costs of choices have to be justified more openly, rather than swept under the technocratic carpet or assumed away theoretically'.[49] This was not driven by anything drawn from Polanyi's writings, but those writings allow us to get a deeper understanding of what is driving the forces now reshaping our society and how we should be responding. They also show that the dominant neoliberal frames of analysis and their value systems are now part of the problem; we urgently need an alternative.

Conclusions

In helping understand the political crisis of our era, Karl Polanyi has much to contribute. He still offers a valuable interpretative lens through which to examine the roots of the stresses and strains of our times, including the global climate crisis. As shown in this chapter, Polanyi offers a much more precise diagnosis than most analysists of the heart of the crisis we are living through, with a focus on the destructive impact on society and on nature of the imposition of the market mechanism. This points to the need for an alternative, which for Polanyi was socialism. The need for this alternative and what might constitute it are the focus of the next two chapters, entitled 'An alternative future?'. Chapter 3 will analyse the contemporary crisis of capitalism while Chapter 4 will draw on Polanyi to outline a response to the crisis of market society.

Part Two

An alternative future?

3

Beyond capitalism

There is an irony at the heart of today's global politics that seems to be largely missed by analysts and commentators. On the one hand, far-right movements and parties are growing in power and influence, as was outlined in Chapter 2, and the future of democracy itself is seen to be under threat. On the other hand, however, disillusion with capitalism is widespread and the appeal of those advocating various versions of socialist alternatives is also growing.[1] The most common reading of this is that it shows evidence not of a lurch to the right but, rather, a greater volatility and the growth of extremes, of both left and right. If the focus is limited to our political systems, there is validity to this reading. But broadening the focus to the economic system raises the question of the future of capitalism itself, a question that is not being as widely debated as is the rise of the 'new populism' despite the recent upsurge of interest in socialism.

Here again, there are parallels with Polanyi. The chapter in *The Great Transformation* (1944) entitled 'Conservative Twenties, Revolutionary Thirties' (Chapter 2) has surprised some readers as it seems to contradict the evidence that the 1920s had been swinging and, indeed, had witnessed significant revolutionary movements at the beginning of that decade whereas the 1930s, far from being revolutionary, were reactionary. There are parallels with our time: the 2000s were exuberant and triumphalist whereas they are being followed by deepening divisions and the systematic undermining of our liberal politico-economic order by a resurgent inward-looking nationalism. Yet, Polanyi labelled the reactionary 1930s revolutionary because they witnessed the final nail in the coffin of the liberal capitalist order. For him, the rise of fascism far from being the *cause* of the crisis of liberal capitalism was, rather, the *result* of the strains generated by handing society over to the self-governing mechanism of the market. It was a symptom that unmasked the deeper unsustainability of the dominant model. Applying this to our time focuses attention away from the new right as the cause of what is threatening our liberal civilization and directs our attention to a more fundamental cause, free-market capitalism itself.

This chapter examines contemporary capitalism as the cause of the stresses and strains that are undermining its sustainability as the dominant way of ordering our economic system and, indeed, our wider society. It begins by examining the state of capitalism today, uncovering some of its systemic disorders. The following section draws in climate change as a fundamental challenge to capitalism, highlighting why it is being increasingly seen as incompatible with the requirement to transition to a low-carbon society over the next three decades. The third section turns again to Polanyi and his views on the incompatibility of capitalism and democracy, asking if his fears are again being realized in our contemporary era.

Capitalism under pressure

The collapse of Lehman Brothers in 2008 triggered a global financial crisis but also sent a message about the future of capitalism: that the next generation will be poorer than this one and that the old economic model is broken and cannot revive growth without also reviving financial fragility. This is the view of journalist Paul Mason who adds that the message was only partially understood at the time.[2] Taking the projections of the Organisation for Economic Cooperation and Development (OECD) for the world economy between now and 2060, Mason sees long-term stagnation as being the future of capitalism as automation kills jobs and drives up inequality, as growth flatlines, as migration explodes and as states go bust due to tax systems collapsing under mass unemployment.

> Allow yourself to imagine the world of 2060 as the OECD predicts it: Los Angeles and Detroit look like Manila today – abject slums alongside guarded skyscrapers; Stockholm and Copenhagen look like the destroyed cities of the American rust belt; the middle-income job has disappeared. Capitalism will be in its fourth decade of stagnation.[3]

This is the future of capitalism *if* the policy prescriptions of today's dominant neoliberalism are followed: make labour more flexible, deepen globalization, privatize higher education and integrate tens of millions of migrants amid collapsing tax systems as the work crisis undermines income tax revenues. But, for some, these are simply the surface symptoms of much deeper systemic disorders. Renowned German sociologist Wolfgang Streeck sees capitalism itself as being in crisis and he asks whether it has seen its day:

> In the 1980s, the idea that 'modern capitalism' could be run as a 'mixed economy', both technocratically managed and democratically controlled, was abandoned. Later, in the neoliberal revolution, social and economic order was reconceived as benevolently emerging from the 'free play of market forces.' But with the crash of 2008, the promise of self-regulating markets attaining equilibrium on their own was discredited as well, without a plausible new formula for political-economic governance coming into view. This alone may be regarded as a symptom of a crisis that has become systemic, the more so the longer it lasts.[4]

And it is not only its critics who are questioning the future of capitalism. Raghuram Rajan, whose views on the ways markets damage community were quoted in Chapter 2, has warned that 'capitalism is under serious threat because it's stopped providing for the many, and when that happens, the many revolt against capitalism'. It is not providing equal opportunity, he says, and 'in fact the people who are falling off are in a much worse situation'. While advocating greater opportunity through education, he acknowledges that this is now much more difficult as 'the very communities that are hit by the forces of global trade and global information tend to be communities which have deteriorating schools, rising crime, rising social illnesses and are unable to prepare their members for the global economy'.[5] Even fund managers in the City of London are calling for a rethink of capitalism (Box 3.1).

Box 3.1 Capitalism borrows from future while destroying the environment

Capitalism must end its obsession with economic growth and giving primacy to the interests of shareholders say two of the world's biggest fund managers. Anne Richards, chief executive of Fidelity International, and Andreas Utermann, CEO of Allianz Global Investors, agree that the current form of capitalism is unsustainable, borrowing from the future while destroying the environment.

Richards called for 'a pivot from the Milton Friedman concept of capitalism and the primacy of shareholders, who may have a very short-term involvement with an individual company, towards a wider stakeholder approach'. Utermann said that 'more sophisticated measures than GDP per capita are required to determine whether capitalism is delivering to all stakeholders'. He added that 'a more holistic approach to "growth" needs to evolve, looking to capture societal and environmental benefits and costs'.

The monthly City Network forum hosted by the *Financial Times* brings together a panel of more than fifty senior figures from across the City. Several participants praised Extinction Rebellion, Greta Thunberg and David Attenborough while agreeing that capitalism needs metrics that measure not only financial performance but also positive or negative impact on society. 'Solving climate change through inclusive capitalism will define our generation,' said Nigel Wilson, chief executive of Legal & General, another big asset manager.[6]

There is therefore quite a widespread view that, as Collier puts it, for many 'capitalism is not working': 'Deep rifts are tearing apart the fabric of our societies. They are bringing new anxieties and new anger to our people, and new passions to our politics.'[7] So a key question is the extent to which capitalism is able to reform itself, serving the needs of society and the environment, rather than giving priority to the interests of capital and shareholders. There are plenty of proposals for reform as illustrated by the views of the City fund managers. In discussing the future of global capitalism, Branko Milanovic highlights its positive capacity to undermine traditional hierarchies based on family or class: 'Money is a great equalizer, and commercial societies provide the best examples of its power.'[8] Yet it also stimulates in individuals 'the most selfish and greedy behaviour' and neither of the two traditional constraints to such behaviour (religion and the social contract) holds in today's globalized capitalism.[9] But he sees no alternative as every system that has been tried to replace it has proven worse. He dismisses fears that robotization will create masses of unemployed people since 'we cannot imagine what new jobs will be required to satisfy the newly created needs'.[10] He doesn't mention climate change but believes that 'our terrestrial limits' are much wider than we generally think: 'The better our technology, the more reserves of everything we discover, and the more efficient we are in using them.[11] Instead of critiquing capitalism, Milanovic speculates on what type of capitalism is likely to evolve, a liberal meritocratic capitalism of the type that currently dominates or a 'people's capitalism' in which wealth and income inequalities would be less, and intergenerational income mobility greater. This could be achieved by relatively simple reforms, he believes: tax advantages for the middle class, increased funding for public schools, the end of the binary division between citizens and non-citizens, and exclusively public funding of political campaigns.[12] He also speculates on whether US-style liberal capitalism or Chinese-style political capitalism will get the upper hand.

Collier's prescriptions for the future of capitalism go much further, drawing on the ethical foundations of social democracy in the co-operative movements of the nineteenth century. These foundations, he argues, have been corroded by the rise of ideologues and populists within our political system, polarizing them and distracting from pragmatic solutions. He sets himself the task of providing 'a basis on which the beleaguered centre of the political spectrum can rebuild'.[13] He thinks this can be done through:

- Political reforms to how party leaders are elected;
- Development policies to reverse the divergence between the metropolis and broken cities, such as taxes on land and skilled workers;
- Restoring the web of reciprocal obligations through state changes to laws, taxes and benefits to restore the ethical family;
- Fostering narratives of shared identity and belonging 'to create the conditions for people to be confident that the obligations they accept will be reciprocated by others'.[14]

These reforms would move capitalism in a more social democratic direction and would require much more state guidance and regulation than has been the case under neoliberal capitalism. It would involve returning to a more Keynesian set of policies.

Streeck goes much further, identifying five systemic disorders of today's advanced capitalism.

1. Stagnation: there is now a widespread view that healthy growth rates in the developed world are a thing of the past. This poses a major problem for capitalism as it seeks to generate the profits that drive the system.

2. Oligarchic redistribution: the swift growth of inequality is destroying the social contract which linked the fate of the marginalized and those on low incomes to the success of elites.

3. Plundering of the public domain: this process has two main drivers: privatization of the public domain, both productive assets and the welfare state; and the many opportunities given the wealthy to evade taxes, hide their wealth and impose competitive pressures on governments.

4. Corruption: this has now become a pervasive feature of contemporary capitalism poisoning the body politic like never before, finding expression in a myriad of ways.[15]

5. Global anarchy: the end of the bi-polar global system in the late 1980s has resulted in more and more zones of the world collapsing into effective anarchy, with resultant terrorist attacks and migration pressures, affecting many poorer countries as well as the developed West.[16]

He concludes that 'the capitalist system is at present stricken with at least five worsening disorders for which no cure is at hand. ... What is to be expected, on the basis of capitalism's recent historical record, is a long and painful period of cumulative decay'.[17] To these can be added a sixth, capitalism's reliance on fossil fuels (see Box 3.2).

Box 3.2 Weaning capitalism off fossil fuels

One dimension of contemporary capitalism that is often taken for granted is its reliance on the availability of extensive and accessible sources of cheap fossil fuels – coal, oil and natural gas – what Di Muzio calls 'carbon capitalism'.[18] From the beginning of the nineteenth century, this reliance on fossil fuels fast accelerated society's capacity to produce, consume and trade, though in highly unequal ways, laying the foundation for today's mass consumer and mobile societies. However, in the early twenty-first century the continuation of carbon capitalism is under severe threat from two different sources. The first is the growing evidence that the supply of fossil fuels on which it is based is in terminal decline, often called 'peak oil'.[19] The second is the urgent need to reduce greenhouse gas emissions to avoid runaway climate change, requiring the widespread move to renewable sources of energy.

Much hope is placed on technologies to help make this transition while maintaining current standards of consumption. The move to electric vehicles is one current example. However, while there is a major growth in renewables, demand for fossil fuels also continues to grow and hit a record high in 2018.[20] This reflects both the continuing power of the fossil fuel industry and the ways in which the technologies that dominate are configured for centralized, extensive systems of energy generation and supply. A collapse in the demand for oil during the coronavirus pandemic was seen by some as the gravest challenge to the fossil fuel industry in its 100-year history. Prices dropped to twenty-year lows and carbon emissions began to decline. With oil companies facing a very uncertain future, investors were looking with more interest to renewables as offering less risk.[21] 'Our analysis argues that the current crisis could accelerate the shift away from fossil fuels,' wrote Jessica Alsford, head of sustainability research at Morgan Stanley.[22]

However, whether this happens depends on how governments and consumers respond. Will fossil fuel subsidies be cut or seen as ways to help an ailing industry? Will cheap fossil fuels lead to more intense consumption? Pirani argues: 'Transition means changing not only the way that energy is produced, but also the technological systems that consume it and the social and economic contexts in which they operate.'[23] This will require 'forms of social organisation that supersede corporate and state control of the economy, advance collective and community control, and, crucially, in which employed labour – a central plank of profit-centred capitalism – is superseded by more meaningful types of human activity'.[24]

Streeck's diagnosis points towards much more radical conclusions than do those of Milanovic or Collier. As a result of the fact that market expansion has faced no opposition since the collapse of communism and the failure of new left-wing forces to curb its excesses, he writes, it now runs the risk of undermining the capitalist system itself. He turns to Polanyi's fictitious commodities to identify three major crisis zones of today's capitalist order. The first is the excessive commodification of money that brought down the global economy in 2008. The second is the commodification of nature which has set up a clash between capitalism's principle of infinite expansion and the finite nature of the natural world. Finally, the commodification of labour has made work ever more precarious. The result has been 'a fundamental disorganisation of the agencies that have, in the modern era, more or less successfully domesticated capitalist "animal spirits", for the sake of society as a whole'.[25] Each of these is examined in Chapters 5, 6 and 7. Paradoxically, however, it is through the even more intense commodification of money (speculation), land (plunder) and labour (precariousness) that capitalism is today seeking to stimulate growth and maintain profits.

The key question arising from this discussion is how far can capitalism be reformed to curb the excesses now widely recognized. Fulcher writes that the essential feature of capitalism is 'the investment of money in order to make a profit', involving the exploitation of wage labour, the mediation of all economic activities by the market and the tendency towards the concentration of enterprises and speculation which may not be productive but is based on mechanisms central to the operation of a capitalist economy.[26] Interestingly, in the early days of the coronavirus pandemic, the *Financial Times* published an editorial comment arguing for policies that point in a very different direction:

> Radical reforms – reversing the prevailing policy direction of the last four decades – will need to be put on the table. Governments will have to accept a more active role in the economy. They must see public services as investments rather than liabilities, and look for ways to make labour markets less insecure. Redistribution will again be on the agenda; the privileges of the elderly and wealthy in question. Policies until recently considered eccentric, such as basic income and wealth taxes, will have to be in the mix.[27]

At the very least, such reforms would result in a much more managed and limited form of capitalism, going back to the heyday of social democracy or an even more radical rebalancing favouring communities over capital. Whether these can provide, in Mason's words, 'an escape route for capitalism' requires that they have the ability to transition speedily and successfully to a low-carbon society, which is now fast emerging as the greatest challenge facing our societies and economic systems.

Capitalism versus the climate

Naomi Klein was among the first who presented the issue of capitalism versus the climate in the subtitle to her book *This Changes Everything* (2014).[28] She sees climate change as a threat to the interests of those who want to keep to

Business As Usual (BAU), examples being US foundations such as the Heritage Foundation, the Cato Institute and the Ayn Rand Institute, which systematically seek to sow doubts about the science behind climate change. But she states clearly: 'Contemporary capitalism has not just accelerated the behaviours that are changing the climate. This economic model has changed a great many of us as individuals, accelerated and uprooted and dematerialized us as surely as it has finance capital.'[29] Therefore, the gradual, incremental options through which climate capitalism addresses the challenges are no longer adequate. The demands of profit-making trump the climate imperative, she concludes, realizing that 'the oligarchs who were minted by the era of deregulation and mass privatization are not, in fact, going to use their vast wealth to save the world on our behalf'.[30]

Yet capitalism remains the dominant means being used to achieve climate goals, employing the mechanisms of the market to this end. This is often called climate capitalism and uses different market-based mechanisms to try to achieve carbon reductions. Principal among these are trading in carbon and the establishment of markets for such trade: emissions trading systems[31] have grown from the first one established by the EU in 2005 to four by 2010 and twenty by 2019, covering twenty-seven jurisdictions and raising $57 billion through the auctioning of allowances.[32] More widely, it has succeeded in making sectors of business and finance see climate as an opportunity for profit-making rather than a threat to it. At a global level, the most influential body promoting climate change as a capitalist growth opportunity is the New Climate Economy (NCE) project established by the Global Commission on the Economy and Climate comprising former heads of government and leading figures in economics and finance. The NCE has mapped out a comprehensive agenda in areas such as multi-stakeholder cooperation to catalyse sustainable economic growth, overcoming barriers to financing sustainable infrastructure and highlighting the economic benefits of climate action.[33]

These are examples of climate capitalism in action, defined as 'a model which squares capitalism's need for continual economic growth with substantial shifts away from carbon-based industrial development'.[34] However, how possible is this without fundamentally changing the nature of capitalism itself? Elliott thinks the dominant Anglo-Saxon variety of capitalism is too short-sighted, thinking only of the here-and-now of profit maximization and resisting any regulations that might restrict profits. Instead he sees the Chinese model of managed and directed capitalism as being better able to scale up the massive investment needed in clean technology, though China has also been criticized for seeking to weaken the requirement for countries reporting emissions under the Paris Agreement.[35] Also needed is a global carbon tax set high enough to keep fossil fuels in the ground.[36] This echoes Newell and Paterson's view that the problem with climate capitalism is its neoliberal laissez-faire character. What is needed is a 'climate Keynesianism':

> This form of climate capitalism, therefore, regulates those areas of the carbon economy that are currently under-regulated. It deepens and strengthens regulation of those areas that are already subject to regulation and tries to steer a nascent carbon economy towards a fully fledged form of climate capitalism that delivers growth (as any form of capitalism must) but in so doing achieves a significant degree of decarbonisation. Importantly, however, it does this in a way that seeks to address inequalities in the carbon economy.[37]

The key question of climate capitalism is the extent to which it is possible to square the circle of growth and emissions reduction: can a growth economy deliver sufficient emissions to meet the targets of the 2015 Paris Agreement? This is what is called decoupling growth from emissions, meaning that an economy can continue to grow and also reduce emissions at the same time. Jackson and Victor unravel the claims for and against this green growth and conclude that, despite some evidence of relative decoupling in some regions, at the global level 'there is no evidence of absolute decoupling at all'. They point out that it is not enough to reduce emissions but that economic activity must also be decoupled from environmental and material resources on which future prosperity depends (it must use less of the planet's finite resources). This is measured by the carbon intensity of economic output (how much carbon is produced by each unit of growth). To prevent climate breakdown, they point out, would require an average annual decline in carbon intensity of around 14 per cent for the next three decades. The highest rate of decline ever experienced by advanced economies was a little under 3 per cent following the oil crisis in the 1970s. The average rate up to the coronavirus pandemic was less than 1 per cent; while emissions fell sharply during it expert opinion was divided on whether the virus would help or hinder decisive climate action.[38] 'In the case of a rich country like the United Kingdom, sufficient absolute decoupling would mean a decline in the nation's carbon footprint at a rate in excess of 20 per cent each year, with a net zero target that might need to be as early as 2030.'[39]

Hickel and Kallis examine empirical evidence about decoupling GDP growth from resource use and carbon emissions and come to similar conclusions: at a global level there was some relative decoupling at the end of the twentieth century but this has not been maintained into the twenty-first century. Even where some decoupling has been found to occur it is unlikely to be maintained over the long-term. The total amounts of emissions did stabilize in 2015 and 2016 only to rise again in 2017 and 2018 and the decoupling that is happening is unlikely to happen fast enough to keep global warming within the limits of the Paris Agreement of 2015 (1.5°C and 2°C). 'Models that do project green growth within the constraints of the Paris agreement rely heavily on negative emissions technologies that are either unproven or dangerous at scale,' they add.[40]

Gough asks whether green growth is a panacea or a chimera and draws damning conclusions based on a rigorous examination of studies and data. Broadening the focus beyond emissions reduction to include reducing inequalities and promoting wellbeing, he finds 'a tragic contradiction between growth, climatic instability and egregious inequality'.[41] Emissions growth over recent decades is fundamentally explained by the drive to accumulate profit while improvements in productivity have only partially and inadequately offset the upward surge in emissions. Consumer preferences and spending power continue to determine what is produced, sidelining issues of equity and justice while the chances of failing to meet climate goals remain high. Reducing poverty through economic growth 'would devastate the planet' and instead require 'either new forms of redistribution or a shift to an alternative economic pathway'.[42] This raises the bar for the proponents of a green capitalism, essentially showing the impossibility of combining three variables – reducing emissions, fostering equitable wellbeing and capitalism. One attempt to try to square this circle and combine goals of equity and justice with climate goals is the Green New Deal, requiring not just massive public investment but also the redistribution of wealth and power (see Box 3.3). How much it is compatible with capitalism is a question that will become clearer over time as it has emerged as a focal point of struggle between governments (including the EU Commission) and climate activists. The former will be seeking to achieve climate goals within the framework of capitalism while the latter will be pushing hard for ever greater ambition. Chapter 9 returns to this issue.

Box 3.3 Reviving the Green New Deal

As one response to the economic crash in 2007–8, a group of progressive economists linked to the New Economic Foundation (NEF) published a proposal for a Green New Deal, inspired by US President Franklin D. Roosevelt's New Deal of the 1930s. Seeking 'the transformation of national economies and the global economy', it was designed to address not just the economic recession but also the urgent need to reduce greenhouse gas emissions. This was to be done through mobilizing public and private expenditure to foster employment and demand through 'targeting environmental projects that will dramatically cut fossil fuel use and hence help to tackle climate change and peak oil'.[43]

While welcomed by the British Labour government at the time, it lost political momentum with the change of government in 2010. Taken up by the Green Party in the United States, it failed to make a political breakthrough until the election of Alexandria Ocasio-Cortez to Congress in 2018. She swiftly moved to introduce a Green New Deal resolution in Congress in early 2019 laying out a specific programme for an ambitious deal. This addresses the jobs crisis as well as the climate and environmental crises in its five goals: achieving net-zero emissions, creating jobs, investing in infrastructure and industry, securing clean air and water in healthy communities, and promoting justice and equity. The means to achieve these is through decarbonizing electricity, transportation and industry, restoring ecosystems, and upgrading buildings and electricity grids. All this is to be paid for by a massive ten-year programme of trillions of dollars of public spending.

While the resolution was defeated by Congress in March 2019, Ocasio-Cortez is moving head to introduce specific bills to implement part of it. Perhaps more important however is that the resolution has generated widespread public debate and a social movement around the concept of a Green New Deal. As one commentator put it: 'It is a vision for a new kind of economy, built around a new set of social and economic relationships. It is not merely a way to reduce emissions, but also to ameliorate the other symptoms and dysfunctions of a late capitalist economy: growing inequality and concentration of power at the top.'[44]

Capitalism or democracy?

Polanyi identifies an essential contradiction between capitalism and democracy arising from the destruction caused by the free market colonizing ever more areas of social and natural life. For him, the options were stark:

either maintain capitalism and sacrifice democracy, as happened with the rise of fascist regimes in the 1920s and 1930s, or save democracy by moving beyond capitalism to socialism. In posing this dilemma, Polanyi reflected the suspicion widespread in his time that the owners of capital and the means of production were unaccountable. If faced with pressures for greater accountability or distribution of their wealth and assets by progressive governments, they would opt for fascism. Certainly, this is what happened in Germany in the 1930s observed at close quarters by Polanyi. Therefore, he concluded that capitalism and democracy are 'irreconcilably antagonistic'.[45] The post-war period of social democratic capitalism seemed to belie this antagonism. Indeed, in this period Polanyi came to be interpreted as a champion of social democratic means of taming capitalism through state regulation and he was convinced that the utopian experiment of the self-regulating market was finished and would not return.[46] However, over recent decades a counter-tendency of capitalism taming democracy has become evident, as both centre-left and centre-right parties have become virtually indistinguishable in imposing market mechanisms on society. The rise of new oppositional movements, both from the right and from the left, has led some to fear again for the fate of democracy itself. Runciman writes that 'populism could turn into fascism as well as social democracy'.[47] Or, more likely today, is that it turns itself into neither, succumbing instead to the constant undermining of democratic values and accountability by the fragmenting tendency of social media, themselves a powerful expression of corporate capitalism. Immersing himself in the new politics of the people, Jack Shenker shares these concerns, echoing Polanyi's fears about the threat of markets to democracy: the questions for journalists, he writes, are not whether democracy can survive the internet but whether 'democracy can survive an internet subordinated to the demands of the market' or, more succinctly, 'whether democracy can survive the elevation of market logics over humanity'.[48]

Behind the concern for democracy lie deeper divisions, also highlighted by Polanyi and relevant to the situation in which we now find ourselves. Writing about England in the early nineteenth century, he stated that 'economic society had emerged as distinct from the political state'.[49] By this he meant that 'a self-regulating market demands nothing less than the institutional separation of society into an economic and a political sphere'. Not only was this a novel development in history but it required that 'such an institutional pattern could not have functioned unless society was somehow subordinated' to the requirements of the economy.[50] While the institutional processes are quite distinct between the two periods, what is striking about today's economy is the extent to which it has succeeded in freeing itself from political controls with the result that society's needs are subordinated to what the economy requires. And, as Polanyi also saw, such a situation quickly leads to a counter-movement by society to protect itself; such a reaction can be seen today in the emergence of political movements, not only of the right but also of the left, whose main motivation is to attack the establishment as outlined in Chapter 2.

The concept Polanyi used to express this subordination of society to the needs of the economy was disembeddedness, as mentioned in the outline of his major themes in Chapter 1. He writes in *The Great Transformation* that 'the control of the economic system by the market is of overwhelming consequence to the whole organisation: it means no less than the running of society as an adjunct to the market'.[51] For, the malaise of capitalism, as analysed in this chapter, arises from the dysfunctional way in which the economy relates to society as the pursuit of individual gain is elevated to the organizing principle of economic life. Monbiot expresses it well: 'At the heart of capitalism is a vast and scarcely examined assumption: you are entitled to as great a share of the world's resources as your money can buy. You can purchase as much land, as much atmospheric space, as many minerals, as much meat and fish as you can afford, regardless of who might be deprived.'[52] Polanyi 'was concerned with what happens to social order and political freedom when economic exchange is organised chiefly through self-regulating markets', writes Beckert.[53] Thus Polanyi's point does not concern the institutionalization of the economy: after all an extensive network of regulatory institutions and legal frameworks characterizes the functioning of the neoliberal market society. The central point relates to the fact that the economy operates according to rules and values of acquisitiveness and self-interest which then come to dominate in the wider society. Polanyi has been criticized for adopting an overly restrictive definition of economy and failing to recognize that it is 'as social a realm of human existence as any other'.[54] But such a critique misses what is distinctive about Polanyi's central insight, namely, that the economy when disembedded from society becomes a realm of human existence that operates according to its own interests and values, and these leave little freedom for society to do other than follow them. Felber's distinction between human values and economic values captures this:

> The values which hold for the economy today are completely different from those which apply to our daily interpersonal relationships. In regard to our friendships and everyday relationships, we thrive when we live in accordance with human values: the building of trust, honesty, esteem, respect, empathy, cooperation, mutual help and sharing. The 'free' market economy is based on the rules of the systematic pursuit of profit and competition. These pursuits promote egoism, greed, avarice, envy, ruthlessness and irresponsibility. This contradiction is not merely a blemish in a complex or multivalent world; rather, it is a cultural catastrophe; it divides us inwardly – as individuals and as a society.[55]

If disembedding the economy from society results in restricting our freedom, then the central task facing us is to re-embed the economy in society. This constitutes the double movement, seen by Polanyi as a fundamental dynamic of social change. Much attention has been paid over recent times to what are seen as manifestations of the double movement in the contemporary world – from the anti-globalization protests that emerged in the late 1990s to the emergence of the new populism in the 2010s. These are acts of spontaneous resistance in Polanyi's view, as society reacts against the damage inflicted on human beings and on nature, seeking to protect society through pressing for greater state interventions to regulate the market or through building counterpower such as social movements and trade unions to resist market power. But it is often forgotten that this is the second part of what is a double movement: the first part is that 'conscious and often violent intervention on the part of government which imposed the market organisation on society for noneconomic ends', which he regards as a 'utopian experiment'.[56] While he believed in the early 1940s that this imposition and the massive social and economic dislocation that it inflicted were on the wane, since the 1970s society has experienced yet again the violent intervention by government imposing the market organization on society for non-economic ends, ends which have much more to do with private profit-making than with social wellbeing. This is one of Polanyi's insights that has attracted the attention of both activists and analysts to his writings in recent times. Yet there are deeper lessons here than the proponents of the double movement often realize.

In describing the double movement, Polanyi was identifying the core contradiction of industrial capitalism, namely the constant tension between the needs of the economy and the needs of society. In a world that 'is arguably more turbulent and dangerous than Polanyi's'[57], the challenge facing humanity now is to transcend this contradiction. If we fail to do it, if the pendulum continues to swing between periods of intense marketization followed by periods in which society manages to embed the market to serve society, we will fast make the planet uninhabitable for humanity. As the United Nations Development Programme (UNDP) has stated: 'Our development model is bumping up against concrete limits.'[58] The 2018 report of the Intergovernmental Panel on Climate Change (IPCC) on the topic of limiting global warming to 1.5°C called for 'strategies for adaptation that are transformational, as well as complex interactions with sustainable development, poverty eradication and reducing inequalities'. It makes clear that what it calls 'past development trajectories' do not go far enough because they 'can constrain adaptation futures by reinforcing dominant political-economic structures and processes, and narrowing option spaces; this leads to maladaptive pathways that preclude alternative, locally relevant and sustainable development initiatives and increase vulnerabilities'.[59] Similarly, the 2019 global assessment report of the Intergovernmental Panel on Biodiversity and Ecosystem Services (IPBES) makes clear that we need 'a change in the definition of what a good quality of life entails – decoupling the idea of a good and meaningful life from ever-increasing material consumption' involving 'alternative models and measures of economic welfare (such as inclusive wealth accounting, natural capital accounts and degrowth models)'.[60] The European Environment Agency's 2019 report states that Europe will not achieve its sustainability goals by continuing to promote economic growth and seeking to manage the environmental and social impacts. Instead it needs fundamental change in the key systems of production and consumption such as food, energy and mobility.[61] Just as Polanyi emphasized the need to supersede capitalism in a new model that embeds the economy in society, which he called socialism, so too do these authoritative reports on the climate crisis point to the urgent need to move to an alternative socio-economic model. However, the outlines of such an alternative model are far from clear. What is clear is that it needs to be an eco-social alternative, weaning society off its addiction to economic growth and ensuring that transformative changes are carried out swiftly to return society to living within the boundaries of the planet.

Conclusions

Following Polanyi, this chapter has shifted the focus from the immediate threats to liberal democracy to examine the state of liberal capitalism since the stresses and strains threatening democracy find their roots there. This focus helps uncover deeper causes associated with the disembedding of the market from society, a process that gathered pace again over recent decades as the communist threat collapsed and social democracy abdicated to the pressures of the free market. The need radically to reduce greenhouse gas emissions and to address the mass extinction of species adds new and urgent pressures, raising growing questions about the future of capitalism itself. Our contemporary period, therefore, reflects in a distinctive and alarming way the conclusions that Polanyi drew almost a century ago about the destructive impact on society and on the natural world when they are made subservient to a self-regulating market mechanism. His response pointed to the need for a socialist future. What this might mean in our contemporary context is the subject of Chapter 4.

4

Mapping an eco-social future

If the ideal of a socialist society dominated progressive politics in the twentieth century, it is ironic that it seemed to disappear from the everyday lexicon of politics in the early twenty-first century just when capitalism began to show signs of self-destruction. As Bregman puts it, 'The left seems to have forgotten the art of politics': 'Sadly the underdog socialist has forgotten that the story of the left ought to be a narrative of hope and progress.'[1] True, recent years have seen the re-emergence of a socialist narrative associated with leaders such as Bernie Sanders in the United States and Jeremy Corbyn in the UK, both of whose legacies continue to exercise major influence even after they leave the centre stage of politics.[2] As mentioned in the last chapter, the idea of socialism seems to be gaining adherents again among the young in particular though what they mean by the term lacks clarity. Yet what this socialist narrative is offering is a return to what would have been mainstream social democratic policies in the 1960s and 1970s – universal healthcare, free education, decent welfare benefits, access to good quality and affordable housing. What it offers is a reformed capitalism at the very time when the system itself is showing signs of fundamental breakdown and society desperately needs new sources of hope amid fears of civilizational collapse. The traditions of socialist thought do remain a rich seedbed to inspire and nourish pathways beyond capitalism, theoretical and practical ideas of how to organize society and the economy to move humanity into a more sustainable future. But what is remarkable is the almost complete absence of any robust socialist alternative from current debates about the rise of the new right and the need to defend liberal democracy. There is a need therefore to critically assess the legacy of socialism and draw from it those elements that can contribute towards transitioning to a more secure, egalitarian and sustainable future.

From the 1920s to the 1960s, Polanyi kept believing in a socialist future and offered rich contributions to mapping out what that might look like. During an era when conceptions of socialism were associated with the dictatorial and repressive societies of 'real existing socialism' in eastern Europe or the accommodations to capitalism that characterized western European social democracy, his conception of socialism remained profoundly democratic, communal and postcapitalist. Although the writings of Karl Marx and his followers were by far the predominant influence on socialist thought throughout the twentieth century, Marx himself offered only the vaguest outline of what a socialist society might look like. By contrast, Polanyi in his extensive writings elaborated on socialist values, individual freedom within socialism and organizing a socialist economy, emphasizing always the centrality of society. This developed a distinctively different understanding to the centralized statist model of socialism that developed in the Soviet Union and other eastern European societies during his lifetime.

This chapter returns to the creative socialist thinking of Polanyi to offer an outline of a distinctive alternative to address the urgent need to move beyond capitalism if we hope to maintain flourishing societies living within planetary boundaries. The chapter begins by examining the crisis of socialism, looking at how and why it ceased to offer a narrative of hope and progress for those on the margins of capitalist society. The following section outlines Polanyi's understanding of socialism, returning to some of the sources that helped him develop his distinctive socialist vision. The third section addresses how Polanyi's ideas offer the basis for a postcapitalist alternative, beyond both Keynesianism and neoliberalism. It discusses an appropriate way to characterize this alternative, whether as a version of socialism or as an eco-social paradigm.

Socialism's demise

The swift demise of socialism as an underlying cultural reference point is well illustrated by Tony Judt's reflection on changes he observed over his teaching career: 'In 1971 almost everyone was, or wanted to be thought, some sort of a "Marxist". By the year 2000, few undergraduates had any idea what that even meant, much less why it was once so appealing.'[3] With the demise of socialism

Mapping an Eco-social Future 61

as a horizon of expectation that society could be fundamentally changed for the better, we are left with a widespread inability to even imagine a better future much less mobilize around achieving it. The German philosopher Axel Honneth draws attention to the puzzling divide in our contemporary societies that has resulted: on the one hand, discontent with capitalism has increased enormously in recent times; yet on the other, this widespread outrage lacks any sense of direction, any capacity 'to think beyond the present and imagine a society beyond capitalism.' This disconnect, which he sees as 'a novel phenomenon in the history of modern societies' he puts down to the fact that socialism has disappeared as the intellectual challenge to capitalism. 'If socialism finds any mention at all in social theory, it is taken for granted that it has outlived its day. It is considered unthinkable that socialism could ever again move the masses or be a viable alternative to contemporary capitalism.'[4] So, why has belief in socialism collapsed so startlingly?

When speaking about the historical legacy of socialism in the twentieth century, it is important to distinguish the state socialism of the communist societies of the USSR and its satellites in eastern Europe from the social democracy that ruled in many western European countries. The collapse of communism in 1989–91, while unexpected at the time, resulted from the rigidities of its state-centric economic model coupled with its declining legitimacy among populations fed up with repression and lack of civil and consumer freedoms. But neither of these reasons applied to social democracy. Yet the decades since communism's collapse have seen the steady decline of support for social democratic parties almost everywhere. The reasons for this warrant some attention as they are widely seen as precluding the possibility of socialism re-emerging as a viable alternative socio-economic project.

Two sets of causes can be identified for the growing crisis of social democracy: firstly fundamental economic changes that undermined its traditional bases of support and, secondly, wider cultural changes that reshaped values and expectations. Among the economic changes was the decline of the traditional working class as manufacturing was replaced by services as the key sector in most industrialized countries and the more liberalized and individualized forms of employment that accompanied this. Meanwhile, following the oil crises of the 1970s and the recessions that followed, more neoliberal ways of governing the economy came to the fore associated with the governments of Margaret Thatcher in the United Kingdom (1979–90) and Ronald Reagan in the United

States (1981–9). These weakened both the base of support for social democratic parties and the power of the state to restrain the market as practised by social democratic governments. A second set of changes was perhaps more decisive for social democracy, as 'fantasies of prosperity and limitless personal advancement displaced all talk of political liberation, social justice or collective action' among a generation that took the benefits of the welfare state for granted but demanded greater personal freedom to pursue goals of self-realization.[5] These found expression in what sometimes was called the 'new left', struggles for women's and gay rights and movements of solidarity with Third World liberation struggles. Although using socialist vocabulary, these attracted a more middle-class base of support very distant from the aspirations and values of traditional working-class militancy.[6] As Nancy Fraser puts it, these movements focused more on recognition than on redistribution and 'were highly critical of the forms of social protection that were institutionalized in the welfare and developmental states of the postwar era': 'Demanding access, as opposed to protection, their paramount aim was not to defend "society" but to overcome domination.'[7] Leaders like Thatcher and Reagan were able to respond discursively to these aspirations, fashioning tropes drawn from Hayek championing individual liberty against the bureaucratic state, and celebrating the consumer free to exercise their choice in the marketplace.[8] This new vision gained hegemony, putting social democracy on the defensive; workers' movements came under sustained attack and engagement in political struggle began to erode as evidenced by declining membership of political parties and turnout in elections in the 1980s.[9] However, the politics of the new social movements proved less stable as a power base to counter the growing power of global market forces, particularly multinational corporations, and the steady erosion of workers' rights as market liberalization advanced. As Judt puts it: 'Laudable goals – fighting climate change, opposing war, advocating public healthcare or penalising bankers – are united by nothing more than the expression of emotion. In our political as in our economic lives, we have become consumers: choosing from a broad gamut of competing objectives, we find it hard to imagine ways or reasons to combine these into a coherent whole.'[10]

Socialist movements responded by initially trying to articulate the liberatory promise of socialism in new ways, such as Eurocommunism in the 1980s marrying communism to democracy, a convergence of Christianity and socialism in liberation theology,[11] or Rudolf Bahro's move from socialist into

Green politics following his expulsion from East Germany in 1979.[12] However, social democratic politics moved in the opposite direction, embracing much of the market-oriented approaches associated with neoliberalism such as labour flexibility, individual choice and bringing the values of private capital into the public sector.[13] This Third Way as it was called[14] particularly influenced the politics of the UK Labour Party under Tony Blair, the US Democratic Party under Bill Clinton and the German Social Democrats under Gerhard Schroeder. However, the result was that social democracy came to be indistinguishable from other neoliberal approaches towards governance. As Judt puts it: 'Without an ideological narrative, and shorn of its self-described "core" constituencies, [Social Democracy] has become something of an orphan in the wake of the euphoric delusions of post-'89.'[15] The essential problem for any of the variants of socialism was the collapse of the core belief that had sustained them, namely that socialism had uncovered the law of history that capitalism would collapse. This secular faith had sustained generations of socialists even when the evidence did not seem to bear it out. However, with the collapse of communism 'there unravelled the whole skein of doctrines which had bound the left together for over a century', writes Judt. 'The absence of a historically-buttressed narrative leaves an empty space' and all that remains is self-interest. 'Without idealism, politics is reduced to a form of social accounting, the day-to-day administration of men and things.' While conservative politics can embrace this approach and even turn it to its advantage, 'for the Left it is a catastrophe'.[16]

However, Judt limits his attention to reviving social democracy, stating explicitly that socialism – as transformative change to replace capitalism with a regime based on a different system of production and ownership – has failed. Amid today's crisis of capitalism and faced with the need to change our systems of production and consumption radically if we are to achieve a low-carbon future, his focus seems a betrayal of the promise of the wider socialist tradition (see Box 4.1 on socialism or barbarism). In this context, what we require is Honneth's objective of refinding socialism's 'vital spark, if only we can manage to extract its core idea from the intellectual context of early industrialism and place it in a new socio-theoretical framework'.[17] To do this, Honneth goes back to what he calls socialism's 'antiquated intellectual structure' to identify its faults and conceptual shortcomings so as to liberate its core insights from the constricting framework in which they originally found expression.

Honneth accepts that the core insight of socialism, turning individual freedom into social freedom through recognizing that human capacities can only flourish in communities, remains entirely valid. Furthermore, he distinguishes this concept of social freedom on the one hand from collectivism, in which individual freedom is extinguished, and on the other from individualism, in which individuals can realize themselves without reference to communities. These ideas were also central to Polanyi's work, as he wrote:

> Socialism is essentially the tendency inherent in an industrial civilization to transcend the self-regulating market by consciously subordinating it to a democratic society. ... From the point of view of the community as a whole, socialism is merely the continuation of that endeavour to make society a distinctively human relationship of persons which in Western Europe was always associated with Christian traditions. From the point of view of the economic system, it is, on the contrary, a radical departure from the immediate past, insofar as it breaks with the attempt to make private money gains the general incentive to productive activities, and does not acknowledge the right of private individuals to dispose of the main instruments of production.[18]

For all the leading socialist thinkers, realizing social freedom required overcoming the constricting nature of the capitalist market economy which was sundering the ties of communal belonging. Yet the problem arises when the socialist aspiration is limited to the workers' struggle to replace capitalism with an economic system based on co-operation rather than private ownership. Honneth identifies three early assumptions that have limited the socialist tradition subsequently: prioritizing the economic sphere as the locus of the struggle for social freedom, identifying an already existing workers' struggle as the means through which social freedom would be achieved and the philosophical conviction that victory was inevitable because it was in line with historical laws that capitalism would be replaced by socialism.[19] The significance of this straitjacket into which the socialist project was born left it with 'a heavy burden that it could no longer so easily shake off'. As a consequence of these assumptions, the socialist movement in its heyday was based on a sense of certainty about historical progress, so that the need for social experimentation and learning was not understood. As Honneth puts it, for decades, this 'deprived socialism of the chance to explore and experiment with different strategies for realising social freedom in the economic sphere'.[20]

Box 4.1 Socialism or barbarism?

'Two spectres are haunting Earth in the twenty-first century: the spectres of ecological catastrophe and automation,' writes Peter Frase in his book *Four Futures: Life after Capitalism* (2016).[21] They point towards opposite futures: climate change towards a future of scarcity, automation towards a future of leisure and of plenty. But many conceptions of what future may emerge are based on a techo-optimism: grand technological schemes such as geo-engineering will solve our emissions problems while robots will do most of the work currently done by humans, allowing us all enjoy life more. What these benign scenarios ignore, says Frase, is that we live in a capitalist society with 'an economy dedicated to maximising profits and growth, and in which money and power are held in the hands of a tiny elite'. Therefore, the futures that emerge will be shaped more by distribution than by technology: 'who will pay the costs of ecological damage and who will enjoy the benefits of a highly productive, automated economy'.[22]

Echoing Honneth and Polanyi on the primacy of community over individual possession, Frase argues that the future therefore depends to a large extent on politics, specifically the politics of power and distribution:

> The question of class power comes down to how we end up tackling the massive inequality of wealth, income, and political power in the world today. To the extent that the rich are able to maintain their power, we will live in a world where they enjoy the benefits of automated production, while the rest of us pay the costs of ecological destruction – if we can survive at all. To the extent that we can move toward a world of greater equality, then the future will be characterised by some combination of shared sacrifice and shared prosperity, depending on where we are on the other ecological dimension.' Frase summarizes the options we face by quoting Rosa Luxemburg: it is either 'transition to socialism or .regression into barbarism.[23]

Bringing society to the fore

A concern for social freedom was at the heart of Polanyi's analysis of the imposition of the market on society and the double movement of reaction to check this. In part, this echoes the early writings of Marx with its emphasis on human alienation as the condition of capitalist society, separating people from one another but also from their own essential nature or being. Polanyi writes that Marx's historic greatness lies in seeing beyond his contemporaries who expressed outrage at the injustice of capitalism since he 'understood that capitalist society is not just unjust but also un-free'.[24] He agreed with Marx that under capitalism workers depend on the means of production which are owned by others and so 'they work under external command' which is degrading. 'Being separated from his product, the worker is in a sense separated from himself,' writes Polanyi.[25] For Marx this is the essence of the lack of freedom under capitalism; however, Polanyi goes much further, broadening the concept of social freedom to include the totality of social relations, the individual freely assuming a responsibility for society:

> Being free therefore no longer means, as in the typical ideology of the bourgeois, to be free *of* duty and responsibility but rather to be free *through* duty and responsibility. ... [I]t is thus not a form of releasing oneself from society but the fundamental form of social connectedness, not the point at which solidarity with others ceases but the point at which we take on the responsibility of social being, which cannot be shifted onto others (emphasis in original).[26]

At the core of Polanyi's understanding of freedom therefore is that it requires assuming the needs of society (see Box 4.2 on Robert Owen and the discovery of society), which finds expression in the many actions that constitute the double movement against the market mechanism. While Polanyi accepts the common socialist understanding that the capitalist market economy undermines society and restricts human wellbeing, his vision of social freedom is not restricted to the productive sphere but focuses on people assuming responsibility for the social effects of their existence which, he says, 'is the final meaning of social freedom'. He illustrates what this involves with the story of the murdered Chinese: if we were given the possibility of immediately having every wish granted by simply pressing a button, but on condition that at each press 400 million people would die in China, he asks how many people would abstain from pressing the button. He says that this story gives a true allegory of the situation in which even the best person finds themselves as they purchase things on the market unaware of the impact this has on peoples and societies far away: today, 'all humanity consists of nameless Chinese whose life he is ready, without batting an eye, to snuff out in order to fulfil his wishes'.[27] While, it can be argued that media saturation today means we are no longer entirely unaware of the consequences of our actions on far-away peoples or on the planet's ecosystems, Polanyi's essential point remains even more valid than ever as we wake up to the devastating impact of human behaviour on our climate and on the planet's biodiversity.[28] The distance between producer and consumer in today's globalized capitalism locks most people into patterns of consumption without assuming responsibility for the consequences of their actions. In reinterpreting freedom to mean social rather than individual freedom, Polanyi therefore offers a strong counter-narrative to the neoliberal focus which reduces freedom to simply a matter of individual choice.

Box 4.2 Robert Owen and the discovery of society

Robert Owen (1771–1858) was, in Dale's words, 'Polanyi's lifelong idol'.[29] This stemmed from seeing him as the first to discover the importance of society. In transforming the village of New Lanark and its cotton mills into a co-operative enterprise, Owen ensured that the profits were invested in improving the lives of the workers and ensuring their health and wellbeing. What impressed Polanyi, and indeed Marx also, was that Owen was pioneering a new form of co-operative socialism, not relying on the state or the market.

As Polanyi wrote about Owen: 'He was deeply aware of the distinction between society and state; while harbouring no prejudice against the latter … he looked to the state merely for that which it could perform: helpful intervention designed to avert harm from the community, emphatically not the organising of society. In the same way he nourished no animosity against the machine the neutral character of which he recognised. Neither the political mechanism of the state, nor the technological apparatus of the machine hid from him *the phenomenon: society*' (emphasis in original).[30]

Owen's innovation of wage tickets, which could be used in the village shop where prices were around 25 per cent lower than elsewhere or exchanged for money, was praised by Marx as a claim to the products of common labour while the co-operative movement which sprang from the example of New Lanark he saw as the 'first examples of the emergence of a new form' the greatest merit of which was 'to practically show the … [possibility of] the republican and beneficent system of the association of free and equal producers'.[31] This was the earliest form of socialism, often called 'utopian socialism'.[32] Polanyi summed up the essential feature of Owen's socialism: 'His socialism, one might say, was based on a reform of human consciousness to be reached through the recognition of the reality of society'.[33]

Polanyi therefore eschewed equating socialism with state power over the economy and society, the dominant view during his time as the Soviet Union institutionalized a highly statist model. Instead, the task that Polanyi sets himself is restoring the fullness of society – its institutions, culture and values – to guide the economy. For Polanyi, socialism is the attempt to build an economic system that will allow a society of rich human relationships to flourish which requires a break with allowing private acquisition to be the main incentive for production. When living in Vienna in the 1920s, he participated in debates where he outlined a functional socialism based on the 'existing capacity of the trade unions, industrial associations, co-operatives and municipalities to contribute to a socialist economy'[34] and to run the economy in a decentralized democratic way.[35] This served clearly to distinguish his conception of socialism from the centrally planned state-run Soviet economy that was emerging at the time. To ensure the economy serves social needs, balancing those of producers and consumers, democratically elected associations of producers would negotiate prices with organized consumer groups under the guidance of what he called the Commune, the organ of central political authority which would own the means of production.[36] He wrote: 'The main point remains that every person present is equally interested in both sides, although his assignment as a negotiating party places him on one side. And now the economic plan is negotiated: one side asks for better and cheaper goods, the other for shorter working times. In the end they agree on a specific working time expressed in minutes and a product series expressed in prices.'[37] In this way, people confront their social problems taking their economic fate directly into their own hands without it being mediated through the state (as in communism) or the market (as in capitalism).

Yet Polanyi also disagreed with what became a widespread suspicion of markets in socialist thought. Although, as outlined in Chapter 1, he saw the commodification of land, labour and money, the 'fictitious commodities', as resulting in the destruction of society, he supports markets for commodities. These would ensure the freedom of the consumer to provide information on demand, to influence producers' income and to serve as an instrument for accounting. It is an economy with markets but not one subservient to the needs of a market system.[38] Thus Polanyi's understanding 'demonstrated quite innovatively how markets could be embedded in, or even *constituted of*, democratic institutions controlled by producers and consumers' (emphasis in original).[39] Furthermore, it is not the state that acts to defend society but, rather, society itself through its self-organizing democratic institutions. Therefore, the free associations of workers, of neighbours, of those in need assume the highest level of responsibility, 'one that only presents itself to the truly free'. This, then, is self-organization in a classless society, with no passing of responsibilities on to other entities. But this 'leap into freedom' is not the end but only the beginning: 'Freedom through social knowledge can never mean a specific state of affairs; rather, it is a programme, a goal which is constantly re-establishing itself. The history of humanity will not have reached its final goal with socialism; humanity's history will, in its true sense, only begin with it.'[40]

This brief outline of some of Polanyi's early ideas shows clearly how they went far beyond social democratic conceptions of taming the excesses of capitalism through the agency of the state. As stated in Chapter 3, one common reading of Polanyi has been to claim him as a champion of the US New Deal or the European welfare state. Block and Somers argue that 'Polanyi's vision depends on the possibility of a political-economic compromise by which businesses would continue to earn profits, but they would accept regulatory restraints, taxation, and the steady expansion of social welfare institutions.'[41] This essentially tames Polanyi, vitiating his critique of its powerful novelty and transformative potential. Furthermore, it reads the double movement as the continuing dynamic of market-state relations rather than as a pendulum to be overcome in the transition to socialism. As Bockman puts it: 'This socialism is not the extension of regulations into the market as in the New Deal and the welfare state, but rather a movement through which the economy and the polity themselves are made social. ... Polanyi seeks to recognise and expand the social, a relational domain. Society *itself* creates markets and democracy simultaneously' (emphasis in original).[42] This expresses well the novelty of Polanyi: it is the self-organizations of society that fashion both state and market ensuring they serve social needs. It is his essential difference from both Keynes and Hayek: it is neither the state's role to hold the market in check as in Keynes, nor the market's role to throw off the constraining hand of the state as in Hayek. It is a totally new vision of the power and potential of society.

Polanyi's socially based conception of socialism helps overcome limitations that Honneth identifies. Its locus is the freedom of the individual as a social being, experimenting with ways to fully assume social responsibility; therefore the working class is just one among many self-organizing associations engaging in a deliberative democracy. Far from being an ultimate victory, this socialism is only the beginning of humans taking their destiny into their own hands. Honneth seeks 'a more universalizable substitute … for all of [socialism's] misleading assumptions about history and social theory'. These he lists as the fact that traditional socialism has limited struggles for social freedom to the economic sphere with no place for recognizing individual rights or intersubjective exploration, it sees the workers' movement as the exclusive vehicle to achieve these and it assumes that laws of history move in this direction. He argues that 'we need complementary ideas that correspond to the more advanced consciousness of our time. Therefore, if socialism is to have a future, it must be revived in a post-Marxist form.'[43] Polanyi's conception of socialism offers such a post-Marxist form, focused as it is on re-embedding the economy in the institutions, values and needs of society, seeing agency as not being limited to workers but taking place through many social movements of both left and right, and setting its face strongly against any view that history is guided by laws. These aren't without their limitations and internal inconsistencies, but they help recapture the 'vital spark' that used to characterize socialism, as shown by the increasing interest in his writings over recent decades.

An eco-social paradigm for a postcapitalist future

We are becoming more and more aware that the defining issues of our times are climate change and biodiversity loss. As the young generation take to the streets demanding actions adequate to the scale of the challenge, Polanyi's words, written almost a century ago, seem remarkably prophetic. Referring to what he calls 'an eerie image' of desperate children in a cage on a cart, rolling towards an abyss, he writes: 'We are all grown-up children of this sort; but we have ourselves built the cage that makes us helpless, and we are also holding up the inclined plane on which the cart rolls, and we have created the gravity, which has become fatal for us. Humanity, even civilised humanity, does not represent a unity. It is not a subject, and if it were then its organisation would not make possible a universal goal nor a development of solidary power.'[44]

Cutting through all the techno-speak that characterizes discourse on climate change,[45] this quote gets us to our essential contemporary reality: we have not shown the ability to undertake the transformations necessary to avoid the grim future that scientists, with ever greater alarm, tell us awaits humanity. If we seem finally to have reached the limits of capitalism, we have also reached the limits of individual freedom, one of the foundations of neoliberal thought and perhaps Hayek's most fundamental assumption. Instead we require a Polanyian understanding of freedom as social responsibility.

Assuming such social responsibility requires new development pathways as the 2018 IPCC report spelled out:

> The profound transformations that would be needed to integrate sustainable development and 1.5°C-compatible pathways call for examining the values, ethics, attitudes and behaviours that underpin societies. Infusing values that promote sustainable development, overcome individual economic interests and go beyond economic growth, encourage desirable and transformative visions, and care for the less fortunate is part and parcel of climate-resilient and sustainable development pathways.[46]

The traditional left-right divide that has provided the organizing principle of political struggle since the French Revolution seems inadequate to address the nature of such a profound transformation. This is partly because of the straitjacket that has limited socialist thought over much of the twentieth century, as outlined in this chapter, and the addiction of both right and left to economic growth, increasingly being recognized as a principal driver of greenhouse gas emissions. Alternative ways of conceiving of the battlelines in contemporary politics are proposed: one of these is migration versus climate,[47] or we might say a right populism versus a climate activism. Shenker writes that 'the politics of space is replacing the traditional politics of class' as 'the old hierarchy of upper, middle and working class, which ranked groups in society as workers and bosses, no longer holds up in the face of a property-based economy where the income from rent far exceeds economic growth and wages'.[48] In this situation, the traditional divide between left and right, socialist and capitalist, seems inadequate to capture the essential nature of the struggle now underway. One way of defining it is through the emerging concept of ecosocialism (see Box 4.3).[49]

Box 4.3 Towards a Red-Green ecosocialism?

The term 'ecosocialism' has emerged to define a form of socialism that seeks to shed the productivism associated with Marxist thought while breaking decisively with central tenets of political ecology that limit themselves to greening capitalism while lacking a radical critique of its political economy.[50] It is sometimes seen as an attempt to combine Red and Green politics into a new synthesis. Löwy defines it as 'an economic policy founded on non-monetary and clearly articulated extra-economic criteria: ecological equilibrium of the earth and fulfilment of the social needs of its people'.[51]

Ecosocialists agree on the need for a new model to replace capitalism with three key elements: socialization of the means of production, democratic economic and social planning, and substantial equality of wealth and income through extensive redistribution.[52] Such a definition, however, hides fundamental difficulties in reconciling socialist and environmentalist approaches.[53] Some of these originate from Marx's central emphasis on liberating productive forces through the workers' struggle to overcome private ownership of the means of production. Environmentalists ask if socialists fully appreciate the need for an equitable downscaling of production and consumption so as to live within planetary boundaries.[54]

In the world of practical politics, the interests of workers' movements to protect jobs and living standards can at times put them in opposition to environmental movements' struggles to close polluting power stations or protect natural habitats from productive exploitation (an example is leaving bogs or forests as carbon sinks instead of utilizing them as productive assets). Differences in political priorities can be another source of tension: is winning state power the priority or creating strong local co-operative economies and cultures? For example, new-left governments in Latin America supported a growth model based on the extraction of natural resources despite rhetorical commitments to the protection of nature.[55]

However, a more Polanyian understanding of socialism seeks to re-embed the market in society through the decommodification of land, labour and money and offers people a secure sense of belonging within flourishing local communities. This has the potential to ground a richer synthesis of the socialist and environmental traditions.

Another way of articulating the central divide in politics today is to use Polanyi's distinction between Improvement and Habitation. Improvement can be summarized as economic progress, fuelled by 'the rich man's desire for a

Mapping an Eco-social Future 73

public improvement which profits him privately' at the price of Habitation or social dislocation, the destruction of the fabric of society 'which the poor had long regarded as theirs and their heirs'.[56] Holmes summarizes them as 'a vision of economic growth, progress and transformation on one hand and of stability and security of livelihood – both physically and psychologically – on the other'.[57] It could simply be stated, in a very Polanyian way, as economy versus society. The pole of Habitation or social flourishing can be well summed up in President Michael D. Higgins's term 'the new ecological-social paradigm' or simply the 'eco-social paradigm'.[58] Paradigms are 'the sources of systems', Donella H. Meadows, one of the authors of the influential 1972 book *Limits to Growth*,[59] reminded us. They are thus harder to change than anything else about systems; paradigm change at a personal level is similar to a conversion experience but systems resist such changes more than anything. So how do you change paradigms she asks, and offers this answer:

> In a nutshell, you keep pointing at the anomalies and failures in the old paradigm, you keep speaking louder and with assurance from the new one, you insert people with the new paradigm in places of public visibility and power. You don't waste time with reactionaries; rather you work with active change agents and with the vast middle ground of people who are open-minded.[60]

It is in fleshing out what this means in practice, based on a deep understanding of human capacities and freedom and on the destructive nature of the market mechanism to society and the human person, that is Polanyi's central contribution. But another theme began to emerge in Polanyi's writings in the post-war period that provides a further and very contemporary strand of analysis, namely the power of technology. 'Industrial technology is showing itself wholly capable of generating suicidal tendencies that strike at the roots of liberty and life itself', he wrote.[61] This echoes Paul Mason's warning of our tendency to give machines autonomy: 'What we do with computers and information networks is only an extension of what we did with windmills, cotton-spinning machines and the combustion engine. But once machines can give themselves instructions, the risk is that humanity steps "to the side" permanently, surrendering control'.[62] And, though Polanyi acknowledged the progress that technology had brought, late in his life he feared that technological civilization was turning 'society itself inside out' as it takes its 'forms and objectives from the needs of the machine'. The only answer for Polanyi was to 'recognise the reality of society and ground our institutional freedoms upon it'.[63] Perhaps the Covid-19 pandemic has given a unique opening for such a fundamental rethinking: 'This is now an opportunity to rethink governance, reclaim agency for communities, build practices of trust and social cohesion, embedded in respect for expert advice,' wrote Australian climate activist Tim Hollo of the pandemic.[64] Neither the state-market pendulum that has dominated society since the Industrial Revolution nor the ever-growing inroads of technology into our lives can provide the basis for human flourishing: only by recognizing the essential requirement for social responsibility, our social freedom, and developing it in social and democratic institutions can we lay the bases for a humane and sustainable future.

Conclusions

This chapter has outlined an eco-social response to the contemporary crisis of capitalism as outlined in Chapter 3. Drawing on Polanyi's distinctive elaboration of what he saw as a socialist alternative, the chapter has shown how it centrally addresses the major limitations of the socialist traditions that have dominated our politics for over a century. Based on a rich understanding of human freedom realized through social responsibility and of the need to re-embed the market so that it serves society rather than destroying it, it offers a narrative to replace the Hayekian narrative that has inspired and underpinned neoliberalism. It thus has the potential to respond to the great crises of our time – climate change and biodiversity loss, and the social dislocations spurring the rise of the new right. At the core of Polanyi's insights were the processes that drive the relationship between state and market, namely commodification and decommodification, particularly the three fictitious commodities of land, labour and money. These are of such central importance to Polanyi's project for society that Part Three devotes a chapter to each. It begins with an introduction outlining what Polanyi meant by commodification and decommodification.

Part Three

From commodification to decommodification

Introduction to Part Three

Commodities are goods produced for sale in the marketplace. Buying such commodities – shopping – is the predominant way in which most people in a modern society gain access to the goods and services necessary for living. We take this so much for granted that we rarely advert to the fact that a tendency exists in capitalist society to extend this practice into more and more areas of life. Where previous generations grew much of the food that the family consumed, made and repaired clothes in the home, and cared in the family for children, the aged and those with disabilities, over time more and more of these activities are provided in the marketplace, purchased with money.[1] The process of commodification, therefore, is an everyday experience in all capitalist societies, shaping the lives of anyone who wishes to participate actively in social activities. The title of this part 'From commodification to decommodification' adverts to this tendency but it does so in a way that suggests the possibility of reversing it, of lessening the dependency of society on markets and on money. As understood by Polanyi, commodification involves a transformation of society based on a change in the motive of action: 'For the motive of subsistence[2] that of gain must be substituted.' Private gain over sufficiency for all therefore lies at the heart of commodification. The introduction of money into all spheres of life is the means:

> All transactions are turned into money transactions, and these in turn require that a medium of exchange be introduced into every articulation of industrial life. All incomes must derive from the sale of something or other, and whatever the actual source of a person's income, it must be regarded as resulting from sale. No less is implied in the simple term 'market system'.[3]

Nancy Fraser draws attention to the consequences of this tendency of market society towards commodification:

> For Polanyi, ... capitalism's inherent tendency to structural crisis is not internal to its economy. It consists, rather, in a set of inter-realm contradictions between the capitalist economy and its natural and social surroundings. In a nutshell: society and nature supply indispensable preconditions for the economy's functioning; yet the latter systematically consumes and degrades them, eventually jeopardising its own operations. What grounds capitalism's propensity for crisis for Polanyi, then, is the inherent tendency of the 'self-regulating market' to destabilize its own conditions of possibility – through the process he calls fictitious commodification.[4]

A central insight of Polanyi's, one that distinguishes him from Marx,[5] is that commodification ends up consuming and degrading the very natural and social conditions required for the economy to function. As we are being alerted with ever-growing alarm to the destructive impact on our ecosystem of the ways many of us live and consume, this central insight of Polanyi takes on added significance. Referring to Polanyi's warnings about the danger of commodifying land and nature, Block and Somers write: 'Today, the scale at which nature is being commodified has expanded to such a degree that planetary annihilation through radical climate change seems almost inevitable.'[6] And as Fraser emphasizes, capitalism's tendency to generate crises arises not from its own internal features but, rather, from how it relates to its natural and social surroundings, systematically consuming and degrading them. The results of this tendency are ever more clearer today as its destructive impacts mount. Yet, Polanyi's major contribution lies in his understanding of the *means* through which this happens. As we saw in Chapter 1, the creation of market society results in social destruction as the commodification of land, labour and money leaves the fate of people and the soil to the market which is tantamount to annihilating them. The central importance of this topic to Polanyi's whole intellectual edifice therefore warrants devoting it greater attention, particularly showing how the process of commodification is key to shaping today's world.

The purpose of this introduction to Part Three is to outline Polanyi's concepts relating to commodification and decommodification. This offers the theoretical framework that will guide the empirical examinations that follow

Introduction to Part Three 79

of land, labour and money in the conditions of contemporary economy and society. In addition to outlining Polanyi's ideas, it also highlights a lack of clarity about their practical application.

Fictitious commodities

For Polanyi, more important than the mechanical inventions of early industrial capitalism was the extension of price-making markets changing land, labour and money into commodities to be bought and sold in the marketplace.[7] It must be remembered that, as Polanyi argued, before the Industrial Revolution markets had never been anything other than 'accessories of economic life ... absorbed in the social system' and compatible with the principles of social behaviour that predominated, such as barter or exchange. Although markets existed, there was no such thing as a market economy 'controlled, regulated, and directed by market prices' and governed by 'this self-regulating mechanism'. The advent of this market mechanism meant that all the elements of industry must be subject to the mechanism of prices and be bought and sold in the marketplace, not just goods but also land, labour and money. Rent is the price for the use of land, wages for the use of labour power and interest for the use of money. This marked 'a complete transformation in the structure of society' since a self-regulating market implied the existence of separate economic institutions rather than the economy being a function of the social order as it had been under all previous economic systems, whether tribal, feudal or mercantile.[8] To include land, labour and money in the market mechanism 'means to subordinate the substance of society itself to the laws of the market'.

The central contradiction for Polanyi is that while the industrial economy needs to treat land, labour and money as commodities, 'they are obviously *not* commodities; the postulate that anything that is bought and sold must have been produced for sale is emphatically untrue in regard to them' (emphasis in original). Labour is only another name for a human activity that goes with life itself, land is another name for nature which is not produced by people, and money is merely a token of exchange and not produced at all but comes into being through banking and state finance. Therefore, 'the commodity description of land, labour and money is entirely fictitious'. And, allowing the market mechanism to be the sole director of human beings, of their natural environment and even of the amount and use of purchasing power 'would result in the demolition of society'. The devastating effects that he foresaw have already been quoted in Chapter 2 and he described them as 'awful beyond description'. 'Human society would have been annihilated but for protective counter-moves which blunted the action of this self-destructive mechanism.'[9] Thus the double movement, already introduced in Chapter 1, was born, namely the self-protective response by forces within society to protect themselves from the destruction being wrought by market forces. As introduced at the end of Chapter 4, this sets up two competing organizing principles for society – the principle of economic liberalism using laissez-faire and free trade as its methods versus the principle of social protection aiming to conserve human beings, nature and productive organizations through the actions of those immediately affected by the market mechanism. Polanyi mentions means such as protective legislation, restrictive associations and other 'instruments of intervention'. He emphasizes class as being important on both sides of this double movement, though he doesn't devote it such central importance as does Marx. The middle classes with their business interests were 'the bearers of the nascent market economy' while the 'labouring people to a small or greater extent became representatives of the common human interests'. To protect land and nature, he saw the landed aristocracy and the peasantry as playing the key role. With the extension of the franchise, he saw these class tensions playing themselves out in government and business, state and industry respectively.[10] However, Polanyi lacks any detailed examination of how social classes drive the double movement, much less any precision about re-embedding the market in society. As Burawoy states, for Polanyi, society is the transcendent historical category, not class. He never addresses how the rupture with market society will take place: 'His failure to interrogate and problematize the transition to socialism is rooted in his failure to appreciate the strength of class *domination*. ... Polanyi overlooks capitalists struggling with all their strength against the abolition of private property or clinging to the pursuit of profit' (emphasis in original).[11] It is somewhat surprising that, while he is very critical of a certain determinism in Marxism emphasizing instead that change comes through the flesh and blood struggles of people, Polanyi himself devoted little attention to the nature of these struggles.[12]

Yet, as Fraser recognizes, 'Polanyi identifies three contradictions of capitalism: the ecological, the social, and the financial, each of which underpins a dimension of crisis. Each contradiction pertains to a necessary condition of production, which the capitalist economy simultaneously needs and tends to erode.'[13] This is what makes his analysis so compelling and so contemporary. He recognized that a fundamental tension lies at the heart of the contending principles he identified and the forces promoting them – the attempts to decommodify land, labour and money through protective measures undermined the efficient workings of the market mechanism and therefore were resisted by those who benefited from it. Polanyi identified three sources of instability between the free market economy and efforts at social protection. The first was that any restrictions on the freedom of the price mechanism introduced rigidity and endangered growth. This has remained a common criticism of socialist policies down to the present day – that they will endanger economic growth. The second divide, that between liberalizing tendencies at international level and national efforts to protect workers and the environment, has emerged as a major tension related to globalization in our day. Indeed, it is central to the famous trilemma of Harvard professor Dani Rodrik that it is impossible to maintain national sovereignty, democratic policies and economic hyperglobalization. Only two can be achieved at any one time.[14] Third is the tension between parliamentary efforts at social protection and business efforts to maintain as much freedom of manoeuvre as possible.[15] As outlined in Chapter 3, the double movement therefore was never overcome and constituted a pendulum which swung between the two extremes throughout the period of industrial capitalism.

However, as critics have pointed out, what Polanyi means by 'the process of decommodification that a socialist transition would entail remained nebulous'.[16] Dale clarifies that Polanyi did not equate decommodification either with re-embedding the market in society or, indeed, with socialism. For example, Polanyi sees the extension of international trade in the 1870s and 1880s as being accompanied by 'protectionist institutions designed to check the all-round action of the market' such as social legislation and customs tariffs.[17] Similarly, he viewed the rise of central banking in the same period as 'essentially a device developed for the purpose of offering protection without which the market would have destroyed its own children, the business enterprises of all kinds'.[18] Clearly this was not socialism, nor does it securely ensure the re-embedding of the market in society since Polanyi traced the ways in which these protective measures failed to avoid 'a complete disorganisation of business and consequent mass unemployment'.[19] Yet, in the aftermath of the Second World War Polanyi seemed more optimistic that the primacy of society over the economy was being secured: while he welcomed the New Deal in the United States he didn't see it as marking a transition to socialism since it was based on private enterprise; however, he was enthusiastic about Labour coming to power in Britain and foresaw 'a rapid transition to a socialist society' there.[20] Although clearly over-optimistic in those predictions, Polanyi was correct in seeing the trend towards what afterwards came to be called 'embedded liberalism', namely the reconciliation of market efficiency with the values of social community.[21] However, by the 1980s it became clear that business interests were beginning again to disembed liberalism. Blyth recognized that by the 1990s 'a new neoliberal institutional order had been established in many advanced capitalist states with remarkable similarities to the regime discredited in the 1930s' so that Polanyi 'had been put into reverse gear'.[22] It therefore remains unclear what would constitute decommodification for Polanyi. More than any clarity on *how* to transition to a society in which again the market was embedded, Polanyi's contribution was to identify three mechanisms through which the economy had been embedded in society. These offer a wider understanding of the market-society relationship that remains very relevant for our times.

Embedding the market in society

Following the writing of *The Great Transformation*, Polanyi spent much of the rest of his life working in Columbia University with a team of economic anthropologists. The purpose was to examine modes of economic organization, specifically the role of markets, money and trade in societies before the advent of the industrial revolution as a way of showing that the imposition of the market mechanism on society at the time of the British Industrial Revolution was an historical novelty. The societies examined included ancient Babylon, classical Greece and Rome, Central and South America before their conquest by Europeans, and Dahomey and the west African slave trade. A primary concern for

Polanyi was to investigate the role the market played and identify what he came to call the 'forms of integration' that embedded the market in society. This work was principally published in three edited books, two of them after Polanyi's death.[23]

This led Polanyi to identify three forms of integration through which the economy was institutionalized to serve society, existing side by side and on different levels in different economic sectors so that it is often impossible to select one as being dominant. He wrote that 'these forms offer a means of describing the economic process in comparatively simple terms, introducing a measure of order into its endless variations'.[24] The three forms of integration are reciprocity, redistribution and exchange. These are different ways in which the exchange of goods and services took place, each requiring different cultural networks and institutional forms. Reciprocity required strong community relationships to exist within a group: 'This was true both of the more permanent communities such as families, tribes, or city states as of those less permanent ones that may be comprised in, and subordinate to, the former,' wrote Polanyi. But it can also exist at least in transitory form, in voluntary or semi-voluntary groupings such as the military, vocational, religious or social groups which 'would form symmetrical groups the members of which practice some sort of mutuality'.[25] Redistribution requires some measure of central power to collect into and distribute from a centre. It occurs 'for many reasons, on all civilizational levels, from the primitive hunting tribe to the vast storage systems of ancient Egypt, Sumeria, Babylonia, or Peru'. It can also take place in smaller groups, such as the Greek estate, the Roman *familia* or the medieval manor. He writes that in non-market societies, these two forms usually occur together. The third form, exchange, requires a system of price-making markets through which the exchange takes place. Polanyi distinguishes this form of market exchange from the operation of the market mechanism:

> Higgling-haggling has been rightly recognised as being of the essence of bargaining behaviour. In order for exchange to be integrative the behaviour of the partners must be oriented on producing a price that is as favourable to each partner as he can make it. Such a behaviour contrasts sharply with that of exchange at a set price.[26]

This form of market exchange, as old as settled human societies, continues to flourish in the bustling markets of towns and cities throughout the developing world, and is beginning to reappear in developed countries in farmers' markets or craft fairs, though perhaps with less 'higgling-haggling' over price. These are markets characterized by human interaction and relationship rather than the impersonal exchange that became dominant in more commodified markets. As Dale summarizes, the locus of reciprocity is the community, the locus of redistribution is the state and the locus of exchange is the market.[27] However, these ideal types are found in very different and intermixed forms in actual practice (see Box III.1 on twentieth-century bureaucracies).

Box III.1 Reciprocity, redistribution and exchange in twentieth-century bureaucracies

Studying the poorly functioning bureaucratic systems of Chile, Mexico and the Soviet Union in the mid-twentieth century, Lomnitz identified informal modes of exchange – reciprocal, redistributive or market modes – as adaptive mechanisms thriving in the interstices of the formal systems. Based on kinship and friendship codes, she writes that these 'may be more essential than ever for gaining an insight into the operation of the economy and the state'.[28]

Examples include the 'debt of honour' in Chile, the *mordita* (bite) in Mexico or the shadow economy in the Soviet Union. Those within the civil service dispense favours to friends and relatives such as jobs, loans, legal preference, bureaucratic favouritism and social introductions. Dispensed without payment, they set up a debt of honour to be discharged in the future. These acquire 'a quasi-ritual character that compensates for the uneasiness the individual is liable to feel about the social system in general'.[29] Where favours are not performed by social equals they exist within a patron-client relationship, a form of redistribution involving 'a downward flow of resources (employment, protection, bureaucratic patronage) in exchange for work and loyalty'.[30] Where bribery is involved, it becomes a market mode of exchange, though one hedged around by social mores, calculated not to embarrass the recipient.

Such modes of exchange not only exist in extensive bureaucratic systems, she argues, but can be found in business and labour groups in developed countries. They exist in liberal democracies, mixed economies dominated by corporative states and in socialist systems. 'In each case, informal-exchange systems based on culturally conditioned forms of sociability have proven surprisingly adaptive and resilient in the face of modernisation and changes in cultural values'.[31] Rooting out such informal modes is one of the purposes of the new managerialism.

Polanyi's categories generated very active debates at the time since they challenged core assumptions in economic history, which equated the existence of money, markets and trade in past historical epochs with the self-regulating market of our time. While some of the empirical details of Polanyi's work have been found faulty, 'he appears to have been more right than he thought about the larger picture'.[32] Over and above debates about the technical nature of forms of integration is the alternative analysis of the role of the economy in social life that he offers, an alternative now finding expression in numerous schemes and projects as the three chapters of this part will outline. Writing in *The Livelihood of Man*, which was published posthumously, Polanyi describes the integrating role the economy can play when embedded in social values and networks rather than dominating them:

> The solidarity of the tribe was cemented by an organisation of the economy that acted to neutralise the disruptive effect of hunger and gain while exploiting to the full the socialising forces inherent in a common economic destiny.[33] The social relations in which the economy was embedded sheltered the disposal over land and labour from the corrosive effects of antagonistic emotions. Thus the integration of man and nature into the economy was largely left to the working of the basic organisation of society, which took care almost incidentally of the economic needs of the group, such as they were.[34]

Conclusion

This introduction has highlighted how, for Polanyi, the commodification of land, labour and money was the central feature of the market society, making society subservient to the needs of the self-regulating economy, and resulting in the devastation of society and nature. Attempts to re-embed the market in society set up the pendulum of the double movement between the laissez-faire economy and efforts at social protection, which has dominated politics since the nineteenth century. In our day we are witnessing efforts to turn back from an intense neoliberalism that has led society to extreme political polarization and is damaging the planet's eco-system to such an extent that the future of human civilization itself is at risk. Examples of these are given in the following chapters before a brief conclusion to Part III summarizes the main lessons.

5

Fictitious commodities: Land

'What we call land is an element of nature inextricably interwoven with man's institutions. To isolate it and form a market for it was perhaps the weirdest of all the undertakings of our ancestors,' wrote Polanyi in *The Great Transformation*.[1] To describe the commodification of land as 'perhaps the weirdest' thing done by our ancestors seems an exaggeration. This may be due to the fact that the significance we attach to land and to our links with nature has grown much weaker as fewer and fewer people live close to the land. More people now live in cities, and even the produce of the land that they consume tends to come from distant places, thereby making obscure any knowledge of who produces it and how. While this serves to cut us off from nature, the climate and biodiversity crises are again highlighting just how dependent we are on nature and its rich ecosystems. The coronavirus also, as George Monbiot has written, 'reminds us that we belong to the material world.[2] This belonging was strongly emphasized in the 2019 IPCC report on land.[3] But the commodification of land and nature is not limited to rural life; this chapter will also examine the impact of land commodification in urban areas and the growing housing crisis that has become a feature of many countries today, the commodification of energy and its consequences, and the commodification of the human person, also a feature of the growing commodification of nature. The chapter will then examine processes of decommodification that are emerging, drawing on a wider set of values beyond the cost-benefit analysis and profit-making that have dominated policy and practice in the neoliberal era.

Commodification and its social consequences

The 2019 IPCC report opens by highlighting the central importance of land for human society:

Land provides the principal basis for human livelihoods and well-being including the supply of food, freshwater and multiple other ecosystem services, as well as biodiversity. Human use directly affects more than 70 per cent of the global, ice-free land surface. Land also plays an important role in the climate system.[4]

Yet the same report provides alarming evidence of how intensive forms of agricultural production are degrading the soil, undermining food security, increasing greenhouse gas emissions, and contributing to declining biodiversity and the loss of natural ecosystems such as forests, grasslands and wetlands. The stability of food supply is expected to decrease as extreme weather events cause greater disruption to food chains while increased atmospheric CO_2 levels can also lower the nutritional quality of crops.

The report identifies the expansion of areas under agriculture and forestry to feed a growing population, including commercial production and enhanced productivity, as the key drivers of the changes they examine. Since 1961, the per capita supply of vegetable oils and meat has more than doubled while that of food calories has increased by about a third; between 25 per cent and 30 per cent of the food produced is lost or wasted. Changes in consumption patterns have contributed to about 2 billion adults being overweight or obese while 821 million people are still undernourished. The report does not explicitly link this to the dominant intensive monocrop agriculture that has been the legacy of Western colonialism and has been further intensified through the liberalization of global trade over recent decades. However, the results it examines derive from what Salleh describes as 'the capitalist economic cycle of extraction > manufacture > transport > market > consumption > disposal [that] creates and maintains a chasm between humans and nature'.[5] This cycle embodies an understanding of the human-nature relationship that she links to commodification:

> Living systems are pulverised into dead matter for turning into commodities. Natural metabolic flows are pulled apart and treated as linear variables. There is little grasp of active human co-evolution with the environment, bypassing the historically gendered, class and racialised origins of economics, to leave a distancing pseudo-scientific vocabulary of 'human capital' and 'natural capital'. The psychology of nature externalisation is assisted by all sorts

of quantifying devices, and this in the face of overwhelming qualitative incommensurables on the ground. This lack of reality testing is exacerbated by the capitalist prioritisation of exchange value and adoption of money as the standard of comparison.[6]

Indian economist Vandana Shiva writes that this industrialization of food and agriculture 'has put the human species on a slippery slope of self-destruction and self-annihilation'. The coronavirus pandemic has dramatically emphasized this: even before it broke out in China in late 2019 research was warning of the links between the unprecedented growth of infectious diseases and industrial scale intensified agricultural methods. Such methods 'have historically come with massive habitat conversion, contamination with animal waste and increasing use of agricultural inputs, such as pesticides and antibiotic growth promoters ... that constitute important sources of emerging infections in humans'.[7] Furthermore, 'The expanded spatial scope and increased frequency, speed and volume of people and agricultural products moving within and among countries necessarily facilitates the spread of pathogens'.[8] Among the steps recommended to combat the growth of diseases is biodiversity conservation, enforcing global regulations to cap antimicrobial use, eating less meat, reducing excess per capita food consumption, and producing food in more urban and suburban environments to enhance local food production.[9] Evolutionary biologist Rob Wallace believes we have been lucky that Covid-19 is not as lethal a virus as others that have emerged such as H7N9 and H5N1 (strains of avian influenza virus) which haven't become pandemics. This gives us time to question our lifestyles and elect politicians who will hold agribusiness to account: 'Hopefully, this will change our notions about agricultural production, land use and conservation'.[10] Shiva argues that biodiverse, ecological and local food systems offer 'security in times of climate insecurity, while producing more food, producing better food, and creating more livelihoods'.[11]

Finally, a shocking example of how commodified agriculture and extractive industries driven by global demand are destroying the planet's ecosystem comes from Brazil (see Box 5.1).

Box 5.1 The Amazon burns: A perfect storm of commodification

The northern hemisphere summer of 2019 saw fires raging throughout the Amazon rainforest with an area of forest the size of Manhattan being lost every day. In August alone more than 30,000 fires were recorded. Travelling almost 2,000 kilometres through the region, journalist Tom Phillips found the main culprits to be soya farmers, mining companies and ranchers availing of the dismantling of Brazil's environmental protections by right-wing President Jair Bolsonaro.[12]

Meanwhile, at the European Parliament in Strasbourg, Members of the European Parliament (MEPs) were debating the EU-Mercosur trade agreement. Some of them made a direct link between the destruction of the Amazon rainforest – the 'lungs of the planet' as one MEP called it – and the demand for Brazilian beef, soya and sugar which will be greatly boosted if the agreement is ratified. Green MEP Yannick Jadot argued that the agreement 'is structurally destructive of Amazonia and structurally climaticide'. Others want to use it to pressure Brazil to reforest, restoring 12 million hectares of forest, and to attain zero illegal deforestation by 2030.[13]

Processes of commodification have also come more and more to reshape our urban landscapes, often to the detriment of local residents. Colin Crouch calls this 'post-democracy' as largely unaccountable, opaque and distant corporate power takes control over the resource and land base of urban areas, as well as over the daily lives of urban dwellers.[14] The evidence is all around us in almost all large cities today as corporate brands such as Starbucks and Nike extend their reach into the urban space, not only resulting in the closure of many local small businesses but also emptying out town centres and changing the very aesthetics of urban landscapes. A large-scale shift of ownership is underway, intensified since the financial crisis of 2008 with global corporate investors buying up large areas of urban space resulting in a shift from largely small private to large corporate ownership.[15] Geographer Paul Chatterton calls this 'the neoliberal city', describing it as 'the corporate takeover of cities'[16] and he identifies its social and environmental impacts:

Cities sit squarely at the heart of a big capital, globalised, competitive, pro-growth economic model. They have increasingly become locked into a fast money, highly volatile inward investment economy, dominated by competition between cities, big brands, zero-hour contracts and low pay, poor skills and educational opportunities. Much of this isn't geared towards the challenges ahead such as community resilience, reducing carbon emissions or narrowing income inequalities. Instead, it instrumentally feeds non-local economies and firms, extracting surplus value from places and stripping them of essential resources.[17]

Inequalities open up therefore both within cities and between them. Those cities which successfully connect to global capital flows experience the gentrification of both commercial and residential areas, catering to the needs of those working in the sectors fuelling economic growth and driving up prices, particularly of housing. But other parts of our cities are increasingly characterized by economic decline and social decay, affecting the quality of life of residents, as seen in poorer health outcomes and higher crime rates. Often there is a racial element to the social divide, with those in the better off areas being predominantly white while more marginalized areas have a more diverse racial makeup.

One of the outcomes of the commodification of our urban spaces that impact on the quality of life of large sectors of the population is what is happening to housing. This begins with the transformation of land from a local resource that could be used for amenities or housing to a speculative asset, often bought up and hoarded in large quantities to be held until maximum profits can be extracted as market conditions permit. This has been greatly intensified as global investors search the globe for profitable locations in which to invest; since the financial crisis of 2008 property has become a very attractive option. Economist Ann Pettifor estimates the value of what she calls 'the Great Wall of Money' at $453 billion (€390 billion) aimed at global markets in real estate. This drives up the price of housing, particularly in countries where prices collapsed due to economic recession. A small country like Ireland is a good example as property prices have been driven to new heights with the influx of global capital. Pettifor says this explains why €4.47 billion was invested in Irish commercial property in 2016, with total turnover 21 per cent higher than the previous year.[18] Average house prices were 56.5 per cent higher by early 2019 from their lowest point in 2013,[19] one of the highest rises in Europe, while average incomes rose by just over 8 per cent over the same period. As a result, the ratio of house prices to average incomes has steadily increased, shutting large sectors of the domestic population out of the housing market. The Irish Central Bank estimates affordability as a ratio of house price to average income of 3:1. By late 2018 this had reached 10:1 in Dublin and up to 14:1 in some areas of the capital.[20] As Irish politician Eoin Ó Broin writes:

> Between the late 1980s and 2018 the decision to invest in building or buying a house was informed as much by considerations of speculative gain as it was home building. As ever expanding financial providers sought out ever more lucrative markets a toxic housing-finance feedback cycle was put in motion, driving up prices and forcing decisions on housing to be made not according to public need or proper planning but on the basis of bottom line return.[21]

Nelson reports how the deterioration in housing affordability is widespread around the world being replicated in the United Kingdom, the United States, Canada, Australia and New Zealand. House prices and household debt multiplied remarkably in Sweden, Norway, France, Chile, Belgium, Israel and Denmark, while dropping in Portugal, Japan and Greece over the period 2000–15. Furthermore, she shows how there are direct connections between housing and the over-use of the Earth's resources. In 2010, she reports, buildings worldwide accounted for 32 per cent of total global energy use, contributing significantly to global warming.[22]

Energy has been the principal driver of global warming, and the consumption and mobility patterns that grew up based on the easy availability of cheap oil, coal and gas have locked society into a deep dependence on fossil fuels. This model has been exported to the developing world with the result that the early 2000s saw the fastest rate of growth in fossil fuel consumption ever recorded, driven by industrial output growth in China and east Asia. Between 1980 and 2015, in the OECD countries industry's share of fossil fuel consumption fell from 40 per cent to 31 per cent while rising from 28 per cent to 52 per cent elsewhere. However, in rich countries, energy consumption continued to rise with electrical and electronic appliances being the main driver. And, while fuel consumption was falling in the developed world, a share of the increased consumption in the developing world is accounted for by the fact that more and more of the goods destined for the developed world are manufactured there. Overall, it is striking that fossil fuels' share of total energy consumption was the same in 2013 as a quarter of a century earlier, at around 82 per cent.[23] A small number of global corporations have controlled the production of fossil fuels, particularly oil and gas, and this has played a central role in ensuring their dominance,[24] though the impact of Covid-19 led analysts to claim the industry faced its gravest challenge in its 100-year history.[25] Indeed, Exxon, then the largest company in the world, was reported to have known as early as 1977 of the link between fossil fuels and global warming yet chose to keep it from the public and from government, though it did share it with other major oil companies, among them Texaco, Shell and Gulf.[26] A decade later, when the issue of global warming came into the public domain, the oil giants funded a campaign to sow doubts about the reliability of the science and to oppose the 1997 Kyoto Protocol to reduce greenhouse gas emissions. McKibbon calls it 'the most consequential cover-up in human history.'[27] It is a classic example of the narrow vested interests that derive from the logic of commodification as neatly summarized by Yeomans: 'The oil industry has dominated global affairs for nearly 150 years. Most of that time, it has been controlled by a small cadre of powerful companies and producing nations that have set prices and production levels to maximize their profits.'[28] Over recent decades, similar processes have been happening to water as global corporations took control of privatized water services. But, as Box 5.2 shows, the fightback has begun.

Box 5.2 Water: From common resource, to economic good, to human right

Water has traditionally been treated as a common resource, access to which is governed by well-established community norms; if these include payment it is for the upkeep of the resource and not for private gain. It was the irrigation commons that has existed in the Swiss village of Törbel for over 500 years that first interested Elinor Ostrom in the issue of the commons for which she was later awarded the Nobel Prize in Economics.

Under the influence of neoliberal thinking water came to be redefined as 'an economic good in all its competing uses' to quote the 1992 Dublin Statement on Water and Sustainable Development. The privatization of water management and services was actively promoted in the developing world by the World Bank, and the EU's Water Directive in 2000 imposed the principle of full cost recovery, imposing cost-benefit criteria on the provision of water services. Defining water as an economic good has been the central justification for the commodification of water services in many countries in both the developing and developed world.

Two UN resolutions in 2010, in the General Assembly and the Council for Human Rights, however, explicitly recognized water as a human right essential for the full enjoyment of life and of all human rights. Implementing such a right in practice is proving contentious despite significant social mobilization in some countries on the issue. A global campaign is seeking an International Protocol to the International Covenant on Economic, Social and Cultural Rights to define international binding norms that states have to apply to implement the human right to water and sanitation, including sanctioning violations.[29] If ratified, this would be a major step in limiting the control of private companies over water resources and services, thus again decommodifying water.

A final dimension of the commodification of nature concerns something that Polanyi could not have imagined: the commodification of parts of the body of a living person. Polanyi saw the commodification of labour as being 'the technical term used for human beings' but he made it clear he was referring to 'the forms of life of the common people', namely human beings in their social context.[30] However, markets have now emerged on which individuals can sell or rent their body parts, which is more correctly seen as another form of the commodification of nature. For example, there is a flourishing market in human kidneys, often sold by desperate people in countries like the Philippines, Brazil, Egypt, Syria and India.[31] Sandel reports that the services of an Indian woman to carry one's baby cost $6,250, about a third of the rate in the United States, and it is perfectly legal. Air New Zealand rented out thirty people to shave their heads and wear temporary tattoos with an ad for the airline.[32] For Sandel, commodifying sex or kidneys allows us to avoid moral judgements: 'Markets don't wag fingers. They don't discriminate between admirable preferences and base ones.' They therefore have served to evacuate public discourse of moral arguments about what constitutes the good life. He goes on: 'But our reluctance to engage in moral and spiritual argument, together with our embrace of markets, has exacted a heavy price: it has drained public discourse of moral and civic energy, and contributed to the technocratic, managerial politics that afflicts many societies today.'[33] Commodification therefore damages society in ways that go beyond its economic impact. Chapter 7 returns to this issue of how commodification corrupts values and our public life.

Decommodification and social wellbeing

Before examining empirically examples of the decommodification of land and nature in today's society, there is a need to clarify what we mean by decommodification. As stated in the introduction to Part Three, Polanyi's writing on the subject is nebulous and he devoted his attention, both theoretically and empirically, to identifying the principles and processes whereby the market could be re-embedded in society, rather than to decommodification per se. However, we can extract from his writings certain principles to inform a more robust understanding of what would constitute processes of decommodification. In outlining his wider understanding of 'the many vital functions of land' over and above the economic function, he is effectively laying out a series of principles as to how society should relate to nature, rather than treating it as a commodity to be bought and sold:

> The economic function is but one of the many vital functions of land. It invests man's life with stability; it is the site of his habitation; it is a condition of his physical safety; it is the landscape and the seasons. We might as well imagine his being born without hands and feet as carrying on his life without land. And yet to separate land from man and to organise a society in such a way as to satisfy the requirements of a real-estate market was a vital part of the utopian concept of a market economy.[34]

We can conclude from this that Polanyi saw land as a public good, the demands of which would require organizing society in a very different way to one organized around its purchase and sale. A second point concerns access to nature as a requirement for people's stability and belonging so that society must ensure this access as much as possible. A third point recognizes the fundamental importance of land and nature to people's personal flourishing, echoing principles of eco-psychology in our time recognizing that personal healing requires healing the land also.[35] A number of principles can be derived from such an understanding of the society-nature relationship:

1. Ownership: while Polanyi does not specify the precise forms of land ownership, his emphasis is on land as a resource for the whole community. He identified the enclosure of the commons in Elizabethan and early modern times in Britain as laying one of the foundations of the market society that emerged with the Industrial Revolution. And, in an article in 1928 on liberal social reforms in England, he juxtaposed contract based on the cash nexus to status based not on money but on social power, rank, influence, respect and responsibility, namely socio-cultural values.[36] So, Polanyi's concern isn't primarily with juridical ownership but with the deeper social value system that governs how people relate to nature.

2. Access: underlying his references to accessing nature is a radically egalitarian ethic, opposed to any forms of enclosure or restrictions of rights for the good of some over the wellbeing of the many. Polanyi's mention of stability, habitation and physical safety implies a rich understanding of personal and communal embeddedness with land and nature which has implications for the links between the production and consumption of the produce of nature. In other words, one can derive a principle of localization, namely that people should have access to the fruits of nature in their locality.

3. Belonging: the word 'habitation' in Polanyi's writings has a particular meaning from which two aspects of decommodification can be derived. Firstly as outlined in Chapter 4, habitation refers to what Hughes calls 'stability and security of livelihood – both physically and psychologically'[37]; Polanyi in his writings dwells more on how this has been destroyed by commodification, which he saw as resulting in 'a catastrophic dislocation of the lives of the common people'.[38] Polanyi therefore emphasizes the need for people to belong securely to a community which provides them not only with a livelihood but also with a sense of respect and belonging. The second aspect derives from the fact that Polanyi counterposed 'improvement' (namely economic progress spurred by the profit motive) and saw it, when not carefully regulated by government, as destroying habitation.

4. Wellbeing: For Polanyi, people's well-being depends on their links to nature. This has implications for urban planning and architecture as well as for leisure activities, and focuses attention on the importance of nature beyond what it produces, thereby providing a value system much broader than that embodied in commodification and the dominance of the cash nexus.

These principles find echoes in the remedies recommended in the 2019 IPCC report on land management and sustainable agriculture. For example, pre-conditions for both reducing greenhouse gas emissions and adapting to the impacts of climate change include reducing inequalities, effective land-use regulation and less resource intensive consumption, including food produced in low-emission systems and lower food waste. The report recognizes that insecure land tenure can affect the ability of people, communities and organizations to make changes to the land that support mitigation and adaptation and, in this context, it recommends such land policies as 'recognition of customary tenure, community mapping, redistribution, decentralisation, co-management and regulation of rental markets' to provide both security and flexibility in responding to climate change.[39] Also recommended is the involvement of local stakeholders in selecting and monitoring land policies, 'particularly those most vulnerable to climate change including indigenous peoples and local communities, women, and the poor and marginalised'.[40]

This points the way to forms of land management and agricultural production that require decommodification. As Badgley states: 'Feeding people receives a lower priority in the current food system than does the profit to be made from the global spread of luxury diets – most of which have deleterious effects on both human and ecosystem health.' She adds that what is required are 'agricultural practices that are more hospitable to native biodiversity than are the industrial methods that prevail today' in order to feed everyone well, to safeguard biodiversity and to provide a decent living for those who produce food.[41] This is consistent with Vandana Shiva's claim, quoted earlier in this chapter, that biodiverse, organic farms and localized food systems offer security in times of climate insecurity and threats of pandemics, producing more and better food, supporting more livelihoods and protecting against new diseases gaining a foothold among humans. This claim has been substantiated by empirical studies: surveying research findings on the benefits of organic farming, Moore finds that in terms of biodiversity, soil, landscape, ground and surface water, climate and air, energy and yield, organic agriculture offers either an alternative to the conventional sector or else lessons for the conventional sector to emulate. Continuing with the conventional model of production and consumption of food 'will continue to add significantly to the transgression of planetary boundaries', he writes.[42] Comparing yields and the use of organically acceptable fertilizers by conventional agriculture and by agro-ecological sustainable practices across a wide range of developed and developing countries, Badgley et al. conclude that 'organic agriculture has the potential to contribute quite substantially to the global food supply while reducing the detrimental environmental impacts of conventional agriculture'.[43] This form of agriculture combines ecological, economic and social regeneration:

> Production per unit area is greater on small farms than on large farms in both developed and developing countries; thus an increase in the number of small farms would also enhance food production. ... [O]rganic production on average requires more hand labour than does conventional production, but the labour is often spread out more evenly over the growing season. This requirement has the potential to alleviate rural unemployment in many areas and to reduce the trend of shantytown construction surrounding many large cities of the developing world. ... Finally production methods are but one component of a sustainable food system. The economic viability of farming methods, land tenure for farmers, accessibility of markets, availability of water, trends in food consumption, and alleviation of poverty are essential to the assessment and promotion of a sustainable food system.[44]

Where can we identify these processes of decommodification happening today? Ecolise is a Europe-wide network of community-led sustainability initiatives with forty-three member organizations in twenty-one countries. Its first Status Report on these initiatives in 2019 offers one overview of the range of such decommodifying processes and their impacts.[45] It describes some of the major networks and movements of community-led initiatives across Europe, many of them linked with networks in other parts of the world. The Transition Towns movement, community-led processes building resilience and self-organization, began in Ireland in the early 2000s but has grown to encompass national hubs in twenty-five countries in Europe, the Americas, Japan, Australia, New Zealand and South Africa. A survey in 2012 identified 1,179 Transition initiatives in twenty-three countries while the Transition Network website reported initiatives in forty-three countries the following year. Ecovillages are intentional communities working to create working models of sustainable living and social wellbeing. It is now a global movement networked as the Global Ecovillage Network which in 2017 listed over 1,000 ecovillages worldwide with 130 of these in Europe. Permaculture is a design system for sustainable and resilient human habitats created in Australia in the 1970s; a global survey in 2016 found it being practised in 141 countries. Community energy initiatives are closely connected with decentralized renewable energy generation; in early 2019 RESCoop, a European federation of renewable energy co-ops, listed 1,500 such co-ops on its website, involving over 1,000,000 citizens though it claims there are around 1,500 other renewable energy co-ops in Europe.

The Social and Solidarity Economy (SSE) is a movement dedicated to creating new economic structures based on cooperation, solidarity and social responsibility, prioritizing social over fiscal goals, and environmental and social ethics over market logic. The Réseau Intercontinental de Promotion de l'Economie Sociale Solidaire is a federation of continental networks in Latin America and the Caribbean, North America, Europe, Africa, Asia and Oceania; a 2015 report studied fifty-five solidarity enterprises in twenty-three EU states most of them in agriculture and the production of organic food, fair trade, critical consumption and sustainable lifestyles. It estimated that the solidarity economy worldwide employs 15 million people, representing 6.5 per cent of the total labour force. SSE also practises the democratic decision-making advocated by Polanyi, as seen in Chapter 4, and operates within 'conceptualisations of economies as embedded, plural institutions that include economic relations based on market exchange, but also redistribution, householding and reciprocity as substantive alternatives to the utopia of the self-regulating free market promoted by neoliberals', writes North.[46] The concept of the commons as 'social spheres of life the main characteristics of which are to provide various degrees of protection from the market' has also come to the fore as a way of grouping such practices as time banks, urban gardens, land and urban squats, food coops, local currencies, 'creative commons' licences, and bartering practices as they represent collective forms of self-reproduction outside the logic of markets.[47] It shows the diversity of forms that decommodification is taking while focusing attention on the many contemporary social struggles constructing and reproducing the commons,[48] an alternative paradigm that one scholar believes 'conforms to the vision of Karl Polanyi'.[49]

Community-led initiatives have been found to have beneficial effects on social capital; social inclusion; participation, volunteering and employment; economic regeneration; skills development and community empowerment. A study of twenty-three ecovillages and co-housing initiatives found that their ecological footprints were on average around half those of similar communities in their regions or countries. The Ecolise report concludes that community-led initiatives are 'actively envisioning, creating and living within alternatives that are rooted in fundamental ethical commitments to sustainability, equality and social justice'. Largely located on the margins of society, 'they are far from realising their potential as catalysts for society-wide transformation'.[50] But they are also showing in practice the transformations that will be required of agriculture and land management as the conventional forms become ever more unsustainable.

Awareness of the unsustainable nature of conventional agriculture is also driving change. As Crabb and Thorogood point out: 'European government policies have created a subsidised farming system that does not recognise locally sustainable farming practises and overlooks environmental and cultural degradation. This, combined with the free market and globalisation polices, has allowed an influx of cheap imported goods that undermine local markets and carry a high carbon cost due to unsustainable production, transport and refrigeration.'[51] This conventional system is now facing multiple pressures coming from rising oil prices, pressures to reduce greenhouse gas emissions, avoiding new disease strains emerging, soil degradation, climate impacts and the vulnerabilities of long supply chains. As Box 5.3 shows, the externalization of costs is also becoming more evident and pressure for change is mounting.

Box 5.3 Public bears costs of industrial-scale farming

Intensive industrial-scale farming is doubling the cost of food for UK consumers according to a report from the Sustainable Food Trust.[52] For every £1 spent on food, an additional 50p is spent on the externalities created by intensive food production such as environmental pollution, soil degradation, biodiversity loss and health impacts. Healthcare costs related to poor diets add another 37p; most of this additional spending is being paid through taxation, water charges, private healthcare and lost income. Overall, the report estimates that, in addition to the £120 billion spent annually on food in the UK, costs totalling an additional £120 billion are generated.

At the report launch in 2017, Professor Jules Pretty of the University of Essex called for a redesign of Britain's agricultural and food systems to set agriculture on a journey towards sustainability and to set food and environmental targets to achieve much wider social benefits. Overall, the report showed that it is more profitable to produce and distribute food in damaging ways while many food producers pass this cost of environmentally damaging practices to the public sector.

One example of this pressure for change is the report written for the UK Labour party in 2019 entitled *Land for the Many*.[53] This traces some of the costs of the commodification of land such that land values in the UK have risen by 412 per cent since 1995 and that planning permission can increase the value of land 250-fold. To address this, the report makes a list of recommendations focusing not only on stabilizing the price of land and reforming the tax system – to discourage the use of homes as financial assets while reducing the tax paid by the majority of households – but also to democratize development and planning, giving citizens much more of a say in creating local land plans; to facilitate community ownership and control of land trusts, and to facilitate co-housing; to give Councils more powers to create more public green spaces; and to widen access to farming.

In urban areas also, pressure for change has resulted in some promising initiatives. Examining responses to the challenges today around access to housing, Nelson traces how, in many countries, governments moved away from providing public housing. Some public authorities began to support types of collaborative housing since the 1980s but Nelson shows how outcomes were very mixed. They depended on whether the community could drive them or whether government allowed developers to cherry pick what would be profitable. She cites Berlin city government's support for eco-collaborative housing responding to grassroots demand as a particularly successful example. But what Nelson calls 'the current state of flux' means that more market-led models have come to the fore over recent times. However, she also identifies grassroots strategies defined by relative autonomy from the market and the state such as Tinkers Bubble in Somerset (UK), Twin Oakes in Virginia (United States), ufaFabrik in Berlin, Christiania in Copenhagen and Calafou in Catalonia. These illustrate how 'alternative communities and neighbourhoods have developed and refined more equitable, income-sharing, financial arrangements, and horizontal decision-making techniques to support their existence to persist, and even blossom, in undoubtedly troubled times'.[54] Thus, in urban areas also, processes of decommodification are emerging on the margins of the dominant system of ownership and regulation, what Chatterton describes as 'the decoupling of work and life in the contemporary city from the logic of capital'.[55] The Covid-19 pandemic may strengthen these, as Shenker writes:

> The vulnerability of many fellow city dwellers has been thrown into sharp relief, from elderly people needing social care to the low-paid and

self-employed without a financial buffer to fall back on, but upon whose work we all rely. A stronger sense of society could lead to a long-term increase in demands for more interventionist measures to protect citizens. This may be harder for governments to resist given their readiness in the midst of coronavirus to override markets.[56]

Conclusions

While the logic of commodification has come to exercise tight control over large sectors of the natural world, a fightback against this is also clearly evident. At the heart of these struggles is the rejection of the principle of private gain as the dominant incentive governing society's relationship to nature; instead a wider value system valuing nature for itself is motivating many different groups to find forms of land management, production and consumption that achieve a regenerative balance between humans and the natural world. This can be called a motive of subsistence, as Polanyi did, if by this we mean achieving sufficient to live while safeguarding balance and regeneration. In many ways this is returning to the society-nature relationship that characterized many societies before the Industrial Revolution. Although the terms 'commodification' and 'decommodification' are unwieldy and can be opaque to many, they serve to make visible the processes that are destroying society and the natural world. This makes clear that nothing less than thorough processes of decommodification, drawing on wider value systems more deeply rooted in the history of humanity, is sufficient at this time of human history. Following Polanyi, the next chapter examines the topic of labour under the same optic.

6

Fictitious commodities: Labour

In discussing labour as a fictitious commodity, Polanyi makes clear that he is referring to far more than workers' conditions of employment. As he writes: 'If labour is to be handled as a commodity then, the vast majority of human society … must be at the disposal of the market on which that fictitious commodity is being bartered. Now, nothing could be more contrary to the traditional organisation of human society than the existence of such a market.'[1] His focus is therefore wider, namely the means through which people earn a livelihood and how society is organized around this. Just as with the commodification of land and nature as discussed in the previous chapter, Polanyi understood that treating workers as commodities selling their labour power on the market was a 'tremendous innovation' since it involved 'the destruction of the traditional organisation of society with its security from starvation.'[2] Here he was referring to the Poor Laws in England which made the parish responsible for ensuring that people didn't starve; their repeal in 1834 did away with this 'right to live' and removed 'this obstacle to the new capitalistic economy'.[3] The result was that people's livelihoods and the wellbeing of society were now dependent on the market mechanism. He made clear that previously there was the occasional hiring of some types of labour and some individuals did earn their living by selling their labour, but for most people 'economic life is embedded in social relations … regulated by a variety of motives none of which bears more than a faint resemblance to profit or gain'. Now, however, the 'social cutting edge' of the system became fear of starvation.[4] With this new situation came 'the incomprehensible fact that poverty seemed to go with plenty' so that 'it was in relation to the problem of poverty that people began to explore the meaning of life in a complex society'.[5]

This, then, was Polanyi's understanding of the commodification of labour. However, a counter-movement in the form of factory legislation and social laws soon emerged to protect society from the destructive impacts of the market mechanism. The purpose of this chapter is to trace this double movement of commodification and decommodification of labour as it has played itself out over the decades of neoliberalism and the attempts to resist and turn it back. It begins by examining debates on the meaning of poverty and how these illuminate the challenge of decommodification. The chapter then traces the attempts at social protection through the extension of the welfare state and how the market mechanism managed to blunt these and integrate them into a marketized logic. The following section turns its attention to various forms of inequality, seeing there a site of struggle in the double movement of commodification and decommodification. The challenges of automation are discussed in the next section before finishing with the emergence of social struggle against marketization.

Poverty amid plenty

The fact of poverty amid plenty was, for Polanyi, one of the 'baffling paradoxes'[6] of industrial society and has been a regular topic of social debate since. For example, the mid-2000s saw a transnational social movement dedicated to 'Make Poverty History'[7] and around the same time the World Bank placed a logo proclaiming 'Our dream is a world free of poverty' on various of its publications.[8] A decade later, the international development agency Oxfam was celebrating the success of halving extreme poverty since 2000 based on the fact that the numbers living on less than $1.25 a day has declined by millions and that more children are going to school and more families have access to healthcare and sanitation.[9] However, from a Polanyian perspective, these claims need to be interrogated in two ways. Firstly, does a measure of poverty based on levels of monetary income tell us anything very important about the quality of life of those most marginalized? For example, the World Bank's measure is not based on whether it is sufficient to meet poor people's basic needs or not. Hickel points out that the World Bank's claim that 700 million live in poverty (based on a poverty line of $1.90 a day) contrasts with the Food and Agriculture Organisation's estimate that 815 million people do not have enough calories to sustain even minimal human activity, that 1.5

billion are food insecure and 2.1 billion suffer from malnutrition.[10] Indeed, the World Bank's own survey of poor people's views found that risk and volatility of incomes on the one hand and lack of political power on the other concerned poor people more than did low incomes.[11] As was noted, 'frequently the idea of a secure livelihood is perceived as more important than maximising income, and thus the local understandings of people about their livelihoods have more to do with vulnerability than poverty'.[12] Polanyi, in contesting arguments that the Industrial Revolution improved the living standards of the poor, shared such an understanding. He argued that 'a social calamity is primarily a cultural not an economic phenomenon that can be measured by income figures or population statistics', being caused much more by 'a change in the position of a class within the confines of society'.[13] Polanyi's understanding therefore is much closer to the lived experience of the poor today than is that of the World Bank echoed by Oxfam, and is based primarily on social exclusion and powerlessness rather than income levels. Secondly, for the World Bank, the way to reduce poverty is to extend economic liberalization which produces economic growth which, in turn, benefits the poor. The World Bank further recommends measures to ensure the poor benefit from growth such as building up their assets and increasing the returns to them, but the central driver of poverty reduction is extending reliance on the market mechanism[14] which, as argued in Chapter 2, is deepening social fragmentation and exclusion.

As this discussion shows, Polanyi was correct to say that poverty is an issue that helps us explore the meaning of life in a complex society. While an income-based approach remains influential, a wider range of approaches has broadened how poverty is understood. The capability approach pioneered by Nobel Economics prizewinner Amartya Sen looks at social and community factors such as healthcare, education, and law and order, all of which affect people's 'capability to lead the kind of lives we have reason to value'.[15] A more social understanding has become influential within the European Union focusing on social inclusion, including employment, access to housing, minimal income, citizenship, democratic rights and social contacts. Finally, a participatory approach seeks to give voice to the poor and empower them to address class barriers and racial discrimination.[16] However, despite a broader understanding of poverty, the means to address it remain constrained by neoliberal approaches to economic management. Mkandawire sees in the focus on 'poverty reduction' a narrowing of the remit of social policy: instead of being a central dimension of socio-economic policies to achieve social development and equity throughout society, social policies are narrowed to a focus on reducing poverty while overall social development is designed to boost economic growth through market liberalization.[17] A focus on poverty therefore is another example of Polanyi's central insight about making the fate of society dependent on market forces. And, as Gough points out, evidence shows that global growth since the mid-1990s has been highly inequitable with the poorest third of the global population receiving just 1.2 per cent of the additional income generated between 1999 and 2008, the poorest 60 per cent receiving just 5 per cent, and the richest 40 per cent receiving 95 per cent. Continuing to reduce poverty in this business-as-usual way 'would devastate the planet', he writes, because it would need global GDP to increase by fifteen times. He concludes: 'Either new forms of redistribution or a shift to an alternative economic pathway is required.'[18] Box 6.1 shows one alternative economic pathway.

Box 6.1 Living well, below the poverty line

US political scientist Karen Litfin visited fourteen ecovillages around the world to research how they 'reinvent life from the ground up', as she put it, weaving together 'the various strands of sustainability into integrated wholes at the level of everyday life'.[19] Among the lessons she learnt was an answer to the question 'What do I need?' Under the logic of consumerism, the normal answer to this is 'more', she writes, but for ecovillagers it is 'more time, more intimacy, more integration – and less stuff'. This is because their needs are best met in community and substantially outside the cash economy.

This has implications for poverty: 'In the affluent countries, many ecovillagers are living comfortably on incomes that place them well below the poverty line. Their secret? A combination of self-sufficiency, sharing, and elegant simplicity.'[20] If humanity is to avoid systemic collapse, she believes that the lessons she learnt have to be upscaled for the whole of society: 'They are creating parallel structures for self-governance within the prevailing social order while demonstrating how to live well with less.'[21] It shows how, within a decommodified community, poverty can morph into simple living.

Re-making the welfare state

While, as Polanyi pointed out, various state initiatives since the late nineteenth century introduced measures to protect people from dislocations caused by commodification, it was the growth of the welfare state in the decades after the Second World War that saw these developed most extensively. These were based on the premise that citizenship confers social rights so that, in Esping-Andersen's words, 'a person can maintain a livelihood without reliance on the market'.[22] While some countries, most especially those in Scandinavia, moved towards this level of decommodification in the late 1960s and 1970s, most developed capitalist countries ended up with a mix of state, market and family provision that fell far short of decommodification. Esping-Andersen developed a typology of the three worlds of welfare capitalism, based on the very different ways in which countries sought to modify complete dependence on the market for people's livelihoods. The liberal welfare state, which predominated in the Anglo-Saxon world, minimized decommodification effects through means-testing assistance, and ensuring universal transfers or social insurance were modest. The corporatist welfare states such as Germany, Austria, France and Italy relied on social insurance and therefore benefits were almost entirely dependent on contributions, again greatly limiting the extent to which the system offered an alternative to the market. The more universalistic social democratic welfare states that offered universal and generous benefits went furthest in decommodifying, though the extent to which they achieved this depended on how far they went in providing an alternative to reliance on the market. Thus welfare states, even at their height, relied on 'qualitatively different arrangements between state, market, and the family'.[23] However, they offer some of the best examples of the principle of redistribution which, as seen in the Introduction to Part Three, was one of the forms of integrating the market into society identified by Polanyi.

According to Esping-Andersen, the extent of decommodification achieved depended on three elements: the rules that govern people's access to benefits, the amount of their market-based income that benefits would replace and the range of entitlements provided, in particular whether they cover the basic social risks of unemployment, disability, sickness and old age. The crucial dimension was the degree of market-independence provided for an average worker. Measuring the extent of decommodification achieved in 1980 by old-age benefits, sickness benefits and unemployment insurance, he drew up a decommodification score for eighteen developed countries, grouping them according to the three types of welfare capitalism as shown in Table 6.1.

Table 6.1 Decommodification index

Decommodification	1980
Australia	13.0
United States	13.8
New Zealand	17.1
Canada	22.0
Ireland	23.3
United Kingdom	23.4
Italy	24.1
Japan	27.1
France	27.5
Germany	27.7
Finland	29.2
Switzerland	29.8
Austria	31.1
Belgium	32.4
Netherlands	32.4
Denmark	38.1
Norway	38.3
Sweden	39.1
Mean	27.2

Data sourced from: Esping-Andersen, 1990: 52.

However, the year 1980 probably marked the high-point of the post-war welfare state. As Gough puts it, 'things began to change in the late 1970s' as a counter-movement against the welfare state began to be seen throughout the OECD countries.[24] This was partly ideological, associated with the Reagan and Thatcher governments' belief in the superiority of markets and seeing the state as a hindrance to economic efficiency. But it was also due to major changes in the organization of work and the globalization of production. Labour markets began to fragment, putting new pressure on welfare systems as new forms of flexible, temporary and atypical employment generated new forms of insecurity. Competition among countries for foreign investment resulted in pressure to reduce tax levels thereby undermining the investment required for generous social benefits. This resulted in reforms to welfare states reversing the process of decommodification and initiating a recommodification, re-instating the discipline of labour market competition on workers but also new forms of administrative control, often through conditions attached to welfare benefits.[25] While social expenditure in the OECD remained substantial at around 20 per cent of GDP,[26] benefits were being re-designed to relieve the state of its responsibility and instead emphasize freedom, choice and individualism, what Holmes calls 'the language of consumerism and the market'.[27] Not only was the relationship between the individual, the state and the market reconfigured but the meaning of welfare was transformed with the individual being pressured to become entrepreneurial, risk-savvy, self-interested, prudent and responsible. Instead of protecting the individual from market pressures, the welfare system came more and more to function as a means of forcing the individual into reliance on the market.

Once the coronavirus hit in early 2020, government responses were initially slow and inept but, under pressure from businesses and trade unions, unprecedented levels of support were quickly introduced giving businesses easy access to credit and income supports to workers. This showed the ability of developed states to step in decisively when required to do so, throwing massive resources to support the economy against what was being feared would be the greatest recession since the Great Depression.[28] This involved not only mobilizing huge sums of money that add greatly to levels of public debt, but also commandeering private facilities for public uses (hospitals and morgues). President Trump even ordered Ford and General Motors to manufacture badly needed ventilators for hospitals. This 'suspension of orthodoxy' was seen as marking a 'once in a generation shift in economic policy reversing the earlier conjunctural shift against state ownership, control and service provision inaugurated by Thatcher and Reagan in the 1980s'.[29] The pandemic also served to make evident the 'systemic fragility and vulnerability' in public services

110   *Karl Polanyi and the Contemporary Political Crisis*

and provision brought about by years of underfunding and austerity, thereby making them unprepared for the crisis when it hit. As the Foundational Economy Collective put it: 'The implication is not only that certain sections of the economy are not suited to marketable provision; but also, that we need a new and different way of thinking about what effectiveness, efficiency or "value for money" looks like',[30] marking a shift in emphasis from commodification to decommodification.

However, this did not overcome tensions between decommodification and recommodification within the welfare system itself. This had been most evident in the world of work as precarious forms of employment are increasingly becoming the norm to which social protection systems must adjust. Precarious work includes part-time, temporary and zero-hours contracts associated with low-pay, insufficient and variable hours and limited social protection rights, often originating in the gig economy but increasingly evident in mainstream employments such as education and healthcare. Rubery et al. study how six countries – Denmark, France, Germany, Slovenia, Spain and the UK – seek to respond. They find that traditional protections tend not to be extended to precarious work or are not flexible enough for the needs of those not able to take up standard employment. Instead, they find people being pushed into precarious employment by welfare conditions that limit benefits or facilitate people to take up work while keeping some benefits. Thus a complex mix of decommodification alongside recommodification is taking place. During the Covid-19 pandemic, it became obvious that the extensive supports given to some economic sectors and workers didn't extend to all. In the United States, for example, it was estimated that more than a quarter of private-sector workers could not claim time off for sickness, forcing them to stay working even if showing symptoms of the virus. Many others lost their health insurance as soon as they were laid off.[31] In the UK, stories of vulnerable workers being laid off by businesses that could avail of government supports led columnist Owen Jones to describe coronavirus as 'not some great leveller: it is an amplifier of existing inequalities, injustices and insecurities. … In the age of Covid-19, the rubble of economic collapse will fall on those who suffered the most from the last crash: the young, the precarious, the low-paid.'[32]

Beyond the technical issues involved, however, these contradictions 'are the consequence of the state's political orientations towards work disciplining of the unemployed or allowing employers to renege on their traditional employment guarantees and responsibilities.'[33] What is being weakened therefore is not just the generosity of benefits but, more significantly, the rationale for such payments so that the welfare system itself acts as a significant agent of recommodification. In this situation, the proposal for a universal basic income has gained momentum (Box 6.2). It was one measure considered during the coronavirus pandemic but in limited form. In the United States, it won favour with both Democrats and Republicans though seen as a once-off payment to households,[34] while in Spain what was agreed in principle by the governing left-wing coalition was far from being a universal payment and was expected to benefit only around 1 million households.[35]

Box 6.2 Decommodification through a basic income for all?

As welfare systems provide less and less protection particularly for vulnerable groups, the idea of the state paying all citizens a Universal Basic Income (UBI) has gained wide adherence. Pilot projects have been introduced in a number of countries, some being funded not by the state but by charities, as in India and Kenya. Alaska pays $1,600 annually to all adults and children from its oil revenues while Finland undertook a two-year trial in 2017–18. The UBI is promoted as a guaranteed income for all, helping reduce poverty and inequality, address the threats of automation and free people from the pressure to take insecure, low-paid jobs.

A 2019 study by Public Services International examined for the first time the sixteen pilot projects already undertaken and found some major problems. Central to these is that most payments are well below the poverty line and therefore were found to do little to reduce poverty, inequality or job insecurity. The International Labour Office estimates that paying a UBI at a level to provide people with a sufficient income would cost between 20 per cent and 30 per cent of GDP, thereby leaving little social expenditure for health, education, housing and other needs.

The report recommends that the money 'would be better spent on reforming social protection systems, and building more and better-quality public services'.[36] As Pavanelli, general secretary of PSI, puts it: 'A UBI without public services is a neoliberal's paradise.'[37] Ann Pettifor endorses this, seeing public services as giving 'the means to build cooperation and solidarity'.[38]

Inequality and its discontents

One of the most striking consequences of the recommodification of labour over recent decades is the growth in inequality, namely the gap between those on highest incomes and the rest. Attention has been focused on the income growth of those at the top, often called the 1 per cent versus the 99 per cent. For example, Piketty finds 'an explosion of US inequality after 1980' due to 'the rise of supersalaries' largely due to 'the emergence of extremely high remunerations at the summit of the wage hierarchy, particularly among top managers of large firms'.[39] He finds similar processes in Anglo-Saxon countries (Canada, UK, Australia and New Zealand), in Japan and in continental Europe though the scale has been less than in the United States. He concludes: 'The higher one climbs in the income hierarchy, the more spectacular the raises.'[40] On wealth inequality (and incomes derived from capital), Piketty finds it greater in the United States today than at the beginning of the nineteenth century and there was far less deconcentration of wealth than in Europe during the twentieth century. In Europe, the concentration of wealth fell substantially in the twentieth century and, though rising again, has not reached the heights of the United States, though he predicts a significant increase this century. These trends can be directly correlated with a decline in redistributive taxation as labour became recommodified and the welfare state reconfigured to serve that end. In the United States, Leonhardt reports that the overall tax rate on the richest 400 households declined from 70 per cent in 1950 to 47 per cent in 1980 to 23 per cent in 2018 while middle income and poor families have seen only a modest decline in income taxes but pay more in taxes to fund health and social security. In twenty developed countries, the top rate of personal income tax declined from 62 per cent in 1970 to 38 per cent in 2013.[41] Meanwhile estate and corporate taxes on wealth and profits have plummeted, as data for twenty developed countries show in Figure 6.1.[42]

In the 1980s the focus on inequality began to change from the rich-poor divide to focus on diversity and the access of women, racial minorities and the LGBTQ community to equal rights, so-called identity politics.[43] The emerging recognition of the 'considerable disparities between how much

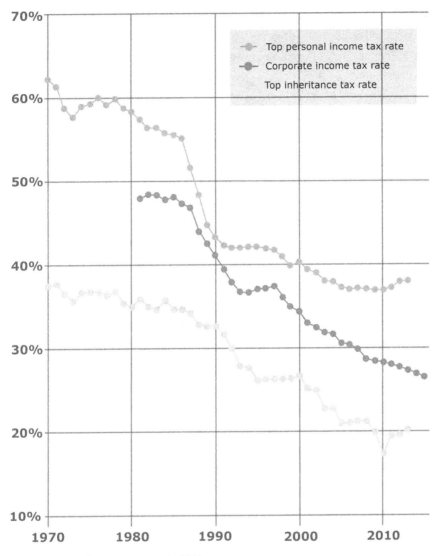

Figure 6.1 Declining taxes, 1970–2012
Source: *Public Good or Private Wealth*, Oxfam, 2019: 24 (Figures 6.1 and 6.2 reproduce material from two Oxfam publications and is used with the permission of Oxfam, Oxfam House, John Smith Drive, Cowley, Oxford OX4 2JY, UK www.oxfam.org.uk. Oxfam does not necessarily endorse any text or activities that accompany the materials).

women contribute to human development and how little they share in its benefits', as the 1995 *Human Development Report* stated, focused attention on the gendered nature of inequality which had been largely hidden.[44] Here too, processes of commodification are evident. Care work, in which women predominate, covers 'an incredibly wide range of social reproduction activities, ranging from highly intimate social, health and sexual care services to less intimate ones such as cooking, cleaning, ironing and general maintenance work offered on a waged and/or non-waged basis in domestic and/or institutional settings'.[45] Yeates traces ways in which this is being commodified as women are seen as a source of cheap and available labour, and emphasizes the role of social policy in facilitating this commodification through, for example, welfare-to-work programmes. Studies show how elder care is being gradually redefined not as a public service but as a commodity increasingly governed by market-like mechanisms.[46] In Australia, elder care is becoming 'more a commodity than a relationship' bringing 'a concern for finance capital and efficiency into one of the most intimate corners of our life'.[47] An often hidden racialized strand is also being uncovered. Women of colour are disproportionately affected by cutbacks since they are more likely to be living in the poorest households, and to be unemployed, underemployed or in low-skilled and low-paid jobs.[48] Migrants are also found to be 'centrally implicated in highly precarious work experiences at the bottom end of labour markets' including being trapped in forced labour, what is called 'hyper-precariety'.[49] These examples bring to visibility the hidden gendered and racialized impacts of commodification.

The rise of the welfare state helped, in its heyday, modify some of the worst excesses of inequality. Writing about the most successful examples, the Nordic countries, Toivanen concludes that this resulted in some of the most equal distributions of income and highest living standards in the world, but this lasted only a generation or two. Since the implementation of neoliberalism, this has been largely reversed:

> State-mechanisms are increasingly used to attack the state owned enterprises: public infrastructure, affordable public housing, pension funds, education, healthcare and so on. Simultaneously, the social security system is cut down and social control of labour is tightened with the result that the already precarious labour force is again increasingly commodified.[50]

As Polanyi recognized, these processes of recommodification impact not just those directly affected but the health of society as a whole. For example, Wilkinson and Pickett have produced extensive data showing the impacts of inequality on levels of trust in society, on mental illness (including drug and alcohol addiction), on life expectancy and infant mortality, on obesity, on children's educational performance, on teenage births, on homicides, on imprisonment rates and on social mobility.[51]

Climate change has also been linked to economic inequality as it has been estimated that the richest 10 per cent of the world's population is responsible for around 50 per cent of global emissions while half the world's population accounts for only 10 per cent as shown in Figure 6.2. Climate scientist Kevin Anderson has said that reducing the carbon emissions of wealthy people to the European average would go a long way to resolving the world's carbon emissions. However, progress is hampered by what he called the 'Davos mentality', characterized by economic growth linked to high inequality and a 'because we're worth it' mentality.[52] This echoes Polanyi writing in 1934–5 about the commodification of labour: 'The anti-working class feeling now hardened into a metaphysical conviction of the moral superiority of the owning classes over the propertyless classes and the corresponding human inferiority of the latter as compared with the former.'[53]

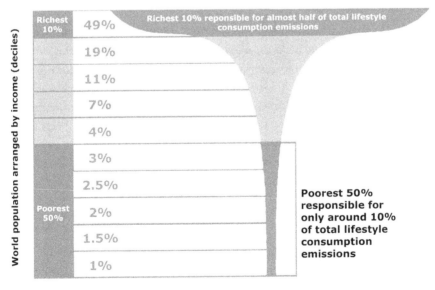

Figure 6.2 Inequality and carbon emissions
Source: 'Extreme Carbon Inequality', Oxfam, 2015: 4.

Machines threaten

As mentioned in Chapter 1, robotization and AI are now widely seen as constituting a major new threat to labour. This echoes Polanyi's warnings about the 'subordination of man to the needs of the machine'.[54] In our time, a similar concern is raised by Paul Mason when he writes about the dangers of 'machine control'; however, he elevates the threat beyond what Polanyi feared. While industrial civilization gave machines 'temporary and limited autonomy', the 'dangers of algorithmic control' pose the challenge 'to place the new technology of intelligent machines under human control, and programme them to achieve human values'.[55] Polanyi focused on the threat to human wellbeing posed by making people subordinate to technological rhythms: 'the fragmentation of man, the standardization of effort, the supremacy of mechanism over organism and of organization over spontaneity'. Perhaps more important, however, was his linking of the factory system to the market mechanism so that technology came to form part of a system which 'revealed its incapacity to satisfy the requirements of a stable society': 'Millions experienced recurrent unemployment and the employed suffered permanent uncertainty of tenure.'[56] In our day, Pope Francis has written of the impacts on the environment and society of the dominant techno-economic paradigm:

> It can be said that many problems of today's world stem from the tendency, at times unconscious, to make the method and aims of science and technology an epistemological paradigm which shapes the lives of individuals and the workings of society. The effects of imposing this model on reality as a whole, human and social, are seen in the deterioration of the environment, but this is just one sign of a reductionism which affects every aspects of human and social life. We have to accept that technological products are not neutral, for they create a framework which ends up conditioning lifestyles and shaping social possibilities along the lines dictated by the interests of certain powerful groups. Decisions which may seem purely instrumental are in reality decisions about the kind of society we want to build.[57]

The clear lesson is that we cannot find answers to the challenges of technology if we neglect the socio-economic system in which technologies are embedded, developed and deployed. Thus commodification, or the 'interests of certain powerful groups' as Pope Francis puts it, sets the context for considering technological threats.

Two different elements need to be distinguished. The first is the threat to employment. Some economists go so far as to say we are at the end of the era of work, that for the first time in human history we have the technological capacity to grow the economy without the need for an organized mass of workers.[58] There is a consensus that technological developments are about to transform our economic and social lives with a particular threat to many middle-class jobs in the medical, legal, educational and financial professions. It has been estimated that up to 47 per cent of total US employment is at risk and, in Europe, from 47 per cent to 62 per cent of jobs.[59] Current trends in all European economies have been described as 'job polarisation or hollowing out' with gains in high-skill and low-skill jobs resulting in increased polarization of incomes.[60] In the past, workers responded to technological changes through reskilling and finding work in the emerging sectors; however today 'the substitution of labour by machines is so far-reaching that in some spheres the workerless factory is becoming a reality'.[61] Yuval Noah Harari predicts that the coronavirus pandemic will lead to the acceleration of automation. With more and more people working from home as workplaces were forced to shut, he sees that robots, AI and automatic learning will replace humans in many workplaces.[62] Meyer advocates 'a significant role for public policy to shape the process so that the sombre "social breakdown" scenario does not come to pass' but acknowledges that 'if only a small part of the well-founded predictions become reality then we are facing the prospect of major political and social upheavals'.[63]

The second element is the threat from AI. This creates a completely new situation for humanity. Up to now, the tools we created were always under our control even if at times they produced results their creators hadn't anticipated. With the rise of AI however we are creating tools 'that have a tendency to escape from human control' and in fact to turn against their creators.[64] This is graphically illustrated in Ian McEwan's novel *Machines Like Me* (2019) in which a robot develops its own life, making decisions and acting on them with major negative consequences for its owners.[65] Mason's fears therefore seem well founded – that AI 'will lead to a technological arms race and that it will arm already powerful elites with the capacity for mind and behaviour control on a new scale'.[66] Nobel Prize winning economist Joseph Stiglitz distinguishes AI that replaces workers and AI that helps people do their jobs better. He writes: 'All the worst tendencies of the private sector in taking advantage of people are heightened by these new technologies.' He advocates fresh policies to curb the monopoly powers of tech giants and a regulatory structure to democratize decisions about who controls data. 'It's a much broader agenda than just redistribution', he says but includes labour bargaining power, intellectual property rights, redefining and enforcing competition laws, corporate governance laws and the way the financial system operates.[67] Similarly, Mason says that 'autonomous artificial intelligences cannot be safely deployed under any form of market-driven capitalism' but need to be brought under ethical human control. This requires a 'comprehensive human-centric ethical system for AI ... to be based on virtue', resolving competing claims through democracy and regulation, and industry standards regulated by law.[68] Addressing the challenges of technology therefore also requires moving beyond the dominance of the market mechanism to ensure it serves the good of society.

Finding agency

While Polanyi rejected the deterministic view that history was inexorably moving towards socialism and instead emphasized the vital importance of social struggles to counter the power of the market, he devotes surprisingly little attention to the issue of agency. By agency we mean the agents of transformation, what social groups are going to bring about change and how. Esping-Andersen was more precise in identifying agency in the developing understanding of social rights within the workers' movement and social democracy, particularly since the Second World War. This resulted in two major breakthroughs: the extension of rights beyond simple survival and the upgrading of benefits to match average earnings and living standards. The former led to payment for care work, for education and even for leisure which he describes as 'in spirit, truly decommodifying'.[69]

Yet it is widely acknowledged that the decline of the trade union movement, under sustained attack by the state particularly in the United States and in Britain for over thirty years and undermined by the fragmentation of employment, has severely blunted attempts to resist recommodification. Therefore, among proposals to counter growing inequality and the erosion of workers' rights, the need to strengthen a 'countervailing power' to the power of capital is recognized. Referring to trade unions, Stiglitz laments that 'there is no recognition of the important role that they can play in countervailing other special interests and in defending the basic social protections that are necessary.'[70] Among the recommendations of social policy academic Anthony Atkinson for reversing inequality is strengthening the power of trade unions to influence policy.[71] However, it is principally through determined struggle that workers can become again a countervailing force to capital and there are some signs that this is beginning to happen in some of the least likely employments, using technology in subversive ways as detailed in Box 6.3.

Box 6.3 McStrike and Rise App: Labour militancy on fresh terrain

When workers in leading British retail and hospitality firms like McDonalds, JD Wetherspoon, Uber Eats and TGI Fridays went on strike in late 2018 they were not only fighting against derisory wages and complete lack of security. They were also fighting fears that they are easily dispensable, feelings that struggle is futile, and the belief that unions are old-fashioned and irrelevant. But the experience of joining with other young people in solidarity kindled a hope that, as one Wetherspoon worker put it, 'we can drive wages and conditions, not just in our industry, but across society in general'.[72]

As employers increasingly use apps to monitor every activity of their workers, an organized resistance is taking place among digitally outsourced workers such as Deliveroo and Uber. 'New apps abound that allow workers to log abuse by managers, read up on their rights, organise their workplace and compare pay rates' and these are helping them to link with one another and turn the system to their advantage:

> Agency staff in maintenance cupboards are busy plotting wildcat walkouts, takeaway couriers are using their bikes to bring major roads to a standstill, gallery openings are being overrun by protesting workers and warehouse operatives are organising clandestinely through WhatsApp. The reality is that labour militancy hasn't died at all. It is simply playing out on fresh terrain.[73]

And this is a global movement. Inspired by the Fight for $15 movement in the United States, the strikes in Britain are linked to similar actions in Belgium, the Netherlands, France, Germany, Australia and Hong Kong.

Conclusions

One of the consequences of the commodification of labour is that monetary motives come to play a greater role in directing human behaviour, the fear of starvation as Polanyi refers to it. To this, he counterposes a 'right to live' by which he seems to mean that society needs to ensure that everyone has sufficient for their livelihood and that this should never be left to market forces. This chapter has shown how far we have moved from such a situation over recent decades. Much of the discussion has centred on mechanisms of protection and redistribution, the traditional mechanisms of the welfare state. While these remain essential elements, there is a growing recognition that 'welfare states have been essentially pro-growth projects' so that ecological limits to growth and the end of cheap energy raise major challenges for generating the resources required to fund them.[74]

Decommodifying labour therefore takes us beyond welfare systems to the ways that society organizes work, indeed to the very meanings it attaches to work. The transition to a low-carbon society as well as the challenges from automation raise these issues in ever-more urgent ways, offering opportunities as well as threats. Yet so often what prevents society grasping the opportunities offered is the dominance of capital and the vested interests that promote it vigorously. This commodification of money is the subject of the next chapter.

7

Fictitious commodities: Money

In turning to the commodification of money, we are turning to the central driver of the commodification process itself. It should be clear from the previous two chapters that the commodification of money or, to put it in more everyday terms, the power of capital explains the constant pressures to treat land and labour as commodities to be bought and sold. Basically stated, it is the driver of capital accumulation or profit maximization that explains why, in Immanuel Wallerstein's words, 'the historical development of capitalism has involved the thrust towards the commodification of everything'.[1] His account of how capitalism developed focuses on how it had to overcome the obstacles that existed to commodifying labour and the production process, since under pre-capitalist social systems it was not considered rational or moral that some of these elements should be commodified. He goes on: 'Historical capitalism involved therefore the widespread commodification of processes – not merely exchange processes, but production processes, distribution processes, and investment processes – that had previously been conducted other than via a "market".[2] This is consistent with Polanyi's account though it lacks the specific focus on the 'fictitious commodities' of land, labour and money.

Commodifying money is the driver of the process. In considering the meaning of capital, Polanyi makes a crucial distinction: 'Capital (with a C) as a fund of money value the ownership of which is a source of income, is a historical phenomenon obtaining only under a definite organization of economic life. Ultimately it is the outcome of the system of private ownership of the tools, plant, machinery and other means of production.'[3]

Therefore, the commodified version of money, Capital with a capital C, is to be distinguished from capital as 'another name for machinery, tools, plant or accumulated resources which are the precondition for production of almost any kind.'[4] What makes money a commodity therefore is that it is a source of income: 'Whether Capital takes the form of plant or raw materials or the abstract form of money and securities, it is the principal agency in economic life.'[5] Yet he regards this as illusionary since the so-called productive capacity of money (that which allows money be a source of income) relies on the private ownership of the machines and the labour which produce the wealth to provide the income. He thus describes it as 'this fantastic concept of Capital'.[6] Against this fantastic concept, he regards money as 'merely a token of purchasing power which, as a rule, is not produced at all, but comes into being through the mechanism of banking or state finance'.[7] When understood in this way, his attitude to money was positive, crediting it with extending 'the scope of our intellectual and moral experience'.[8]

The subject of this chapter therefore is the process of transforming this token of purchasing power into an income-generating commodity, the financial system that has developed based on this commodification, and its impacts on society and on nature. The first section distinguishes further the different meanings of money, the consequences of basing monetary systems on commodity money and Polanyi's analysis of the role that this played in the collapse of the liberal order in the inter-war years. The following section traces the contemporary manifestation of this in the financialization of capitalism and how this is implicated in the contemporary global crisis. Section three 'Money and its Values' turns to the central issue of use value versus exchange value using this as a way of discussing how the commodification of money has had profound effects on narrowing and warping our personal and social values. The penultimate section examines means of decommodifying money through reining in our financial system.

'Money makes the world go 'round', but can also make it collapse

The central distinction to which Polanyi draws attention is 'between money as a means of payment to facilitate productive organisation, and money as a market-traded commodity'.[9] His work helps us to see the longer-term impacts on society of these two different types of money, what he called 'token money' and 'commodity money'. Commodity money grew as a medium of exchange between countries with the growth of international trade. National currencies became convertible through linking their value to gold, known as the gold standard, which came into being in the 1860s. This was thought to shield the value of currencies from political pressures and it was seen as a self-regulating system adjusting prices and demand in participating countries through the operation of the market mechanism. Maintaining the value of a country's currency when under pressure required the imposition of austerity to lower domestic prices, resulting in pressure on wages and on employment, processes which became all too familiar since the financial collapse in 2008. As Polanyi states: 'Currency had become the pivot of national politics ... populations became currency-conscious [and] men and women everywhere appeared to regard stable money as the supreme need of human society'[10] even though it led to domestic unrest and protectionist policies to try to protect the national economy. Instead of international peace and harmony which liberals predicted, this system meant that countries were caught in a vice between the needs of domestic society for protection and the efforts to maintain the value of national currencies. 'Mounting internal tensions, in turn, translated into growing global tensions as political leaders blamed the machinations of foreign leaders for their domestic difficulties.'[11] For Polanyi, these pressures lay behind what led to the First World War and, following the return to the gold standard in the 1920s, to the rise of fascism. He wrote that 'the origins of the cataclysm lay in the utopian endeavour of economic liberalism to set up a self-regulating market system. ... It implies no less than that the balance of power, the gold standard, and the liberal state, these fundamentals of the civilization of the nineteenth century, were, in the last resort, shaped in one common matrix, the self-regulating market.'[12]

If Polanyi's work has shown how the commodification of money led to 'disruptive strains' and the collapse of the liberal order in the 1930s, he has also shown how novel this was in history. The economic anthropology to which he devoted his final years helped show that trade, money and markets could exist in societies without being coordinated by a market mechanism. In other words, society functioned with systems of money that didn't enable its commodification, not allowing money in itself become a source of income. Central to his findings is that, unlike modern societies in which the various uses of money are interdependent, in earlier societies different objects were used to fulfil different functions of money and these were institutionalized separately and mostly independently of one another. There was therefore no such thing as modern society's all-purpose money since different objects – among them slaves, cattle, cowrie shells, gold dust – were used as means of payment, as units of account or as a store of value including as status symbols.[13] 'The internal use of money in exchange in the ancient oriental empires of Egypt, Sumer, Babylonia, and China was, on the whole, very restricted,' he writes.[14] Most importantly, non-economic institutions rather than a market mechanism were what integrated society. The institution of kinship was the setting for reciprocal forms of exchange; how this functioned is well expressed by Fleming: 'The distribution of goods and services is integrated into the tissue of social interdependence. Deals are not closed with the payment of an invoice, and the network of open-ended, unsettled obligation joins people together and sustains the social order.'[15] In more centralized states, political administration practised different forms of redistribution. The emergence of community forms of exchange (e.g. community-supported agriculture (CSA)[16]), local currencies and cryptocurrencies can be seen as modern variants on these ancient practices of institutionalizing the different functions of money separately. They also point to different forms of social institutionalization beyond the market mechanism. This is further discussed later in this chapter.

For Polanyi, the collapse of the gold standard and the cataclysm of the Second World War marked the end of the market mechanism. The Bretton Woods conference in 1944 replaced the gold standard with an international exchange system managed by the International Monetary Fund (IMF) and based on fixed exchange rates and strict regulation of global capital flows. This gave stability to the international financial system ensuring 'national finance served its economic role of channelling savings into investment in the expansion of real productive capacity.'[17] The result was thirty years of growth in both developed and developing countries, with improved employment and rising living standards. Yet, with the decoupling of the dollar from gold in 1971, a new volatility entered the system again as governments dismantled controls over international capital movements and exchange rates floated. The power of finance grew as foreign exchange trading expanded enormously and new financial instruments were created to intensify the commodification of finance. Polanyi's daughter saw the similarities with the 1920s:

We are living Keynes' nightmare of a 'casino economy' of speculators and rentier capitalists and Polanyi's false utopia of the self-regulating market. This 'neo-liberal' economic order favours creditors over debtors, finance over production, and the rich over the poor. A growing underclass of marginalized persons is excluded from formal circuits of employment, production and consumption. Hundreds of millions of poor people in poor countries are simply redundant to the requirements of the global capitalist economy. The system is chronically inequitable and endemically unstable. Ultimately, it is politically unsustainable.[18]

It marks the financialization of capitalism with 'the increasing dominance of financial practices and the fusion of business enterprise with "financial engineering".[19] It returns us to the highly commodified financial system of the late nineteenth and early twentieth century that so interested Polanyi, but with many features very different from that period, one of them being the easy availability of credit to all (see Box 7.1).

Box 7.1 Enticing workers to live on credit

When English journalist Paul Mason returned to his home town of Leigh, a coal mining town in Greater Manchester, and asked people what was the biggest thing that had changed working-class attitudes in the past thirty years, the unanimous reply he got was 'credit'. 'Credit destroyed people's attachment to the one thing that had kept communities like this together for 200 years: work,' he writes.

From around the mid-1990s, work lost its intrinsic value and became something you did to keep your credit card going, pay your mortgage and maintain your mobile phone topped up. 'Under all previous forms of capitalism, for a poor person to borrow vast amounts of money was seen as stupid. Under neoliberalism in its heyday, not to borrow vast amounts of money was seen as stupid.'[20]

Suddenly the coronavirus pandemic plunged this credit-based system into meltdown. Overnight in March 2020 the world faced the largest increase in deficits and government debt since the Second World War, raising the question of who to borrow from:

Banks, financial markets and money markets provide the financial fuel of the world economy. Normally, credit is sustained by the optimistic promise of growth. When that dissolves, you face a self-reinforcing cycle of collapsing confidence, contracting credit, unemployment and bankruptcy, which spreads a poison cloud of pessimism. Like an epidemic, if left uncontrolled, it will sweep all before it, destroying first the financially fragile and then much else besides. It is not for nothing that we speak of financial contagion.[21]

The world's financial sector again turned to governments to survive but the difference with 2008 was twofold – the global extent of the crisis and the uncertainty about when and how it might be resolved. The untested nature of the extraordinary supports given by governments bought time for the banking sector but bankers worried that it could result in 'an old-fashioned credit loss crisis, but on a scale not seen before'.[22]

Financialization: Today's form of capitalism

Financialization was driven by the significant expansion in the financial sectors of leading capitalist countries from the mid-1970s onwards aided by the deregulation of the sector in the 1970s and 1980s particularly in the United States and the United Kingdom and the subsequent 'light touch' regulation that became commonplace. This resulted in a 'vast growth in the supply of credit-money' and 'the proliferation of new financial assets that were "derived" from underlying commodities' adding an increasing fragility to the system. These new instruments are of 'bewilderingly arcane complexity' so that even participants in the system 'struggle to comprehend the astonishing proliferation of specialized markets by which money is mutated, by what is known as "financial engineering" into a complex array of ever-changing tradable financial assets and instruments', some of them essentially 'forms of organised speculative gambling'.[23] The size of the US financial industry's debt grew from 1.35 per cent of GDP in 1946 to almost 110 per cent in 2009 while, in the UK, bank debt grew from around 50 per cent of GDP in the 1970s to over 500 per cent in 2001.[24]

Driving this was a change in the theoretical understanding of financial markets with the emergence of what was called the 'efficient markets hypothesis'. This claimed that the very complexity of the many financial instruments now dominating the sector would counterbalance risks emerging in any particular area. It led to the belief that risk was minimized and that 'no difficult political choices had to be made between the interests of financiers and those of the rest of society or between financial industry-propelled improvement and the stability of the economy for everyone else'.[25] Therefore, there was no need for strong state regulation of the sector as the very workings of the market mechanism itself functioned to minimize risk, and state regulation would interfere with the efficient workings of the system. Rather similar to the way that welfare states were reconfigured to promote market-based responses to need, as seen in Chapter 6, so too the financial sector relied more and more on the market rather than on the state to manage risk. All of this fuelled a huge expansion of risk-taking as illustrated by the growth of hedge funds. These are private funds that engage in speculation using credit or borrowed capital: in 1990 there were fewer than 1,000 funds managing $25 billion in assets but this had grown to over 8,000 by 2004, managing almost $1,000 billion annually, and by 2008 hedge funds were estimated to be managing around $2.5 to $2.7 trillion of funds.[26] This is an indication of just how much private interests, rather than the public good, are the driver of the whole system. The collapse of the financial sector in 2008, particularly in the United States and the United Kingdom where deregulation and liberalization had gone furthest, bore similarities to the collapse of the financial system in the 1929 crash, the Great Depression and the end of the gold standard. The main difference was that the recommodification of the global financial system since the 1970s was driven, not by neglecting the needs of society as happened in Polanyi's time, but by the perverse belief that the market mechanism was the most efficient way of meeting the needs of society. Returning to the terms taken from Polanyi and used in Chapters 4 and 5, instead of finding a balance between improvement (economic growth and efficiency) and habitation (stability and security of livelihood), the theoretical underpinning of today's financial system simply denies the need for any balance – growth and efficiency are all that society needs.

While the 2008–9 financial collapse did focus attention on the need for greater regulation of the sector, the results have been modest and have not fundamentally altered the nature of financialization. Some of the new accounting rules had to be set aside once the coronavirus hit to avoid added strain on banks' ability to lend. One element that has remained largely unchanged is the 'orientation of business management that gives priority to shareholder value over other concerns, such as labour rights, human rights and environmental and social responsibilities.' The Bank of England had to pressure the large banks to suspend all dividend payments at the outbreak of Covid-19, a move that shocked investors.[27] Within this system, therefore, money appears 'as the prime vehicle for inequality and domination, and the global financial industry is indeed often signalled, more precisely, as a threat to social progress'. Furthermore, it is those countries such as China and India that are weakly integrated into this global system that have had higher economic growth and poverty reduction whereas those regions most integrated such as the United States, Europe and Japan have had low growth and a big increase in inequality.[28] Overall, the financial system is failing to serve social progress and is characterized by falling commodity prices, low growth and low returns on investments:

> Global investment in production is one third of what it was before the financial crisis. Stock markets are falling everywhere in spite of extraordinary financial machinations such as Quantitative Easing to share repurchases. The resulting squeeze on labour has reduced demand while household debt continues to rise.[29]

A more hidden dimension of financialization is what Moore has called the 'cheap nature model', driving down the costs of labour, food, energy and raw materials. A central part of capitalism's financial model has been to make nature cheap, writes Moore, but this is now reaching its limits. While neoliberalism did succeed in restoring cheap nature with falling food prices, the stabilization of oil prices in the early 1980s and rolling back labour costs, it has failed to restore agricultural productivity growth through agro-biotechnology. Since the 1990s there has been a steady deceleration of agricultural productivity growth: 'It's not only that the capitalist agricultural model is broken and resisted. It's also that climate change renders both geographical and technical fixes to the agro-ecological crisis a dead letter.' Climate change is already supressing the four big cereal crops (soya beans, rice, maize and wheat) and rising CO_2 concentrations is reducing the protein, zinc and iron content of cereal crops exacerbating nutrient deficiencies that affect about 3 billion people. Therefore 'there will be no effective politics of climate justice without putting agriculture at the centre' and this now requires an end to cheap nature.[30] The coronavirus pandemic revealed overnight the extreme vulnerability of the food supply chains that the cheap food model depends on. International food policy expert Tim Lang highlighted the massive fragility of just-in-time supply chains and dependence on international markets.[31] The overnight closure of restaurants, schools and entertainment left growers with a massive surplus of highly perishable food stock while demand grew for local suppliers to deliver directly to households who worried about purchasing from supermarkets. In the United States, it was estimated that this breakdown of supply chains put at risk half the food grown.[32] This needs to be added to the risks on the minds of the governors of the Bank of England and the Banque de France as recounted in Box 7.2.

Box 7.2 Bankers, 'we cannot ignore the obvious risks before our eyes'

The whole financial sector has a crucial role to play in addressing climate change, stated the governors of the Bank of England, Mark Carney (who has since stepped down), and the Banque de France, François Villeroy de Galhau, and this is going to require 'a massive reallocation of capital'. 'If some companies and industries fail to adjust to this new world, they will fail to exist.'

In an article written with Frank Elderson, the chair of the Network for Greening the Financial System (NGFS), the governors recognized that 'the challenges we face are unprecedented, urgent and analytically difficult'. The NGFS was established in 2017 by thirty-four central banks and supervisors and released its first report in April 2019. This made four recommendations about the monitoring of climate-related financial risks, integrating sustainability into portfolio management, collaborating to bridge data gaps and building capacity with stakeholders to manage risks.

The report encourages regulators to identify 'which economic activities contribute to the transition to a green and low-carbon economy'. The commitment of all actors in the financial system to act on these recommendations will help avoid a sudden climate-driven collapse in asset prices, wrote the governors.[33] It remains to be seen to what extent concern over the future of humanity on the planet can dislodge profit-making as the driver of today's financial system.

'Overall, the global financial industry seems to be confronted today to a series of moral and political critiques that locate in its most defining rationales the engine of both the widening of social inequalities and the endangering of democratic order.'[34] To this could be added environmental challenges. These draw attention to the issue of values that mostly remains hidden in discussions on monetary matters.

Money and its values

New Zealand feminist economist Marilyn Waring lists what she values about life in her country, access to the beauty of nature as well as the absence of nuclear power and energy. She draws attention to the fact that none of this is accounted for in private consumption expenditure, general government expenditure or gross domestic capital formation. She adds: 'Yet these accounting systems were used to determine all public policy. Since the environment effectively counted for nothing, there could be no "value" on policy measures that would ensure its preservation.'[35] Money therefore is not simply a technical tool but embodies values so that 'different kinds of money or monetary systems produce very different effects in society and serve to illustrate how we can't take money for granted.'[36] Di Muzio and Robbins consider 'one of the most significant consequences of a monetary system that uses money as a unit of value is the continual commodification of nature, power and social relations.'[37] However, though 'money can buy almost everything we want – the problem [is] that we tend to want only the things that money can buy.'[38] We need to be aware therefore that commodifying money influences our personal and social values. One person who examined this by living without money for a year in London was Mark Boyle and he learnt disturbing lessons about the damage that money does to society (see Box 7.3).

Box 7.3 Living without money and realizing the real value of things

'Money no longer works for us, we work for it. Money has taken over the world,' writes Mark Boyle.[39] Boyle's year living without money, recounted in his book *The Moneyless Man* (2010), was in some respects difficult and in other respects 'the happiest time of my life', he writes.[40] Among the important lessons he learnt were the value of community and the ability to give and receive: 'My experience has been that when you give freely, with no thought of what you'll get in return, you receive freely, without fail.'[41]

Concerned at the fact that most people are unaware of the destruction their daily shopping habits are causing, Boyle identified money as the tool which 'enables us to be completely disconnected from what we consume and from the people who make the products we use.'[42] The widespread reliance on money is what weakens the bonds that hold society together: 'When you give freely, for no other reason than the fact that you can make someone's life more enjoyable, it builds bonds, friendships and, eventually, resilient communities. When something is done merely to get something in return, that bond isn't created.'[43]

'We're at a crucial point in history,' he writes. 'We cannot have fast cars, computers the size of credit cards, and modern conveniences, whilst simultaneously having clean air, abundant rainforests, fresh drinking water and a stable climate. Humanity must make a choice.'[44]

One approach to how money impacts our values is the distinction between use value and exchange value. Polanyi traces this back to Aristotle whom he considered produced 'the best analysis of the subject we possess: Aristotle insists on the production for use as against production for gain':

> Only a genius of common sense could have maintained, as he did, that gain was a motive peculiar to production for the market, and that the money factor introduced a new element into the situation, yet nevertheless, as long as markets and money were mere accessories to an otherwise self-sufficient household, the principle of production for use could operate.[45]

For Marx also, the distinction between use value and exchange value was central to his analysis of capitalism and influenced socialist thought for decades. For example, the distinction found expression in debates about material versus moral incentives in Cuba after the 1959 Revolution, with Che Guevara arguing that material incentives such as profit would result in a 'dead end' and that new attitudes were needed, a sense of social duty, a collectivist consciousness and a 'new man'.[46] The distinction surfaces again in our time in debates about the social economy. Sayer argues that the concept of investment hides the important difference between wealth extraction and wealth creation: he distinguishes between a use value-oriented meaning that focuses on what is invested *in* and an exchange value-oriented meaning that focuses on 'the financial gains of the "investor" from any kind of spending, lending, saving, purchase of financial assets or speculation' (emphasis in original).[47] Clark and Johansson argue that the distinction fails to be made in much social enterprise literature with the result that many social enterprises end up trying to achieve use value goals through exchange value means. 'This is conducive neither to sustainability nor to welfare,' they add.[48]

One of the consequences of the dominance of market reasoning, therefore, is that it 'empties public life of moral argument', argues Michael J. Sandel in his book on the moral limits of markets.[49] Writing about the United States, he says that 'serious debate about the role and reach of markets remains largely absent from our political life'.[50] Analysing a wide range of day-to-day activities that have become increasingly marketized (paying someone to stand in a queue for a Congressional hearing access to which is free so as to guarantee the payee a place, paying to get the mobile number of your doctor so as to get priority access to medical attention, buying the life insurance of an elderly person so as to collect the benefit when they die), Sandel identifies two main social consequences: firstly, the lack of fairness since it gives those with money privileged access to social goods thereby deepening inequality; secondly, corruption since buying and selling certain goods degrades them thereby affecting the quality of social relationships. Extending advertising leads to a society in which everything is 'brought to you' by MasterCard or McDonald's and this is 'a kind of degradation'.[51] Referring to the few limitations on markets still observed and the moral judgements that lie behind them, such as not allowing parents sell their children or citizens their votes, he concludes:

> Thinking through the moral limits of markets makes these questions unavoidable. It requires that we reason together, in public, about how to value the social goods we prize. It would be folly to expect that a morally more robust public discourse, even at its best, would lead to agreement on every contested question. But it would make for a healthier public life. And it would make us more aware of the price we pay for living in a society where everything is up for sale.[52]

Sandel's argument is very far-reaching since it applies not just to economic activities but to the moral quality of our private and public lives. The commodification of money has effectively robbed society of the need to decide what is the good life and how best to organize to achieve this. The next section turns to examples of how to undo this extensive corruption of society.

Decommodifying money

In his own writings, Polanyi took the view that central banking and management of the monetary system constituted part of the double movement effectively protecting the productive economy 'from the harm involved in the commodify fiction as applied to money'.[53] In more recent decades, various followers of Polanyi have identified the German Bundesbank, the European Monetary System and the Bank for International Settlements as counter-movements against the commodification of money.[54] Yet Kari Polanyi Levitt took a different view, likening the disciplines imposed by the euro to those of the gold standard and arguing that 'escape from the Eurozone may be the only way to reclaim democratic control over economic livelihoods'.[55] The system breakdown of our time, as outlined in Chapter 1, raises in a more acute form what might constitute a more thoroughgoing decommodification of money. A place to begin are the findings of Polanyi's own research later in his life about how the different functions of money were institutionalized separately and mostly independently of one another. How this is happening today in various alternative economic forms therefore provides a foundation on which a decommodified monetary system could be developed.

Writing in 1933 about the Great Depression, Polanyi placed emphasis on the growth of 'the most gigantic financial transactions' through 'the new modalities of credit'.[56] Again in our times, the IMF is alerting to the dramatic rise in global debt since 1950 and to 'the financial vulnerabilities that have grown over years of accommodative monetary policy'.[57] Overall, global debt has risen from around 200 per cent of GDP a decade ago to almost 250 per cent by 2018 and exceeds $86,000 per capita, more than 2.5 times average income per capita. Private sector debt has tripled since 1950 and is now the main driver of debt.[58] This illustrates the fact that the central feature of today's dominant money system is that it is a credit system created by commercial banks which make interest-bearing loans. As Di Muzio and Robbins put it: 'Our entire money supply is effectively on loan from the banks. Interest must be paid on most of the money in the economy. This interest transfers wealth and income from the bottom to the top.'[59] Curbing this debt-driven system, 'the most important change needed in the monetary system' as Dietz and O'Neill state, would require raising banks' reserve requirement to 100 per cent and making illegal the creation of money as debt.[60] This would effectively end the privatization of money creation, opening spaces for local currencies to play a more central role in fostering strongly integrated local economies. Local currencies are, in Boyle's term, 'a form of formalised barter' and 'a huge step towards relocalisation of economies' and reducing the separation between consumers and producers.[61] One value of local currencies is experimentation, allowing locales learn from one another. For example, the Austrian town of Wörgl issued free money notes whose value decreased the longer they were held, thus giving people an incentive to spend them productively.[62] A strong sector of local currencies would therefore be a step in breaking the stranglehold of commodity and credit money over our economic and social lives. Claims have also been made that the rise of cryptocurrencies offers opportunities for decommodification (see Box 7.4).

Box 7.4 Can cryptocurrencies decommodify money?

Many claims have been made that the exploding world of cryptocurrencies helps to by-pass banks and governments, putting power back into people's hands thus facilitating social solidarity and mutual aid. The electronic database on which they are based and which records transactions, known as blockchain, is public hence offering transparency, while the intermediaries are a decentralized network of people. Bitcoin is the best known of the public cryptocurrencies but hundreds now exist, among them Ethereum and Holochain, while banks and governments have developed private chains. Yet, as Brett puts it, they 'have become associated with the hyper-individualism of conservative libertarianism' and regarded as a more efficient way of keeping government and regulators at bay.[63]

However, the technology need not determine the design and use of the currency. Sardex is an electronic currency that started operating in Sardinia in 2009 alongside the euro and offers a mutual zero-interest credit circuit to participating small and medium enterprises. By 2018 it included 3,200 member companies with a transaction volume of €43 million. What distinguishes Sardex is not its blockchain-based transactional platform but rather the financial model within which this is embedded and sets the rules by which it operates. Central to this are by-passing the banking system and distributing the power to create money to the participating small and medium enterprises (SMEs). Since it is a zero-interest circuit, it protects against financial speculation and operates within social norms serving the local economy. Thus Dini and Kioupkiolis see Sardex as 'a very different form of finance to the one engendered by neoliberal capitalism'.[64]

A thorough decommodification of money will require a complete overhaul of our financial system. What this would entail has been comprehensively outlined by Austrian economist, Christian Felber, with the backing of ethical banks in Germany, Switzerland, Italy, the Netherlands and Austria. The banking system, which would be in public ownership and democratically controlled, would be limited to deposit and lending business so that people would live on earned income not on income from capital. Regional common-good stock markets would replace central capitalist ones and would finance enterprises but not trade them. Many of today's financial instruments would no longer exist and commodity prices would be fixed democratically by producers, consumers and representatives of future generations. A new 'globo' or 'terra' currency would be created for world trade and the exchange rates of national currencies flexibly fixed to it. The Democratic Bank 'would be committed to the common good rather than to profit gain'.[65] Felber's proposals would go much further to decommodifying money that anything Polanyi proposed and are just one comprehensive example of the sort of innovative thinking about banking that has followed the 2008 collapse focusing, for example, on community banks, green banks and regional banks.[66] The coronavirus pandemic and its impact on the global financial system has the potential to generate momentum for fundamental reforms that would seek to address the system's vulnerability. However, as the Foundational Economy Collective points out, this will require 'a positive vision of a different set of priorities which embody the collective values that underlie foundational provision'.[67] To this we return in Chapters 8 and 9.

Conclusions

This chapter has shown that, when considering the commodification of money, the central issue is not so much the money per se but the wider social structures within which it is embedded and the purposes for which it is used. It is this that allows us distinguish money as a token of exchange from money as a commodity which can be a means for making more money, and money as credit which requires that it be repaid with interest to a lender. It is this wider context that also determines whether money is institutionalized in a way that requires it to play multiple roles such as a unit of account and as a store of value or whether the different roles are separated. A further crucial dimension as to whether money is commodified or decommodified relates to whether it is a private or a public good, created by private banks for speculative purposes or kept under forms of public scrutiny and control.

Informing the ways in which money is institutionalized are value systems that again tip the balance in favour of either private gain or public good. Social values therefore lie at the heart of our monetary and financial systems. It is not surprising that Polanyi emphasized again and again the motive of gain as the driver of commodification. The dominance of this value finds expression in the identification of corruption as one of the systemic disorders of contemporary capitalism, as we saw in Chapter 3. This theme of values helps unite the very different topics covered in the chapters of Part Three on Polanyi's fictitious commodities of land, labour and money. We now move to a brief conclusion to Part Three before turning to where we go from here which is the subject of Part Four: 'Whither and how?'

Conclusion to Part Three

After examining the pendulum swing between commodification and decommodification as it applies to Polanyi's three fictitious commodities, the nature of the transition signalled in Chapter 1 becomes clearer. The three chapters in Part Three have identified many social disruptions caused by multiple pressure points in many key economic and social sectors – conventional agriculture, greenhouse gas emissions, housing, energy, welfare systems, employment, inequality, automation and AI, debt, speculative finance, marketization – all pointing to the urgent need for radical and broad transformation of the economy and society. Many of these pressure points have been further highlighted by the Covid-19 pandemic. Furthermore, in all these realms radical alternatives are emerging based on much broader value systems than simply value for money. What unites them is the need for a sense of belonging to nature and to one another, rejecting the radical individualism that has sundered social ties of mutual interdependence with such devastating consequences. As economist Charles Eisenstein put it: 'For a long time ... the symptoms of civilizational malaise in the developed world are plain to see, but we have been stuck in the systems and patterns that cause them. Now Covid has gifted us a reset.'[1] Already, before the pandemic struck, as the decade of the 2010s was ending it was clear that more and more people were rising up in anger at the social, economic, climate and financial injustices of real existing capitalism.[2] They were clearly rejecting the Hayekian narrative of freedom through market rule – the rising generation are deeply angry at neoliberalism. But neither were they embracing the Keynesian solution of the state playing a central role in market regulation as the state is often seen more as an enemy than as a protective friend. Instead, they are turning to the power of society, as the many alternatives mentioned in these three chapters make clear. Taking the fundamental division between market liberalism and social protection, Polanyi's duo of Improvement versus Habitation (outlined in Chapters 4 and 5 and illustrated in Box 2.3), it is the pole of Habitation that inspires the alternative being sought. Eisenstein writes, 'Covid-19 is showing us that when humanity is united in common cause, phenomenally rapid change is possible.'[3] Chapter 5 drew out from Polanyi's writings of some of the key elements – public good over private gain, personal and communal embeddedness in land and nature, the localization of economies, secure belonging to communities providing livelihoods but also respect. The vital importance of all of these in our public life was brought to the fore during the coronavirus pandemic. It is this that shows the Polanyian moment has arrived, that his writings offer the inspiration, values and analytical frameworks to make sense of what is being so decisively rejected and so tentatively sought at this crucial time in human history. In Gramscian terms, it offers the basis for a counter-hegemony to the hegemony of neoliberal capitalism.[4] For the 2010s have been 'the age of perpetual crisis', disrupting everything but resolving nothing.[5] Chapter 8 elaborates on the key elements of a Polanyian alternative.

The chapters in Part Three have also brought to visibility that at the heart of the many struggles to transform society lie the three forms of social integration that Polanyi identified: reciprocity, redistribution and exchange. Each depends on different institutional supports. Reciprocity is based on robust communities characterized by strong ties of interdependence; Chapter 5 gave some examples of how communities are reviving local economies to maximize social wellbeing while Chapter 7 touched on how reciprocity also finds expression in local currencies. Redistribution was the key principle behind the welfare state as seen in Chapter 6 but can also find expression when public authorities support local community initiatives as in some of the housing projects outlined in Chapter 5. Exchange takes place in local markets and is central to the success of local and ecological food systems as well as localized artisan production. Polanyi elaborates well the institutional support for reciprocity in his rich insights into community (outlined in Chapter 8) while his distinction between markets as social institutions and the market mechanism (outlined in the Introduction to Part Three) grounds his notion of exchange. Where he is weakest is in his concept of the state which provides the institutional support for redistribution. Burawoy writes that the state was of secondary importance for Polanyi since his view of how to oppose the self-regulating market was essentially a bottom-up one.[6] Polanyi did not see the purpose as being to take control of the state even though he saw government as an important means to regulate the market and to introduce measures of social protection. Dale writes that, in his later years, Polanyi 'conceived of the state as an organ for the self-regulation of society as a whole',[7] and we have seen in Chapter 4 that his conception of the state, like that of Robert Owen, was to protect society from harm and not for the organization of society (see Box 4.2). Such a view of the state is probably much closer to that of most of those organizing and protesting against the dislocations and injustices of today's capitalist order than any traditionally socialist view of the state protecting society; the final chapters will return to this issue.

But Polanyi also recognized that actions promoting Habitation interfere with the efficient working of the economy and he saw a constant tension between it and the principle of Improvement (economic growth and efficiency). As outlined in the Introduction to Part III, he identified three sources of instability that lay at the heart of these tensions. These can be summarized as growth versus rigidity, the international versus the national, and market versus state, all of them as operative today as in Polanyi's time. The corporate growth model defends itself on the basis of its ability to achieve growth through breaking down barriers and keeping markets as free as possible from regulation. The assumption that the first of each of these dualities is superior to the second has been challenged by the coronavirus: it has made visible the profound vulnerabilities on which the growth model is based, the international connections that spread the virus and the impotence of the market mechanism to deal with it. It highlights what Eisenstein has called 'the bankruptcy of the economics of the separate self'.[8] Beyond these lies a more fundamental issue. As Arrighi puts it, Polanyi argued that 'a slowing down of the rate of change may be the best way of keeping change going in a given direction without causing social disruptions that would result in chaos rather than change'.[9] This serves to identify some of the key battle lines in building an alternative requiring a new and inspiring narrative which articulates the central elements of that alternative, a new story for the future beyond that of Hayekian neoliberalism. Where we go and how we might get there are the subject of Part Four.

Part Four

Whither and how?

8

Towards a new public philosophy

We live 'in an age of bewilderment, when the old stories have collapsed, and no new story has emerged so far to replace them', writes Yuval Noah Harari.[1] George Monbiot also believes stories to be very important. His book on grand narratives for a new politics of belonging begins: 'You cannot take away someone's story without giving them a new one. It is not enough to challenge an old narrative, however outdated and discredited it may be. Change happens only when you replace it with another.' The old world, which looked so stable, is collapsing and a new era has begun, loaded with hazard. 'Whether the systems that emerge from this rupture are better or worse than the current dispensation depends on our ability to tell a new story, a story that learns from the past, places us in the present and guides the future.'[2] President Michael D. Higgins of Ireland emphasizes again and again that 'there is now an intellectual crisis that is far more serious than the economic one.'[3] Referring to Europe, he has spoken of us having 'arrived at a crisis as great or greater than that faced by previous generations of political and social theorists,'[4] while urging that 'we must not miss this opportunity to seek, together, a new set of principles by which we might live ethically as a society.'[5]

Such new stories embodying new sets of principles emerged at two key moments during the past century, decisively reshaping the socio-economic system – Keynesianism in the inter-war years and Hayek's neoliberalism in the post-war era.[6] It is clear that a new story is now urgently needed to shape whatever socio-economic system emerges to replace the system currently in breakdown. Such a new story is what Karl Polanyi offers. Block and Somers call this his 'new public philosophy' based on the core principles of freedom and rights. This challenges the narrowness, individualism and anti-statist stance of classical political and economic liberalism, all of them implicated as causes of today's global crisis. 'Nothing obscures our social vision as effectively as the economistic prejudice,' wrote Polanyi[7] and overcoming this prejudice is therefore an essential precondition for developing a new story. As Polanyi elaborated:

> We find ourselves stultified by the legacy of a market-economy which bequeathed us oversimplified views of the function and role of the economic system in society. If the crisis is to be overcome, we must recapture a more realistic vision of the human world and shape our common purpose in the light of that recognition.[8]

Central to this more realistic vision is Polanyi's recognition of 'social interdependence as the foundation of humanity' and the knowledge 'that freedom and rights must be deliberately built on that foundation' so that 'new freedoms will develop by accommodating ourselves to the constraints imposed on us by our complex interdependencies.'[9] Such a recognition was brought forcefully home to many by the Covid-19 crisis.[10] The chapter begins with economics. It elaborates Polanyi's distinction between formal and substantive economics. The following section elaborates on four key challenges for embedding the economy in society – degrowth, limits, community and glocalization. These show how new social freedoms can be developed within the constraints of our complex interdependencies. The penultimate section summarizes the new story offered by Polanyi as the recovery of the public world.

Economics: From formal to substantive

The new story must be grounded in a new understanding of economics. For too long, progressives have limited themselves to focusing on how to use state power to regulate the economy rather than focusing on the economy itself and how to transform it, embedding it again at the service of society. Polanyi aspired 'to take the social decisions made behind our backs into our own hands – not into the hands of any sort of state power.'[11] This breaks decisively with the legacy both of Keynes and of Hayek. This Polanyi does by delineating two different meanings of the term 'economic', the substantive and the formal which for him have nothing in common. The substantive meaning relates to human livelihood, namely the person's 'interchange with his natural and social environment, insofar as this results in supplying him with the means of material want-satisfaction'.[12] The formal meaning which dominates mainstream economics derives from the relationship between ends and means and 'implies a set of rules referring to choice between the alternative uses of insufficient means'. He went on: 'The laws of the one are those of the mind; the laws of the other are those of nature. The two meanings could not be further apart.'[13] The difficulty for Polanyi lay in the fact that all considerations of satisfying people's material needs (the substantive meaning of economics) have been reduced to a formal decision-making method presupposing constant scarcity and relying on the mechanism of prices to balance supply and demand (see discussion of limits below). In other words, the formal meaning reduces all economic thinking to a situation which requires a market system.[14] But this is far too restrictive as it fails to appreciate that the human economy, in the substantive sense of the ways in which people satisfy their material needs, 'is embedded and enmeshed in institutions, economic and non-economic': 'For religion or government may be as important for the structure and functioning of the economy as monetary institutions or the availability of tools and machines.'[15] Elaborating on this distinction, Polanyi's most interesting work in his later years examined empirically how very different societies institutionalized a variety of ways of satisfying material needs whereas mainstream economics, being restricted to a formal definition of its task, severely limited its focus:

> Since market situations do not, in principle, know wants and needs other than those expressed by individuals, and wants and needs are here restricted to things that can be supplied in a market, any discussion of the nature of human wants and needs in general was without substance. In terms of wants and needs, only utilitarian value scales of isolated individuals operating in markets were considered.[16]

Any new story therefore needs to break out of this straitjacket and foster much more creative ways of satisfying material needs through a variety of different means, including those outside the cash nexus (which Polanyi regards as 'a means of estrangement'[17]). Economics must cease marginalizing and dismissing non-market approaches to provisioning society; it must contribute to rethinking the ways in which satisfying our material needs can strengthen rather than weaken social bonds, and regenerate rather than destroy the natural world on which we depend. Gough's work on human needs and sustainable wellbeing does this through setting out an objective conception of wellbeing based on human needs and providing guidelines to address global warming, fleshing out and developing Polanyian themes in some detail.[18]

Kate Raworth's doughnut economics is also based on an understanding of economics similar to that of Polanyi[19]: economics as 'the practice of household management as an art'. Raworth writes that 'it is absolutely essential to have a compelling alternative frame if the old one is ever to be debunked' and she warns that simply rebutting the dominant frame will only serve to reinforce it.[20] Her 'seven ways to think like a 21st century economist'[21] focus on key features of what a new economics needs to address:

1. The goal: from GDP to providing a secure living for all within the limits of the planet.
2. The script: from a self-contained market to an embedded economy.
3. The protagonists: from the self-interested isolated individual to interdependent and altruistic cooperators.
4. The system: from a stable mechanical system to a complex adaptive one.
5. The design: from growth to distribution.
6. The motion: from waste to regeneration.
7. The belief: from growth addiction to growth agnosticism.

Raworth ends by stating that we are all economists now, echoing Polanyi's desire 'to take the social decisions made behind our backs into our own hands' rather than handing them over to the state. Raworth writes: 'Ours is the first generation to properly understand the damage we have been doing to our planetary household, and probably the last generation with the chance to do something transformative about it.' She acknowledges that her's is a work in progress, but she hopes it will start 'erasing the old economic graffiti that has for so long occupied our minds,'[22] moving from economic models to human dignity (see Box 8.1). This is an essential precondition for developing a robust socio-economic alternative, as Polanyi well understood.

Box 8.1 From economic models to human dignity

In surveying 10,000 Americans on a range of current economic issues, 2019 Nobel Economics prizewinners Esther Duflo and Abhijit Banerjee found them to be mostly at odds with the views of economists. It's not that the economists are always right: 'We, the economists, are often too wrapped up in our models and methods and sometimes forget where science ends and ideology begins.' They continue:

> Economists have a tendency to adopt a notion of wellbeing that is often too narrow – some version of income or material consumption. Yet we know in our guts that a fulfilling life needs much more than that: the respect of the community, the comforts of family and friends, dignity, lightness, pleasure. The focus on income alone is not just a convenient shortcut – it is a distorting lens that has often led the smartest economists down the wrong path, and policymakers to the wrong decisions.

They conclude that 'restoring human dignity to its central place has the potential to set off a profound rethinking of economic priorities and the ways in which societies care for their members, particularly when they are in need'.[23] As Yanis Varoufakis, in reviewing Duflo and Banerjee's book *Good Economics for Hard Times* (2019), writes, the authors 'shed much-needed light upon the distortions that bad economics bring to public debates while methodically deconstructing their false assumptions'.[24]

Embedding economy in society: Four key challenges

The new story begins with economics not because the economy is of supreme importance but in order to demystify its power over our social and political lives, to free our social vision from the economistic prejudice. The task now is to re-embed the economy as a key contributor to a flourishing society and this requires consideration of a number of challenges. These distinguish the Polanyian story very clearly from both Keynes and Hayek.

Degrowth: breaking the addiction to growth

'Growth is the child of capitalism,' writes Giorgos Kallis.[25] The means to measure it, GDP, was only developed in the 1930s while only in the 1950s did it come to be widely seen as shorthand for progress and betterment.[26]

For Kallis, growth disguises the underlying processes involved: 'capital accumulation by states or capitalists who appropriate nature and exploit the labour of others'. Despite this, it has taken on a life and power of its own with governments of left, right and centre justifying their actions – whether regulating or deregulating, investing and taxing, or imposing austerity and cutbacks – by their effects on growth. 'People's lives literally depend on GDP.'[27] "'Degrowth" marks a ruthless critique of the dogma of more – the dogma of economic growth,' he writes.[28] Kallis distinguishes degrowth from negative growth and makes clear that degrowth is not advocating recession. 'In economic terms, degrowth refers to a trajectory where the "throughput" (energy, materials and waste flows) of an economy decreases while welfare, or well-being, improves. The hypothesis is that degrowing throughput will in all likelihood come with degrowing output, and that these can only be outcomes of a social transformation in an egalitarian direction.'[29] While proponents of degrowth made clear that 'the sudden, un-planned, and chaotic downscaling of social and economic activity due to Covid-19 is categorically *not* degrowth', in showing 'the unsustainability and fragility of our current way of life' the pandemic illustrated the need for degrowth while also showing how possible it is 'because society (and the state) has demonstrated an ability to dramatically change the modus operandi in response to a major crisis' (emphasis in original).[30]

Kallis makes the point that, at least in the developed part of the world, we already produce more than enough but 'yet we are stuck in a one-way future in which all we can think of is producing even more'.[31] And, particularly since the 2008 crash, more attention is being paid to evidence that shows the effects of growth on social and personal wellbeing go into reverse after a certain income level is reached. This leads Wilkinson and Pickett to conclude: 'Economic growth, for so long the great engine of progress, has, in the rich countries, largely finished its work. Not only have measures of wellbeing and happiness ceased to rise with economic growth but, as affluent societies have grown richer, there have been long-term rises in rates of anxiety, depression and numerous other social problems.'[32] After a certain level, therefore, growth can be bad for society while the proponents of degrowth[33] claim that economic activity can be reduced while maintaining or even improving human development (see Box 8.2).

Box 8.2 Degrowth: Improving wellbeing while reducing economic activity

Degrowth is effectively a strategy of radical redistribution. Hickel summarizes it as a series of integrated policy reforms to reduce aggregate economic activity in high-income countries while at the same time maintaining and even improving indicators of human development and wellbeing:

> For instance, as dirty and socially unnecessary industries close down and aggregate economic activity contracts, unemployment can be prevented by shortening the working week and redistributing necessary labour (into cleaner, more socially useful sectors) with a job guarantee. Wage losses due to a reduction in working hours can be prevented by increasing hourly wages with a living wage policy. To protect small businesses that may find it difficult to pay significantly higher hourly wages, a universal basic income scheme could be introduced, with dividends funded by taxation on carbon, wealth, land value, resource extraction, and corporate profits.[34]

Degrowth also recognizes that capitalist growth is based on a practice of privatizing public goods, from the enclose of the commons in the late Middle Ages to the privatization of water and public services in our own day. This both creates artificial scarcity and foments competition, systematically dismantling the support systems that people rely on. Hickel calls it a 'theory of radical abundance':

> By de-enclosing and expanding the commons, and by redistributing existing income more fairly, we can enable people to access the goods that they need to live well without needing high levels of income (and therefore additional growth) in order to do so. People would be able to work less without any loss to their quality of life, thus producing less unnecessary stuff and therefore generating less pressure for unnecessary consumption.[35]

A second major problem with growth, generating much debate, is its relationship to greenhouse gas emissions. It is becoming ever clearer that achieving a low-carbon transition while continuing to grow the economy is not currently possible. Demand for energy is predicted to outpace the development of renewable sources, decarbonization cannot happen at the levels required if GDP continues to grow, and the technological solutions proposed remain currently highly speculative. In this situation, the 2018 IPCC report developed an alternative scenario called Low Energy Demand based on reducing global energy consumption by over 40 per cent by 2050, effectively a degrowth scenario. The concept of 'green growth' is also being actively promoted, as was outlined in Chapter 3. However, Hickel gives details of three major reports since 2012 showing that even with extreme measures (e.g. raising the price of carbon from $50 a ton to between $236 and $573 a ton) no absolute decoupling of growth from resource use is possible.[36] As *Financial Times* columnist Simon Kuper puts it, 'We can be green or we can have growth, but we can't have both together' (see Box 8.3).

Box 8.3 'Only way now is degrowth'

'We need to slash emissions while feeding and fueling more people,' writes *Financial Times* columnist Simon Kuper. 'But those people are also getting richer: global income per capita typically grows about 2 per cent a year. And when people have money, they convert it into emissions. What's what wealth is.'

There are signs that growth and emissions are being decoupled: the amount of carbon required to produce one dollar of GDP has been dropping by about 0.4 per cent a year while in Europe emissions have been falling although economies have been growing. Yet the reality is not quite so rosy: the carbon intensity of the global economy will have to fall at least ten times faster to meet emissions reduction targets while the European figures fail to include emissions generated in producing the region's imports; when included this adds about 19 per cent to European emissions.

'The sad truth is that moving from dirty to green growth will take much more time than we have,' he writes. The infrastructure we'll be using in these next crucial decades has largely already been built, and it isn't green. Most of today's planes and container ships will still be in use by 2040 and no green alternatives yet exist for these. Even electric vehicles won't save us as their lifetime emissions are far too high. Kuper concludes: 'If green growth doesn't exist, the only way to prevent climate catastrophe is "degrowth" now.'[37]

There is therefore a strong case to be made that weaning humanity off its addiction to growth must be a crucial part of the new post-neoliberal narrative. But degrowth is about more than economics: rather it is a new social imaginary, 'a society of frugal abundance' as Serge Latouche calls it, a society that constantly reflects, questions and makes its own laws.[38] It thus echoes major themes of Polanyi who wrote early in *The Great Transformation*: 'It should need no elaboration that a process of undirected change, the pace of which is deemed too fast, should be slowed down, if possible, so as to safeguard the welfare of the community.'[39] And degrowth offers a space free of the economistic prejudice in which debates, experiments and research can take place on how to avoid planetary disaster and live well within planetary boundaries. Nothing seems more urgent today. Yet, while a lot of funding goes into research on technological and economic options within the mindset of today's formal economy, 'very little goes to studying how, and under what conditions, we could transform society in a degrowth direction.'[40]

Limits: Freeing from the delusion of money

Today's capitalism 'has released the expression of insatiability from its previous restraints', write Robert and Edward Skidelsky, and they identify the commodification of money (bringing 'an increasing range of goods and services under the sway of money exchange') as 'inflaming the love of money itself'. 'So what can we do to free ourselves from this delusion?', they ask.[41] This question, which in previous eras was considered the concern of religious preachers urging repentance and self-discipline, has now become crucial to the survival of human societies on this planet. 'How much is enough?'[42] has therefore been transformed from a question of personal ethics to a collective project to find ways of living well within the carrying capacity of our surrounding ecosystems. This must also become a central theme of the new story.

Like degrowth, the issue of limits fundamentally challenges the theoretical framework of mainstream economics. For the concept of scarcity, a grounding assumption of formal economics, justifies endless growth to transcend it since this form of economics admits of no limits to wants, wealth, natural resources, energy or debt. As Wendell Berry put it: 'The idea of a limitless economy implies and requires a doctrine of general human limitlessness: *all* are entitled to pursue without limit whatever they conceive as desirable' (emphasis in original).[43] But, as Polanyi perceptively saw, 'This means the fullness of freedom for those whose income, leisure, and security need no enhancing, and a mere pittance of liberty for the people, who may in vain attempt to make use of their democratic rights to gain shelter from the power of the owners of property.'[44] For, in pursuing accumulation without limits, a minority imposes limits on the many thereby constraining their ability to live well.

What needs changing is 'a system that wants us to want without limits', as Kallis puts it. 'To free ourselves from the bondage of this system and avert its consequences, we must limit the wants that feed it.'[45] In our consumer-driven capitalism, we are overwhelmed with a self-destructive pursuit of more, and we learn that life is not worth living without engaging in these pursuits even though 'rather than liberating, limitless possibility can be debilitating and a constant source of frustration'.[46] It requires democratic deliberation to create limits to this system, and a good starting point would be to regulate the sophisticated and psychologically manipulative advertising that creates the wants that drive it. But the issue of limits needs to be taken further, to create a new collective culture of self-limitation, based on an appreciation of living in ways that foster a regenerative balance with the eco-systems on which we depend. It has been done before. Some are learning from wartime Britain to discover practices that can be adopted for the transition to a low-carbon society. For example, the 'dig for victory' campaign initiated in 1939 as part of the war effort has been drawn on in more recent years to stimulate debate about land use and localized food production.[47] The concept of austerity has been reformulated as an eco-austerity, returning to its core meaning of sufficiency so as to foster a sense of living within limits, and, in the words of Ruth Levitas, carrying 'the desire for an alternative society'.[48] The coronavirus also, in the words of Jonathan Freedland, stripped public life 'to its essentials. We've come to see what's indispensable and what is not.'[49] But in considering these collective limits, whether imposed or freely chosen, Kallis reminds us that we need to avoid 'accepting unjust ones'.[50] The culture of self-limitation must be radically egalitarian avoiding any attempt to scapegoat outsiders as threatening people's living standards as is happening in Trump's United States and some European countries. As Pope Francis has written:

> The time has come to pay renewed attention to reality and the limits it imposes; this in turn is the condition for a more sound and fruitful development of individuals and society.[51]

Community: Linking wellbeing with place

The economic system, particularly in its current neoliberal form, undermines and divides communities, robbing them of the material conditions to thrive. This creates fertile soil for right-wing populists to propagate nationalist and ethno-supremacist messages of a return to some idealized past of white working-class solidarity. Jack Shenker encounters again and again in his visits to broken communities around today's Britain how 'place matters far more than the high priests of globalism have reckoned for in recent years' and that 'attempts to rescue the notion of "community" from political purgatory need not depend on the construction of imaginary white idylls, as many nationalists would have us believe'.[52] He wonders what alternative path is possible for post-industrial communities like Tilbury close to London: it continues to be home to many institutions 'that have clung on amid the free market's atomising storms, and from which a grass-roots vision of something more collective might yet be forged'.[53] This is why community has to be a key part of the new story, not as romantic nostalgia as is often the case, but as the site from which the foundations can be laid for a new global system that offers real possibilities of belonging and flourishing. Covid-19 showed not just the vital importance of strong community bonds but also the remarkable creativity and solidarity that can emerge almost instantaneously within local communities.

For Polanyi, the aspiration to community is central to his emphasis on society. While the term 'community' is widely used in everyday discourse, he sees this as 'community in name only' as long as society is divided into classes. Instead of community, we have its denial:

> Malnutrition for some amidst the affluence of others, unforced idleness for some amidst the voluntary idleness of the leisured few, lack of opportunity for education and training for some alongside the monopoly of an expensive class education for others, become equivalent to deliberate wrong-doing and crime. It is on account of this denial of community that our society is in process of being destroyed.[54]

McKnight and Block write that 'a community based on scarcity, dependent on systems, with citizens competing and living in isolation from one another, threatens democracy'.[55] Instead, abundant community needs to be the purpose of democracy, allowing us 'to be citizens once again, knowing that we have the power to define our own possibilities, decide what choices reside in our own hands, and choose our own future'.[56] This view of community bears resemblances to that of the communitarian movement with its emphasis on countering excessive individualism by focusing on the common good, the importance of social responsibility and the role of social institutions as counterpoints to market pressures and state coercion. However, Polanyi warns that 'community for community's sake is a poisonous beverage' since it fails to acknowledge that the reality of community is impeded by our present market system which 'acts like an invisible boundary isolating all individuals in their day to day activities'.

Achieving community, therefore, requires 'a transformation of society through a change in the economic system' by abolishing the private ownership of the means of production. Instead 'the means of production must be owned by the community' so that the people as a whole have responsibility for the productive system rather than this responsibility being limited to its private owners while the rest of society has no such responsibility. People as a whole must participate in 'the massive economic adjustments needed to make an international community possible today. The ultimate reason for the helpless drift of the world towards destruction is the denial of community within the nations expressed in the retention of the capitalist system'.[57] What we need to work for is an international community based on local communities that control their means of production.[58] Put in today's terms, the goal is not localization in place of globalization but a globalization based on flourishing local communities and curbing global corporations.

Glocalization: Using global power structures to ensure local flourishing

The form of globalization that has so transformed the world over recent decades is now being seen as one of the principal causes of economic and social disruption in many local communities – 'a system that seemingly recognised no decisions and no authority other than those determined by aggregated market forces'.[59] While it has connected the world, these very webs of intense interconnectedness have themselves deepened vulnerabilities at all levels – economic, political, social, environmental, financial and even personal identities. 'It all adds up to a volatile mix, leaving many with no secure sense of what lies in store.'[60] Since the 1990s, globalization has played a leading part in the discourse of many of our political leaders, presented often as a benign force bringing growth and increased opportunities for those countries which succeeded in linking up to it.[61] However, since the financial crash of 2008, globalization has come to be seen more and more as a threat to livelihoods and local economies, and some see it as being on the wane. But to avoid a toxic xenophobia, it needs to be part of our new story, but playing a very different role to the one it has played in the neoliberal story that brought us to our present impasse (see Box 8.4).

Box 8.4 From private capitalist to public statist globalization?

Even before the coronavirus pandemic, globalization was in retreat under the impact of a populist nationalism. Once Covid-19 struck, spurred by the intense connectedness of our globalized world, countries enforced unprecedented limits on travel while supply chains weakened. Co-ordinated international responses proved much more difficult than at the time of the 2008 financial crisis. Was globalization finally in retreat?

Yet, the pandemic also showed the vital importance of global institutions, particularly for poorer states. President Trump's decision to withhold US funding for the World Health Organisation (WHO) was severely criticized around the world as the WHO's role in gathering data, publishing research and coordinating a global response was recognized as essential to combating the virus. Coronavirus was serving to highlight the shared challenges that cannot be successfully addressed by countries going it alone.

Tackling the effects of the virus on the international order, wrote journalist Paul Gillespie, 'overlaps with how it disrupts or reverses private capitalist globalisation by pushing it in a more public, statist direction'. Most important of all is 'how the promise of an alternative world ... provides lessons that must be applied to climate breakdown'.[62] As Mason puts it: much will depend on the voices of the 99 per cent, reaching across borders and enmities to build a collaborative global order that prioritizes human life, prosperity and wellbeing.[63]

As seen in the previous section, Polanyi saw local communities as having a responsibility to help build an international community. He saw the double movement as happening at local, national and international levels, through local responses to protect labour and the poor, through state actions at national level such as welfare legislation, tariffs and land laws, and through countries' withdrawal from the international system.[64] But he remained a committed internationalist, advocating a system of managed regionalism and fearing the United States' attempts to create a 'universal capitalism'. For example, in 1945 he proposed that Britain follow a form of 'planned foreign economy' with its overseas dominions 'to abolish unemployment, periodically to adjust currencies, to organize bulk imports, to direct her foreign investment, to arrange for large-scale barter, to finance heavy industrial exports, to conclude long-term contracts of industrial collaboration with other governments'.[65] However he feared that Britain would instead succumb to US efforts 'for re-establishing market methods in the liberated countries', the use of which 'must tend to produce starvation and unemployment'.[66] Polanyi, then, advocated something closer to what came to be the European Union, though he never showed any interest in its earliest manifestations during his lifetime. But he clearly feared the form of liberalized globalization that has dominated over recent decades. For him, the promise of regionalism was to ensure the opportunities it opened were used for the good of society rather than the imposition of neoliberal disciplines on member states, as has happened in the EU more recently.[67]

Rather than a retreat from globalization, a Polanyian approach to the present moment would be to seek to create conditions for flourishing local communities through enforcing strong international regulatory standards and through curbing corporate power. This can best be called glocalization, distinguishing what is best supplied locally (much of our food, essential equipment such as that required by hospitals during the Covid-19 outbreak) and networks of regional suppliers for more sophisticated manufactured goods. Addressing the crises of climate change, extreme inequality, automation and social decay is forcing new issues on the international agenda such as fair trade structures, global minimum wage standards and working conditions, and measures to rehabilitate the environment. As the programme of the Red-Green Alliance puts it, 'There must be institutions and bodies that can implement and monitor the new global framework and that can sanction infringements'.[68] Corporate tax avoidance is another major issue requiring globalized responses. Both the OECD and the EU are taking action even if it is still not sufficient to curb the sophisticated avoidance practices of global giants such as Apple, Starbucks, Google and Amazon. As Joseph Stiglitz reports, the IMF estimates that governments lose at least $500 billion a year due to corporate tax shifting. He proposes a global minimum tax to end the current race to the bottom which benefits no one other than corporations, and this should be set at around 25 per cent to ensure global corporate tax rates don't converge on a minimum.[69]

Towards recovery of the public world

At the heart of the new story is paradigm change. Nothing less captures adequately the central thrust of Polanyi's analysis: as we saw in the Conclusion to Part III, he was well aware that efforts to protect society from the destructive inroads of the market mechanism were in constant tension with the efficient workings of that system. The only way forward therefore would be a decisive break.[70] The division between politics and economics would have to be overcome and the economic system become again 'a mere function of social organization'.[71] It is for this momentous task that a new narrative is needed. This chapter has outlined some of the decisive differences that must now guide political action, breaking with the economistic prejudice that has so limited political and social vision, particularly over the decades of neoliberal hegemony. As Irish President Michael D. Higgins has argued, 'A radical paradigm shift is required in the connection between ecology, economics and society. The mere placing of a new lens on the existing orthodox growth model will not suffice.'[72]

Perhaps Covid-19 has done us a service in reminding us of the vital importance of the public world when society hits a crisis. As former US labour secretary Robert Reich wrote, when the virus struck, 'America is waking up to the fact that it has almost no public capacity to deal with it'. It has a private for-profit health system, and 'a rickety social insurance system' for those in employment, both serving individual needs but not the common good. No institutions were in place to administer tests to tens of millions of people as 'local and state health departments [were] already bare bones, having lost nearly a quarter of their workforce since 2008'.[73] In various European countries also, cutbacks were blamed for having undermined the capacity of public systems to address the crisis. Yet, has the capacity of the state been so weakened that private corporations may be the ones to gain? Technology reporter Julia Carrie Wong argued that Amazon was likely to become one of the major winners from the virus: 'As smaller businesses (even those that are not in any sense of the word small) falter and fail, Amazon is expanding its dominance over American commerce and society'.[74] However, in France, the company was forced to close its six distribution centres after a court ruled that it wasn't doing enough to protect its workers from the virus.[75] This highlights the difference that growth models play when threats strike: Blyth draws attention to the fact that the Anglo-American models 'tend to have weaker states, lower taxes and large financial sectors'. The US instinct 'to protect the big players and let workers take the hit' is a key reason why coronavirus 'is a disaster amplifier for the US growth model' in a way that is not true for those European countries with larger welfare states.[76] Recovery of the public world therefore requires challenging dominant growth models.

This chapter has outlined some essential differences that distinguish a Polanyian narrative from a Keynesian or Heyakian one. The account is not meant to be comprehensive and obviously requires extensive elaboration into practical polices of taxation, investment, regulation, supports for local communities and co-operative enterprises, and a radical overhaul of the financial system to name but some of the key elements.[77] Uniting them all is the recovery of the public world. This lies at the heart of Polanyi's writings and actions throughout his life: substituting what he called 'the general interests of the community'[78] for private gain. But telling a new story, while an essential starting point, isn't enough. Recovery of the public world needs to be the focus of a new politics, mobilizing society to create the institutions that will give form to a circular and regenerative economy under public control, weaned off an addiction to growth, attentive to the limits of the ecosystem on which it depends, breaking the stranglehold of corporate capital on the global system, and firmly embedding the economy at the service of flourishing local communities. Chapter 9 will examine where we can identify such a new politics emerging in today's world.

Conclusions

The story that underpinned the neoliberal era is no longer credible to a younger generation, writes Shenker.[79] This was a story of home ownership, private-sector jobs and the dynamism of free enterprise. However, the experience of large sections of young people today is that they are being shut out of home ownership, they lack job security and they see a private sector more interested in its own profits than in offering them the means to a better life. The mainstream is left with no story to tell. We are indebted to Italian Marxist writer and activist Antonio Gramsci for understanding that those who win the battle of ideas go on to shape the 'common sense' of society, thereby cementing their hegemony. This is what happened with the emergence of neoliberal ideas from the margins, first with the Chilean military coup in 1973 when the 'Chicago boys', Chilean graduates of the economics department of the University of Chicago, were given free rein to transform the country's economy. When Margaret Thatcher became UK prime minister in 1979 and Ronald Reagan reached the US presidency in 1981, these ideas went mainstream, reshaping not only policies but individual and social values.

Today the ideas that are shaping a new narrative come from the nationalist and populist right. If an alternative story more adequate to laying the foundations of a just and egalitarian society living within planetary boundaries is not more forcefully elaborated and articulated, humankind faces a bleak future. The present moment of system breakdown calls for a new alternative narrative, opening radical possibilities of fundamental transformation. The days of TINA ('There Is No Alternative', a favourite expression of Margaret Thatcher) are over; Polanyi advocated pluralist approaches to social transformation and already many different ways of organizing society are being proposed and implemented, some from the nationalist right but many also from progressive ecological and social forces as detailed in the chapters of Part Three. Politics itself is changing under the pressure of marginalized groups who find little by way of adequate responses from the mainstream political system. Inevitably, those advocating a radical alternative will be accused of being unrealistic. But the rise of the new right and the coronavirus pandemic show how quickly the neoliberal consensus has been broken. The final chapter examines how a progressive pluralist alternative is also emerging.

9

Beyond market society

The concept of 'tipping points' in climate science indicates the potential of small changes in climate to tip into more fundamental and irreversible changes in the climate system as a whole.[1] In politics too, the concept can be applied to those moments when, often unexpectedly, a succession of small incremental changes tips over into wider system change. In the past, these periods have been called revolutionary but the term 'paradigm shift' may more accurately describe what is needed today as our time requires not just a change of political leadership but deep changes in economy, society and most especially in the ways humanity relates to the ecosystem on which all life depends. As academic and activist Rebecca Willis has written: 'Power also manifests itself in what is said, what is not said, and what is assumed. Immersed in a high-carbon society, it is very difficult to think differently.'[2] President Higgins argues: 'If we are to achieve a paradigm shift, it will be necessary to combine the radicalism that is in the consciousness of climate activism, with the consciousness of egalitarianism and the programmes of inclusion activists and feminists ... We must combine and co-operate for the recovery of the public world.'[3] Having drawn extensively on the work of Karl Polanyi to understand the nature of the system breakdown being widely experienced in our times, and having shown how his core insights help identify and inform the paradigm shift we need to undertake, we now need to interrogate the likelihood of it happening.

The fact that media attention is obsessively fixed on the politics of the new right – from Trump's daily tweets to the anti-liberal measures of the Hungarian and Polish governments, from the obscenities of Bolsonaro to the entanglements of Brexit – can distract attention from the possibilities opening up for systemic change. Climate scientist and activist Kevin

Anderson asks if rapid change can ever be more than a romantic illusion. By way of answer he points to the deep upheavals that have characterized the first two decades of this millennium, though not necessarily in a favourable direction. But he points out that the financial crisis showed how massive resources could be mobilized at the stroke of a pen to save the banking system, and that the power of unaccountable media barons is being challenged by social media. The demands of climate change are forcing governments to consider more transformative actions while the cost of renewables is showing how reliance on fossil fuels has serious consequences for health and security.[4] Michael Jacobs who was an advisor to former British Prime Minister Gordon Brown writes in a similar vein: 'It cannot now be taboo, anywhere, to talk about capitalism, the huge inequities of income and wealth, the unsustainability of the economic system, the power of corporations and media empires to set the limits of debate and govern policy, and how all these need to be radically reformed.'[5] Even more than these rapid changes of the past two decades, Covid-19 has exposed the extreme vulnerabilities of our present situation and the vital necessity of building resilience. As Mason has written, the time is ripe for transformation:

> The utopian socialist communities of the mid-nineteenth century failed because the economy, technology and the levels of human capital were not sufficiently developed. With info-tech, large parts of the utopian socialist project become possible: from cooperatives, to communes, to outbreaks of liberated behaviour that redefine human freedom.[6]

In examining the evidence that paradigm change is underway, this chapter focuses on three central themes. The next section looks at how, amid the crisis of electoral politics, a new politics is emerging in the gaps. The following section examines the ways in which the proposal for a New Green Deal is emerging as a central focus for transformative change combining the environmental, the social and the economic. The third theme is automation, and the discussion here centres on how its potentials are being realized within new organizational practices challenging dominant private ownership structures. The chapter ends by drawing together the central argument of the book under the heading 'Transforming Market Society'.

Politics flourishing in the gaps

In examining 'the new politics of the people', Shenker identifies that it is the gap between radical electoral politics and civil society activism where the new politics can flourish, taking the fight to remake the future to the 'crevices neglected by market liberalism'.[7] This echoes Erik Olin Wright's focus on the interstitial as one of his three strategic logics for transforming capitalism: interstitial transformations 'build new forms of social empowerment in the niches and margins of capitalist society'. Examples of these have been already given in the networks of community-led initiatives outlined in Chapter 5 and many more emerged during the coronavirus pandemic. If Shenker focuses on social empowerment in interstitial spaces, this is not to overlook Olin Wright's two other strategic logics for transformation – the symbiotic and ruptural. The symbiotic refers to state-led projects that extend and deepen social empowerment without threatening capitalist power structures; the welfare state, in its heyday, embodied many such projects, as does some state investment in local community projects today. However, as long as these remain on the margins of capitalism's power structures, they never threaten to become ruptural, in other words to create 'new emancipatory institutions through a sharp break with existing institutions and social structures'.[8] Yet, Shenker powerfully uncovers, as the centre ground implodes, a new 'fractious and volatile' politics is being unleashed in the search for alternatives to a system in crisis unable to meet the basic needs of people and their communities.[9] As in Polanyi's time, this is both of the right and of the left, and in places it is far from clear which vision will win out. But there is a feature common to both and this is that 'the collapse of technocratic authority that has been precipitated by the financial crisis and furthered by the rise of digital technologies has, if nothing else, exposed a stubborn determination on the part of many citizens to defy the old political status quo and see themselves as agents of their own future rather than captives of somebody else's'.[10] The sudden explosion of children's school strikes and of Extinction Rebellion in 2019 expresses a similar stubborn determination. And there is a common feature of all these movements, common even to those who articulate hard-right stories, and that is the need to subdue market logics. On the commodification/decommodification spectrum, they are actively pushing back against commodification.

Box 9.1 The emerging decentralized democratic economy

'Spread across Britain are people and places united by a common condition,' writes journalist Aditya Chakrabortty, 'they are largely powerless. Their economies have been emptied out, their services cut to the bone, their incomes under threat. The market discards them; the media ignores them; the state disregards them.'[11] Yet, in visiting such places he found numerous examples of alternatives emerging, showing what a decentralized democratic economy might look like. He identified some strong common threads:

1. Roots: community bonds are strongly rooted.
2. Emerged from the financial crash: 'a society thrown into an emergency of which it is still trying to make sense'.
3. Basics: dealing with fundamental needs like decent food for children and housing.
4. Values: 'most of the Alternatives challenge how the market measures value'.
5. Participation: 'these are noisy and energetic organisations'.

Altogether he estimates some 100,000 social enterprises with a total of 2 million employees. For example, the Lancashire city of Preston seeks to build an inclusive economy, with advice from the US city of Cleveland, by keeping most of the profits in the locality. This is done by facilitating workers' co-ops to supply big institutions such as hospitals, the university, the police and the councils. Led by the city council, this has become a model for other deprived cities and towns.[12]

Yet, 'two big shackles hold in check the growth of more alternatives', writes Chakrabortty: the first is capital as ventures such as co-ops struggle to raise the necessary cash; the second is that 'the overwhelming centralisation of the British state can stifle development of bottom-up alternatives'. He concludes: 'Such serious constraints prevent our Alternatives from becoming mainstream. They block too many people from authoring a different future for themselves and their home towns.'

The contrast between this new politics emerging from the bottom-up and the dominant electoral politics, particularly in the democratic West, is striking. For while the former is incubating many transformative projects in the interstices of the dominant system (see Box 9.1), the latter is in deep crisis. As we saw in Box 2.2, the hollowing out of electoral politics has been underway for decades, and the years since the financial crash in 2008 have seen a swift erosion of the mainstream centrist parties that gave stability and predictability to the system. In their place a new volatility has emerged as voters move in unpredictable ways (including, as in the 2019 UK election, across the left-right divide that traditionally marked a deep dividing line) resulting in fragmentation and severe problems of governability. Multiple elections in Spain and Israel have failed to provide stable bases for government formation; illiberal governments in Poland, Slovakia, Hungary and the Czech Republic erode democratic checks and balances; centre-right and centre-left coalesce to keep the far-right out of power in Germany as centre-right and far-right coalesce in Austria, while the world watched in amazement as UK politics was collapsing amid a jungle of shifting veto points on Brexit. A poll by George Soros's Open Societies Foundation found between 51 per cent and 61 per cent in six eastern European countries fearful for the future of democracy itself.[13]

But it is in the intersection between electoral politics in decomposition and local politics fighting for jobs and services at local level that the potential for both symbiotic and ruptural transformations is beginning to emerge. And these reveal wider potentials than those envisaged by Olin Wright. For, while the predictable centre of electoral politics shatters as little of substance seems to emerge from there, more radical ideas are emerging through the cracks. In the UK, Harris has noticed 'a renewed sense of something too often overlooked: the fact that our national meltdown is full of political complexities; and that amid the mess, there are also the stirrings of a politics that might eventually answer the 21st century's challenges'. At the Labour Party's 2019 annual conference he found 'a sense of an embryonic leftwing politics that might at last speak to a future oriented around three key things: the roots of inequality in society and the economy; the upturning of life and work by technology; and the need for a green approach to almost everything.'[14] Proposals in the party's manifesto for that year's election included a Green New Deal (GND) to move substantially to zero carbon by 2030, a £250 billion Green Transformation Fund, forcing large companies to set aside 10 per cent of shares over ten years to be owned by employees, one-third of a company's directors to be elected by workers, outlawing zero-hour contracts, introducing a 32-hour working week and making sectoral collective bargaining mandatory across the economy. In the US primaries for the 2020 election, Will Hutton found that Senators Elizabeth Warren and Bernie Sanders were 'getting a growing hearing, even in Republican heartlands and among Fox News commentators ... with their calls for a wealth tax, an industrial policy targeted at the regionally disadvantaged, a new charter compelling responsible business, universal healthcare, a higher minimum wage and mobilisation of education and training'.[15] Warren also proposed laws to break up the big tech companies Amazon, Google and Facebook and requiring that 40 per cent of the directors of all large corporations (with an annual revenue of over $1 billion) be elected by their employees.[16] These proposals move beyond the symbiotic and point to ruptural transformations, at least of neoliberal capitalism. Even if not immediately realized, their proposal by contenders for high office shows that the neoliberal TINA straitjacket is, at long last, history.

Proposals in themselves won't return electoral politics to health but they are a sign that attempts are being made from within electoral systems to offer some responses to the pressures from the new politics. Meanwhile the pressures from below are mounting. Addressing the UN climate summit in September 2019, Greta Thunberg stated: 'We are in the beginning of a mass extinction. And all you can talk about is money and fairytales of eternal economic growth.' This shows how the political consciousness being generated among the young people taking to the streets in the school strikes and Extinction Rebellion takes for granted a different set of realities and priorities than does the politics of the mainstream – this is system change not climate change as emblazoned on the banners they carry. One of the leaders of the UK climate strike movement put it, 'For us, politics is not a game, it's reality, and that's reflected in the way we organise – relentlessly, radically, as if our lives depend on it.'[17] And it's not just climate change that is making people angry enough to take to the streets in large numbers and show a determination in confronting the system: 2019 saw some of the most determined waves of protest for years – in Santiago, Hong Kong, Barcelona, Beirut, Baghdad and Delhi to name just some of the most noteworthy. The triggers are various but behind them all lie 'deep-rooted disillusionment at how millions of citizens have been frozen out of the country's economic rise' as was written about the Chilean protests.[18] A new politics is on the rise and if there is one unifying thread it is to confront a system run in the interests of capital. 'The problem for governments is that there is no longer an established centre ground to snap back to, and their opponents know it – which is why so many of those involved in the current mobilisations will not settle for token concessions from the authorities.'[19] As in the sudden rise of the citizens' Sardines movement in Italy[20] against the new right and Matteo Salvini's populist politics in particular, there is potential here to reshape electoral politics in a more radical direction, though it is far too early to know how this will develop nor how the experience of the coronavirus pandemic is going to play out politically.[21]

Mobilizing around a new project: Green New Deal

The spectre of a highly volatile politics being pushed in both rightward and leftward directions by counter-systemic grassroots mobilizing requires a project around which to organize. This returns us to the GND, already introduced in Box 3.3 and swiftly establishing itself as a way of addressing simultaneously environment (decarbonizing the energy system), social (promoting justice and equity in flourishing healthy local communities) and economic (investing in infrastructure and renewables) needs in a joined-up way. It is being actively promoted in US politics, has emerged as a central plank of European social democracy (as, e.g. in the 2019 UK and Spanish general elections), was adopted by the European Commission in 2018 and is central to the agenda of Commission president Ursula van der Leyen, who took office at the end of 2019 and appointed Frans Timmermans as vice-president for the European Green Deal. Within days of their takeover, details of a comprehensive European Green Deal were announced covering how food is grown, air quality, travel and buildings.[22] Even the plans of the Chinese government to establish what it calls an 'ecological civilization' have been treated as a version of a GND.[23] Inevitably, such a widely endorsed concept will mean very different things to different people, inviting easy dismissal from both left and right. Riofrancos reports how, for left-wing critics, the GND saves capitalism from itself and leaves growth intact while the right sees it as a socialist monster involving state planning, rationing and enforced limits to consumption. But she emphasizes that what will decide which version wins out – the green capitalist or the ecosocialist or the many gradations in between – is politics: 'At every node in this global chain, the technical and the political are intimately entangled. Declaring by fiat that decarbonization is unlikely or impossible amounts to an avoidance of the complex, historic, world-making tasks ahead of us.'[24] It is this potential of the GND to become the battlefield around which version of the future wins out that makes it so significant. Riofrancos sees the GND as providing a historic opening for the left involving three key tasks: shifting the discussion, gathering political will and underscoring the urgency of the climate crisis, adding that 'it's unclear to me how a pathway to radical transformation wouldn't pass through these three crucial tests of political capacity'.[25]

The very fact that the concept of a GND is emerging as a vehicle for parties and countries to define how to address the transition to a low-carbon society, has already decisively shifted and defined the discussion. It broadens beyond a technocratic project focused on renewable energies coupled with individual lifestyle changes, to a social and economic transformation. This is evident in the two main versions, the UK one formulated in 2008 and the United States one formulated in 2018. As Pettifor, one of the original architects of the UK version, puts it: 'The Green New Deal demands major system change: both economic and ecological system change ... not just behavioural, community or technological change. ... In addition, as in the 1930s, such change must be driven by a radical structural transformation of the economy, particularly the financial sector.'[26] This would be driven by a new partnership between the state, local communities and workers: both the UK and the US versions emphasize the potential for creating large numbers of well-paid jobs by reskilling workers to undertake the infrastructural transformations required; the US GND emphasizes justice and equity for marginalized communities and the UK version sees the potential for local communities to generate their own energy through a decentralized low-carbon system while protecting low-income individuals and families. The GND therefore shifts the discussion to a whole-system approach to the low-carbon transition, moving far beyond the static focus on mitigation and adaptation that has so dominated policy on climate change up to now, narrowing it to a silo divorced from wider economic and social policies. A difference between both versions relates to finance: the US GND focuses on the state leveraging adequate capital resources but leaves the details deliberately vague whereas the UK version puts the transformation of the global financial system at the centre of its plan. Yet, the implications of each version for the financial system are far-reaching (see Box 9.2).

Box 9.2 Taming finance: Capital controls and stranded assets

Perhaps the most radical potential of the GND lies in its implications for the financial sector. Pettifor is very clear: 'Financing the hugely costly overhaul of the economy away from its dependence on fossil fuels cannot be achieved without the subordination of the finance sector to the interests of society and the planet.'[27] Polanyi would be pleased; yet, how is this to be done as the sector is likely to threaten a mass exodus of capital if it fears decisive action to curb it?

States need to begin by challenging the ideology that private interests prevail over public ones and that mobile capital should remain unregulated. Pettifor points to China to disprove the widely held view that capital controls are impossible in today's high-tech world. Although highly globalized, China deploys capital and exchange controls all the time, restricting Chinese investment in foreign companies and overseas property. Taxing capital would slow down the large 'hot' flows of capital while central banks could promote productive rather than speculative activity. Managing international capital flows is fundamental not just to finance the low-carbon transition but for the very survival of the planet, she writes.[28]

Rifkin sees global finance in deep trouble already as it faces a growing problem of stranded assets since investments are locked into fossil fuel extraction and infrastructure for decades ahead at a time when the transition to renewables has begun. The banking system is failing to understand the risks, he writes; these could reach $12 trillion of stranded fossil fuel assets by 2035, estimates the Global Commission on the Economy and Climate.[29] Rifkin expects global pension funds worth an estimated $41.3 trillion in 2017 to supply a good deal of the financing for the GND, as governments and public sector unions are already divesting their pension funds from fossil fuels and moving into renewables.[30] In the United States, taxing the super rich, redeploying some of the Pentagon's massive budget and terminating the almost $15 billion annual US federal subsidies to fossil fuels will generate further assets, he writes. Green banks, advocated by both Rifkin and Pettifor, are already established both in the United States and other countries.[31]

Pettifor reports that roughly $7 trillion per annum could be currently available for investment in transformative infrastructure whereas conservative estimates of the annual social costs of inaction amount to around $22 trillion, more than 25 per cent of global income. She concludes: 'Our monetary system and vast quantities of global savings make financing the transformation of the economy away from fossil fuels eminently affordable.' But citizens need to use our power as taxpayers 'to demand that public financial assets be used for public, not private benefit, and be deployed in the service of humanity and the ecosystem.'[32]

At a time when most countries' climate plans are regarded as being completely inadequate to meet the pledges they signed up to under the Paris Agreement in 2015,[33] and yet when two thirds of Americans regard climate change as either a crisis or a serious problem and want urgent action to address it,[34] the GND can serve to garner political will and underscore the urgency of the climate crisis, opening pathways towards the sorts of radical changes now required. For Rifkin, it needs to be transformed into a powerful narrative to take us forward to a great paradigm change equivalent to the Neolithic or the Industrial revolutions, involving 'infrastructure revolutions that change our temporal/spatial orientation, our economic models, our forms of governance, our orientation, our cognition, and our very worldview'.[35] A social movement Green New Deal for Europe was established in April 2019 and has published a *Blueprint for Europe's Just Transition*, offering an alternative to that of the European Commission.[36] In these ways, the GND is fast becoming the vehicle for a radically transformative vision involving a partnership between the state at all levels, local communities and businesses. But the energy to realize its transformative potential requires massive and sustained mobilization of the kind that Extinction Rebellion and the school strikes movement are beginning to show.

Harnessing automation

Automation, particularly in the guise of robotization and AI, has already featured in previous chapters, both as threat and as opportunity. Chapter 3 quoted Paul Mason's view that automation risks long-term stagnation as it destroys jobs and fuels yet greater inequality while Box 4.1 reported Peter Frase's discussion of how to realize technology's promise of leisure and plenty. Again, what will make the difference is politics, prising technology 'from the clutches of capital' in the words of Wendy Liu a writer on the politics of technology.[37] Yet unlike the struggles against the new right or against climate change, the very ubiquity of technology in structuring the ways we live makes this a very different struggle to mount. After all, in using social media we are handing over vast amounts of personal information which not only is used to target us as consumers or as voters, but runs the risk of such information falling into the hands of cybercriminals to be used against us. The emergence of what is being called the rentership society is locking our consumption patterns ever more deeply into high-tech devices with consequences for labour. More and more of the goods and services we require on a daily basis are being rented rather than being purchased, including cars, accommodation, music, books, furniture, electrodomestic goods, DIY tools, storage, even jewellery, shoes and clothes.[38] These trends are likely to intensify as a result of the enforced isolation caused by the Covid-19 pandemic which greatly boosted online shopping. This may be ushering in a circular economy which is cheaper for consumers and less carbon-intensive but contributes also to precarious and flexible work and to undermining local economies. AI raises even greater threats, as McKibben recognizes: 'As intelligence explodes, and the AI gains the ability to improve itself, it will soon outstrip our ability to control it.'[39] Much of the utopian hope held out for technology seems not to see these dark sides, and our dependence on it is in many ways a Faustian pact.

This is why putting the focus of struggle on prising technology from the clutches of capital is a good place to begin. Just like the economistic prejudice that framed the discussion in Chapter 8, so too there is a technological bias that blunts our critical facilities. As Shenker reminds us:

> If the current model feels like an inevitable outgrowth of technological progress, it is only because we are making the category error of conflating digital technologies with the logics of capitalism that currently control them, and of viewing ourselves as merely economic consumers rather than political subjects; only because our political imaginations have been foreclosed.[40]

We have seen evidence in Box 6.3 on McStrike and the Rise App of how technologies used by employers to control workers can instead be used in imaginative and subversive ways to turn the tables and create a common struggle against employers and managers. It is this very mutability that offers potential for harnessing automation, if used with political imagination. Indeed, the potential of technologies to subvert commodified capitalist uses is already being shown in creative ways through peer-to-peer practices creating 'novel configurations of working and producing together within a framework of openness, equity and sustainability'[41] (see Box 9.3) and through the design of novel forms of cybercurrencies such as Sardex, by-passing the banking system, distributing power to SMEs, protecting against financial speculation and strengthening the local economy (see Box 7.4). These are examples of ways in which the struggle to harness automation is already being waged.

Box 9.3 Using technologies to transition from capitalism

Commons-based peer production uses information and communication technologies to share creative outputs in an open-source way. One well-known example is the open-access encyclopaedia Wikipedia to which users are free to contribute. However, this model of production is now being applied to hardware as well, thus breaking with the industrial logic of intellectual property and promoting global access to industrial knowledge and localized physical construction. Known as Design Global – Manufacture Local (DG-ML), it helps overcome the often hostile environment of markets and empowers local communities. Examples include:

- Farm Hack: a network of farmers, primarily in the United States, who develop and openly share designs for agricultural tools, methods and machinery. It allows for entrepreneurial activity not driven by profit maximization but rather by relationships based on mutual values, understanding and support.
- L'atelier paysan: a non-profit cooperative that openly shares tools for small-scale organic agriculture. Based in France, funding allows it provide training workshops throughout the country that teach skills and build tools and machinery that participants can take away with them. It allows intensive research and development without relying on a model of commercialization.
- Sensorica: an open collaborative network of software developers, engineers, researchers, lawyers and others in Montreal, Canada, revolving around the design and deployment of open source sensors and sense-making systems. The network pools resources and develops projects driven more by intrinsic goals than financial remuneration.
- Enspiral: describes itself as 'a DIY collective of social enterprises, ventures, and individuals working collaboratively across the world' delivering professional services and products to support participatory organizing. Made up of the Enspiral Foundation, Enspiral Services and Startup Ventures, the collective open-sources solutions and creates apps so others can do the same.

DG-ML is pioneering innovative ways to develop business and organizational practices geared towards social goals. It thus presents a vision of alternative modes of economic relations and social sharing.[42]

Apart from subversive and creative actions, Mason identifies that the technology itself is subversive of the structures and assumptions of capitalism thus creating the terrain for moving beyond it. This is due to the fact that it uses a raw material – data – which is unlike any other ever used within the capitalist system as it is available in abundance rather than being scarce as is every other raw material. This then undermines the ability of the free market to set prices and make profits. Harnessing technology to the logic of capitalism has meant that companies seek to make data their private property, giving them exclusive control over it. Companies are building vast monopolies, gobbling up competitors so as to eradicate competition and maintain their control.[43] This is the current situation of Facebook, Yahoo, Google, Apple and Amazon which are driving record levels of mergers and acquisitions.[44] But this situation is also creating a new site of struggle around four key issues: (1) combating monopolies and price fixing, socializing the digital infrastructure in non-profit companies or state utilities; (2) combating precarious work and stagnant wages through a combination of a universal income and basic universal services; (3) legislating to make data a public good with each individual having the right to control their own; and (4) outlawing all business models based on asymmetric access to information. As Mason concludes:

> The end-state we should try to achieve is technological abundance: a world in which machines do most of the work, even most of the innovation; in which our massively expanded leisure time allows us to experience a rich cultural life; and in which our economic activity moves into harmony with what the earth can sustain.[45]

This lays out the agenda that would go a long way to harnessing automation to put it at the service of personal and social wellbeing and would certainly be a ruptural transformation. But there is another dark side as revealed by Foroohar. The big tech companies built up significant amounts of debt and many could become vulnerable if interest rates begin to rise. 'Apple and the other purveyors of intangibles have benefited more than other companies from this environment of low rates, cheap debt and high stock prices over the past 10 years,' she writes. 'But their power has also sowed the seeds of what could be the next big swing in the markets.'[46] This is because the $1 trillion in corporate savings parked in offshore accounts, 80 per cent of it owned by ICT companies like Apple, Microsoft, Cisco, Oracle and Google, if sold or downgraded, could topple the markets themselves. These companies have become 'the apex of the shift towards financialisation' but their valuations depend in part to the market's expectations that they will remain lightly regulated, lightly taxed monopoly powers. With growing scrutiny of antitrust and monopoly issues among Washington power elites, this may be under threat.

Conclusions: Transforming market society

The transformation of market society is already underway. One major reason why this isn't as obvious as it should be is that the old Hayekian story of individual liberty and free markets, of 'freedom of choice in a competitive society'[47] still holds the public imagination. This is for want of an alternative account of how to better order society and the economy for human wellbeing and flourishing. Polanyi offers such an account and this book has taken some of his key insights from his writings, insights to which more and more people have been drawn since the 1990s because of their explanatory power. Polanyi's narrative invests significance to innovations and practices that otherwise seem marginal and of little significance, joining the dots as it were to reveal that an alternative is already being built in a myriad of initiatives, struggles and practices all over the world, as shown in these pages. The central thread that unites them is combating and overcoming the rule of capital over our personal and public lives, freeing society in all its richness from the straitjacket of the market mechanism. Many see the sorts of struggles and initiatives recounted here as evidence of the double movement but this is to reduce Polanyi's radical and emancipatory potential, seeing history as a permanent pendulum swing between the poles of commodification and decommodification. Instead Polanyi believed after the Second World War that the market was again embedded in society and he didn't expect the utopian experiment of the self-governing market would return. Yet the socialist society he aspired to was not yet achieved and so more needed to be done. Therefore the emphasis here has been on placing the decommodification of land, labour and money at the centre of the struggle to overcome market society, thereby addressing the triple crisis of our age – environmental, social and financial. This is the pathway to the sort of free society Polanyi wanted, characterized by people freely assuming their social responsibilities. Polanyi never believed that there was any inevitability of victory; he didn't share the widespread Marxist determinism of his age. Instead he believed in the struggle of ordinary people, particularly those who could put the common interest beyond any particular interests, and in places he identified the working class in a particular though not exclusive way as doing this. Thus, the new future is built from the bottom-up, through local creativity and ambition. This is the rich institutional setting for a reciprocal gift-giving economy, so vitiated and undermined by the power of the market mechanism over our economic lives. But it still lives on in the many social networks of interdependence that support our lives, particularly during times of vulnerability, as Covid-19 so powerfully revealed.[48] But state support is also important and provides the institutional basis for redistribution, not just of monetary supports but of life chances, of social capacities, of skills and of creativity. And it is always under the control of the people, fostering their self-organization. Finally, Polanyi recognized the importance of markets as social institutions bringing producers and consumers together in ways that strengthen social bonds and local economies. The markets Polanyi set his face against were those of land, labour and money, because they were based on a fiction and ended up destroying society and the natural world on which we all depend.

Polanyi certainly doesn't have all the answers. His work is characterized by an optimism about social collaboration that fails to address the ways in which divisions can often hinder success at local community level. In this, the criticism levelled at theorists of the commons for neglecting 'the ways that different dimensions of inequality and relations of power interact with the commons'[49] could also apply to Polanyi despite the fact that he did recognize the deep class divisions within communities and he reminds us that community cannot be community unless it overcomes the wider structural impediments of the market society in which it is embedded. In our times, his theory of the state seems rather threadbare, and his work could be richly complemented by consideration of the ways in which the state can build social power, such as the Carnegie Trust project on the enabling state.[50] As has emerged in various examples given in this book, a partnership between the state and local community initiatives can be crucial in providing routes to the non-commodified provision of key community goods such as housing.

In essence, Polanyi's focus is on reconciling the individual with the community and this is a contribution of immense contemporary importance. Dale describes Polanyi's 'genealogy of socialism' as follows:

> It is a movement that aspires to the integration of individual autonomy and moral community; this goal requires a commitment to the values of individuality, community, democracy, equality and freedom. Ultimately, these shared liberal-socialist values have their roots in Christianity ... Socialism, in short, inherits the values of Christianity and carries out a social transformation such that these can flourish in a post-liberal world.[51]

Polanyi's understanding of freedom as social freedom directly challenges and expands Hayek's reduction of freedom to individual choice, an understanding that has done great damage to the contemporary world. Restoring an understanding of freedom as assuming one's social responsibility is therefore a grounding principle of the Polanyian narrative. One unlikely place where we see this finding expression today is in the thinking of Pope Francis[52] whose encyclical letter *Laudato Sí* on 'Care for our Common Home' has many Polanyian emphases, not least on the essentially social nature of the human person.[53] Pope Francis also shares a Polanyian view of technology being constrained by a techno-economic paradigm to serve the needs of 'certain powerful groups'[54] rather than those of society and, in general, he shares Polanyi's view of liberation from the dominant technocratic paradigm coming from grassroots projects like small producers' cooperatives who opt 'for a non-consumerist model of life, recreation and community'.[55]

Humanity is moving into a time of fundamental social change. Climate change and its intensifying impacts on people and their livelihoods throughout the world assures us of this. Yet as novelist Amitav Ghosh puts it, 'It is increasingly clear to me that the formal political structures of our time are incapable of confronting this crisis on their own.'[56] Society will be forced to assume much greater responsibility than has been the case for decades, something more akin to how society has to mobilize in wartime. But war is a temporary phase whereas we now face decades of the most fundamental re-orientation of our societies, our economies and our values if we are to move back within the safe carrying capacity of the planet we inhabit. This is the transition we must undertake and while we might speak of the end goal as a low- or post-carbon society, we have very little idea of what kind of society this is going to be. We will be thrown back on ourselves, our imagination, our creativity and our networks of interdependency, in ways that we got a foretaste of during the coronavirus pandemic. Society will be rebuilt on a basis of strong local communities which will be the bulwark against collapse. In this situation, Polanyi provides essential elements of the values and orientation we need, awakening us to the fact that formal economics and the market mechanism have led us to this crisis point and we need now to set out on a new path to re-create an economy that strengthens the resources, capacity and resilience of local communities, rebuilding society from that base. In the final letter he wrote before he died, Polanyi expressed this lifelong vision: 'The heart of the socialist nation is the people, where collective existence is the enjoyment of a community culture. I myself have never lived in such a society.'[57] Now the time is ripe to make it a reality.

Appendix

Karl Polanyi (1886–1964) A biographical note

Karl Polanyi's life spanned the major defining struggles of the first half of the twentieth century, from the end of the imperial division of power that dominated Europe in the nineteenth century, through the collapse of the liberal order in the First World War and subsequently the rise of communism and fascism. Following the Second World War, he saw the re-emergence of a stable trans-Atlantic liberal order as a key constituent feature of a world divided into a First, a Second and, following decolonization, a Third World. These were all firmly in place by the time of his death in 1964. But Polanyi did more than observe these momentous changes as his life was repeatedly shaped by them. Born in Vienna in 1886, his family had links with early Russian revolutionary socialists through his mother who had come from Tsarist Russia. His father was a Jewish-Hungarian engineer and he moved the family to Budapest in the early 1890s where Karl was given what his daughter described as 'a first-class home education', fostering an early love of classical Greek and a lifelong interest in the philosophy of Aristotle.[1] As a law student in Budapest, he became involved in student politics and was the founding president of a Hungarian student movement, the Galilei Circle, challenging the backwardness of Hungarian society and holding literacy classes for peasants and workers, inspired by the Russian student movements of the 1880s. He was a cavalry officer on the Russian front during the First World War but contracted typhus and was seriously injured when his horse fell on him. He witnessed but did not support the short-lived Hungarian Soviet Republic in 1919 and moved to Vienna for medical treatment later that year.

Polanyi lived in Vienna until 1933 working from 1924 as a senior editor of *Der Oesterreichische Volkswirt*, the most important economic and financial weekly of the German-speaking world at the time, closely observing and commenting on the momentous international events of the period. Living in 'red Vienna' with its strong labour movement, socialist municipality and consumer co-operatives awakened in Polanyi an interest in guild socialism, a subject on which he lectured in the Socialist People's University. He immersed himself in the intellectual ferment of the time, and its active debates on the feasibility of a socialist economy. As a young man, Polanyi had engaged in a debate in the pages of the most important social science journal in the German-speaking world with the liberal economist Ludwig von Mises who argued that socialism was not only undesirable but impossible.[2] Interestingly, Friedrich Hayek, later to be seen as the father of neoliberalism, attended the private seminars of von Mises in Vienna in the 1920s and spread the individualist, anti-interventionist and anti-socialist ideas of the latter in the English-speaking world when he was appointed to a chair at the London School of Economics in 1931. Other key figures contributing to economic debates in Vienna at this time included Joseph Schumpeter, Otto Bauer, a founder of Austro-Marxism, and Paul Rosenstein-Rodan who went on to be a major influence on the emergence of development economics. Polanyi was later to be quoted as saying that the socialist experiments led by the Austrian social democrats in Vienna in the 1920s were 'one of the highpoints of western civilization'[3] and the city was the seedbed of many of the key ideas that were to shape the rest of the twentieth century, including social democracy and neoliberalism. As Block and Somers write: 'Despite being much less well known than other major economic thinkers, Karl Polanyi provides us with the most incisive intellectual apparatus available to understand the actual workings and consequences of market economies.'[4]

It was in Vienna that Polanyi had begun to develop his understanding of socialism and to distinguish it from the dominant Marxism of his milieu. Even before moving to Vienna, Polanyi had clearly parted company with core tenets of Marxism, elaborating a critique that he held to throughout his life. What troubled him about Marxism helps to identify themes that were to inform his life's work. A central issue was determinism, namely that Marx saw political processes and revolution itself as emerging from historical necessity rather than from the activities of living people. For Marx, a revolutionary epoch is ushered in when the development of productive forces (slavery, serfdom, wage labour) enters into contradiction with existing relations of production. For Polanyi, this neglected people's beliefs and values which in his view are what drive social change. Marxist inevitability, he wrote, mirrors a laissez-faire inevitability about capitalist development, both of them being 'a materialistic legacy of the nineteenth century which economic history does not bear out.'[5]

And Marx's labour theory of value he saw as being bourgeois in origin and close to the views of some of the key theorists of mainstream economics, Adam Smith and David Ricardo.[6] Instead, the theme of freedom was, for Polanyi, the core of socialism to which he returned again and again:

> Never has there been such an absurd superstition as the belief that the history of man is governed by laws which are independent of his will and action. The concept of a future which awaits us somewhere is senseless because the future does not exist, not now or later. This future is constantly being remade by those who live in the present. The present only is reality. There is no future that gives validity to our actions in the present.[7]

Related to this was his fear of how technology threatens human freedom, what he called the 'subordination of man to the needs of the machine'.[8] This was to become another major theme of his work. Neither did Polanyi agree with Marx's view of the state as an appendage of the capitalist economy and the consequent need to dismantle it. Instead he saw how the state could defend the interests of the people, protecting society from the inroads of the market.

However, in the early 1920s 'Polanyi's attitude to Marxism was at its frostiest but it rapidly thawed'.[9] This was due to his experience of the transformation of working-class culture in Vienna under the influence of the Austro-Marxist Social Democratic Party. Not only did this convince him that the values of the mass of the population could be fundamentally changed through the restructuring of social conditions but it also led him back to Marx's theories of alienation and commodity fetishism, finding them consistent with and, indeed, 'deeply indebted to Christianity, to the substance of its moral aims'.[10] Polanyi's conception of socialism, as elaborated over this period, rejected both the market economy and the centralized command economy emerging in the Soviet Union. Instead, as his daughter Kari Polanyi Levitt writes, he considered both of these to be forms of 'unfreedom':

> His model was essentially one of cooperative associations of producers, consumers and communities (municipalities etc.) jointly determining the allocation and distribution of resources in a process of negotiation whereby economic efficiency criteria would be consciously moderated by social policy as determined by the members of these associations. This was not a market-less economy, nor an economy without money.[11]

It was essentially a self-reliant, bottom-up, participatory socialism, in which producers and consumers negotiated to ensure the needs of society were met as far as possible.

When he moved to England in 1933, Polanyi encountered the world of the working class through his work with the Workers Education Association. Here he moved in Christian Left circles where he introduced the early and more humanistic writings of Marx. He also began to study the origins of industrial capitalism in England, a study that was to result in the writing of his best-known work *The Great Transformation*, published in the United States in 1944 (the same year that Hayek published *The Road to Serfdom* in Britain). Granted British citizenship in 1940, he was able to travel between Britain and the United States and he accepted a teaching post in Bennington College in Vermont in 1940. However, the fact that he didn't fit easily into any of the accepted divisions of the social sciences resulted in the termination of his contract and he returned to England in 1943, where himself and his wife, Ilona, herself a distinguished academic and activist, participated in discussions on the post-war order that were to influence the two final chapters of *The Great Transformation*. The election of the Labour government in 1945 he saw as opening a possible socialist future for Britain. But, while advocating a system of managed trade for the world's major regions, 'he clearly underestimated the capacity of the United States to impose universal capitalism on the world', as his daughter put it.[12] An appointment to Columbia University in 1947 opened a final and very productive phase of Polanyi's life where he worked with a team of anthropologists studying the role of markets, trade and money in pre-industrial societies around the world. These studies sought to challenge the belief that the mechanism of a self-governing market, which Polanyi saw as a novelty introduced at the time of the British Industrial Revolution in the nineteenth century, was a feature of economic systems before that time. Instead, Polanyi and his team found evidence that economic life was integrated or embedded in society through the mechanisms of reciprocity, redistribution and exchange. Polanyi's wife, Ilona, who had been a communist party member earlier in her life, was denied entry to the United States during the McCarthy anti-communist purges, and so the couple established a home outside Toronto while Karl worked in New York. Diagnosed with cancer in 1957, he continued to work and helped establish a journal *Co-Existence* with the support of eminent economists which sought to encourage communication across the Cold War divide and to provide a platform for the international community of socialist intellectuals. The couple received many Hungarian exiles who emigrated to Canada following the Hungarian Revolution in 1956, and they visited Budapest a year before Karl's death. In 1986, both were reburied in a Budapest cemetery.

Notes

Chapter 1

1   Polanyi, Karl: 'General Economic History', in Giorgio Resta and Mariavittoria Catanzariti, eds: *Karl Polanyi: For a New West: Essays, 1919–1958*, Polity, 2014: 133–47, quote at p. 136 [written as an introductory lecture for a course on General Economic History at Columbia University, 1950–52].

2   Dale, Gareth: *Reconstructing Karl Polanyi*, Pluto Press, 2016, p. 1.

3   Mouffe, Chantal: *For a Left Populism*, Verso, 2018, p. 12. She takes the term from Gramsci and defines it as 'a period of crisis during which several tenets of the consensus established around a hegemonic project are challenged'.

4   Harari, Yuval Noah: *21 Lessons for the 21st Century*, Jonathan Cape, 2018, p. xiii.

5   Polanyi Levitt, Kari: 'The Power of Ideas: Keynes, Hayek, and Polanyi', in *International Journal of Political Economy*, Vol. 41, No. 4, Winter 2012–13: 5–15, quote on p. 14.

6   Chakrabortty, Aditya: 'The End Is Nigh for Davos Man and His Way of Doing Business', *The Guardian Weekly*, 1st February 2019, p. 48.

7   Bregman, Rutger: *Utopia for Realists: And How We Can Get There*, Bloomsbury, 2017, p. 11.

8   The lack of a category related to insecurity may surprise some readers. Clearly insecurity is an abiding concern in today's global order. Violent attacks by people motivated by either a white supremacist or a radical Islamist political worldview have killed and injured many innocent civilians in a range of countries, both developing and developed. Geopolitical instability is also a feature of today's world as alliances erode, new power vacuums open up (Syria, Libya and Yemen at the moment) and the militarization of a more assertive China all generate a new unpredictability. Yet, in many ways these are contemporary manifestations of tendencies that have emerged again and again in the capitalist global order and, while destabilizing that order, are difficult to label as threats to the capitalist order.

9   Kirby, Peadar: *Vulnerability and Violence: The Impact of Globalisation*, Pluto Press, 2006.

10 Harris, Nigel: *The End of the Third World*, Penguin, 1987

11 Lizoain Bennett, David: *Fin del Primer Mundo*, Catarata, 2017.

12 Luce, Edward: *The Retreat of Western Liberalism*, Little, Brown, 2017, p. 191.

13 Mair, Peter: *Ruling the Void: The Hollowing-out of Western Democracy*, Verso, 2013.

14 For introductions to neoliberalism, see Manfred B. Steger and Ravi K. Roy: *Neoliberalism: A Very Short Introduction*, Oxford University Press, 2010; and David Harvey: *A Brief History of Neoliberalism*, Oxford University Press, 2005.

15 Streeck, Wolfgang: 'The Return of the Repressed as the Beginning of the End of Neoliberal Capitalism', in Heinrich Geiselberger, ed.: *The Great Regression*, Polity, 2017: 157–72, quote at p. 158.

16 Zielonka, Jan: *Counter-Revolution: Liberal Europe in Retreat*, Oxford University Press, 2018, pp. 9, 13.

17 Ibid. p. 131.

18 See Benjamin Thomas White: 'Talk of an "unprecedented" number of refugees is wrong – and dangerous', in the *New Humanitarian*, 3rd October 2019.

19 Bauman, Zygmunt: 'Symptoms in Search of an Object and a Name', in Heinrich Geiselberger, ed.: *The Great Regression*, Polity, 2017: 13–25, quote at p. 21.

20 Ibid., p. 24.

21 Ther, Philipp: *The Outsiders: Refugees in Europe since 1492*, Princeton University Press, 2016.

22 Harari, Yuval Noah: *21 Lessons for the 21st Century*, Jonathan Cape, 2018, pp. 154–5.

23 Bridle, James: *New Dark Age: Technology and the End of the Future*, Verso, 2018, p. 2.

24 Ford, Martin: *The Rise of the Robots: Technology and the Treat of Mass Unemployment*, Oneworld Publications, 2016, p. 27.

25 Ibid., p. 109.

26 Hariri, ibid., p. 48.

27 Collins, Randall: 'The End of Middle-Class Work: No More Escapes', in Immanuel Wallerstein, Randall Collins, Michael Mann, Georgi Derluguian and Craig Calhoun: *Does Capitalism Have a Future?*, Oxford University Press, 2013: 37–69, quote at p. 68.

28 Intergovernmental Panel on Climate Change (IPCC): *Special Report on Global Warming of 1.5°C*, IPCC, 2018, Par. B5.

29 Guterres is referring to the slew of scientific reports on aspects of climate change and biodiversity loss being published. For example, in one three-day period in February 2019, *The Guardian* reported on four major reports: on 4th February a report revealed that at least a third of the huge ice fields in Asia's mountain chain is doomed to melt due to climate change, on 6th February US scientists revealed that global temperatures in 2018 were the fourth warmest on record, on the same day the UK's Met Office forecast that global warming could temporarily reach

1.5°C above pre-industrial levels between now and 2023, while on the following day scientists revealed they had discovered a giant cavity beneath a disintegrating glacier in Antarctica, sparking concerns that the ice sheet is melting more rapidly than expected with severe consequences for rising sea levels around the world. See *The Guardian Weekly*, 15th February 2019, p. 11.

30 WWF: *Living Planet Report 2018: Aiming Higher*, WWF, 2018, p. 11.

31 IPPR: *This Is a Crisis: Facing Up to the Age of Environmental Breakdown*, IPPR, 2019, pp. 19, 20.

32 Ibid., p. 17.

33 Monbiot, George: *How Did We Get into This Mess?*, Verso, 2016, pp. 9–13.

34 Patel, Vikram et al.: The Lancet Commission on Global Mental Health and Sustainable Development, in *The Lancet*, Vol. 392, No. 10157, pp. 1553–98.

35 Garcés, Marina: *Nueva ilustración radical*, Editorial Anagrama, 2017, p. 9. Translation by P. Kirby.

36 Ibid., p. 26.

37 Ibid., p. 56.

38 Taylor, Steven: 'For the Generation Shaped by Coronavirus, Life May Never Fully Return to "Normal"', in the *Guardian*, 7th April 2020.

39 Conroy, Catherine: 'This Is Not the Fall of the Roman Empire, This Is a Larger Scale', the *Irish Times*, 17th October 2018, p. 12.

40 Oreskes, Naomi and Erik M. Conway: *The Collapse of Western Civilization: A View from the Future*, Columbia University Press, 2014, p. ix.

41 Ibid., p. 77.

42 Ibid., p. 79.

43 Meadows, Donella, Jorgen Randers and Dennis Meadows: *Limits to Growth: The 30-Year Update*, Chelsea Green Publishing Company, 2004

44 Latouche, Serge (with Susan George, Jean-Pierre Dupuy, and Yves Cochet): *Hacia Dónde Va el Mundo?* Icaria, 2012, pp. 64–5.

45 Trisos, Christopher H., Cory Merow and Alex L. Pigot: 'The Projected Timing of Abrupt Ecological Disruption from Climate Change' in *Nature*, April 2020, https://doi.org/10.1038/s41586-020-2189-9, accessed 15th April 2020.

46 Raskin, Paul: *Journey to Earthland: The Great Transition to Planetary Civilization*, Tellus Institute, 2016, p. 21.

47 Ibid., pp. 111–12.

48 Rendueles, César: 'From Global Regression to Post-capitalist Counter-Movements', in Heinrich Geiselberger, ed.: *The Great Regression*, Polity, 2017: 142–56, quote at p. 146.

Notes

49 Joseph Stiglitz wrote the foreword to a new edition of *The Great Transformation*, published in 2001.

50 Block, Fred and Margaret R. Somers: *The Power of Market Fundamentalism: Karl Polanyi's Critique*, Harvard University Press, 2014, quotes at pp. 8, 9.

51 Polanyi, Karl: *The Great Transformation: The Political and Economic Origins of Our Time*, Beacon Press, 2001, p. 257.

52 Ibid., p. 60.

53 Ibid., p. 89.

54 Ibid., p. 137.

55 Ibid., p. 138.

56 When the New Economics Foundation published a report on how to redesign the economy to address systemic challenges by 2050 it called it *The Great Transition* 'as a deliberate echo' of Karl Polanyi's *The Great Transformation,* since his work offers 'a balance between the market and the non-market; the private and the public; the individual and the community'. See *The Great Transition*, NEF, 2009, p. 1. The German Advisory Council on Global Change (WBGU), an advisory body to the German Chancellor, also explicitly describes its work on climate change as the Great Transformation 'not least with reference to Karl Polanyi's *Great Transformation* to describe an all-encompassing transition'. See WBGU: *World in Transition: A Social Contract for Sustainability*, Berlin, 2011, p. 83.

Chapter 2

1 See the early pages of Gareth Dale: *Karl Polanyi*, Polity, 2010.

2 Snyder, Timothy: *On Tyranny: Twenty Lessons from the Twentieth Century*, Bodley Head, 2017.

3 Runciman, David: *How Democracy Ends*, Profile Books, 2018.

4 Inevitably, the selection of these themes is selective and subjective, reflecting one person's attempt to give an overview of some dominant forces reshaping our world.

5 Luce, Edward: *The Retreat of Western Liberalism*, Little, Brown, 2017, p. 184.

6 Ibid., p. 203.

7 Levitsky, Steven and Daniel Ziblatt: *How Democracies Die: What History Reveals about Our Future*, Penguin, 2018.

8 Murray, Douglas: *The Strange Death of Europe: Immigration, Identity, Islam*, Bloomsbury, 2017.

Notes

9   Runciman, David: 'Coronavirus Is Revealing the True Nature of Political Power', in the *Guardian*, 27th March 2020.

10   Zielonka, Jan: *Counter-Revolution: Liberal Europe in Retreat*, Oxford University Press, 2018, p. 25.

11   Ibid., p. 31.

12   Ignatieff, Michael: *The Ordinary Virtues: Moral Order in a Divided World*, Harvard University Press, 2017, p. 30.

13   Ibid., p. 199.

14   Ibid., p. 204.

15   Ibid., p. 207.

16   Ibid., p. 220.

17   The term 'new populism' is the title of a series of investigative reports by the *Guardian*. See the cover story of the *Guardian Weekly*, Vol. 199, No. 26, 30th November 2018.

18   Judis, John B.: *The Populist Explosion*, Columbia Global Reports, 2016.

19   Eatwell, Roger and Matthew Goodwin: *National Populism: The Revolt against Liberal Democracy*, Pelican, 2018, p. 43.

20   Muddle, Cas and Cristóbal Rovira Kaltwasser: *Populism: A Very Short Introduction*, Oxford University Press, 2017, pp. 9–19.

21   Muller, Jan-Werner: *What Is Populism?*, Penguin, 2017.

22   Eatwell and Goodwin, op. cit., p. 39.

23   Runciman, David: *How Democracy Ends*, Profile Books, 2018, pp. 65 and 66.

24   Ibid., p. 63.

25   Castells, Manuel: *Ruptura: La Crisis de la Democracia Liberal*, Alianza Editorial, 2017, p. 21. Translation by PK.

26   Goodhart, David: *The Road to Somewhere: The Populist Revolt and the Future of Politics*, Hurst and Company, 2017, p. 19

27   Luce, op. cit., p. 193.

28   Runciman, op. cit., p. 70.

29   Mishra, Pankaj: *Age of Anger: A History of the Present*, Penguin, 2017, p. 11.

30   Ibid., pp. 13–14.

31   Mair, Peter: *Ruling the Void: The Hollowing of Western Democracy*, Verso, 2013, pp. 75–89.

32   Runciman, op. cit., p. 73.

33   See 'In Europe, Right-wing Parties Are Offering Bigger Handouts than Traditional Ones', in the *Economist*, 25th January 2018; Max Holleran: 'The Opportunistic Rise of Europe's Far Right', in *New Republic*, 16th February 2018; and Emily Schultheis: 'How Italy's Fire-star Movement Is Winning the Youth Vote', in the *Atlantic*, 2nd March 2018.

34 Lewis, Paul, Seán Clarke and Caelainn Barr: 'People Power: Do Populist Leaders Actually Reduce Inequality?' in the *Guardian Weekly*, 15th March 2019, p. 18.

35 Coman, Julian: 'Law and Justice and the Fight for the Soul of Poland', in the *Guardian Weekly*, 11th October 2019.

36 Runciman, op. cit., p. 79.

37 Dale, Gareth: *Karl Polanyi*, op. cit., p. 48.

38 See Anthony Payne: *The Global Politics of Unequal Development*, Palgrave Macmillan, 2005.

39 Dale, op. cit., p. 249.

40 Rajan, Raghuram: *The Third Pillar: The Revival of Community in a Polarised World*, William Collins, 2019, p. 131.

41 Ibid., p. 243.

42 Ibid., p. xiii.

43 Ibid., p. 373.

44 Ibid., p. 392.

45 Polanyi, Karl: *The Great Transformation*, op. cit., p. 76.

46 Ibid., pp. 164–5.

47 Homes, Christopher: *Polanyi in Times of Populism: Vision and Contradiction in the History of Economic Ideas*, Routledge, 2018, p. 139.

48 Ibid., pp. 145–6.

49 Ibid., p. 147.

Chapter 3

1 A US Gallup poll in August 2018 found that among Democratic voters, 47 per cent view capitalism positively, a decline from 56 per cent in 2016, while 57 per cent view socialism positively, a drop of 1 per cent since 2016 but an increase from 53 per cent in 2010. Negative views of capitalism are higher among younger voters (18–29 years old). The terms 'capitalism' and 'socialism' were not defined in the poll. See Frank Newport: 'Democrats More Positive about Socialism than Capitalism' in *Gallup News*, 13th August 2018.

2 Mason, Paul: *Postcapitalism: A Guide to Our Future*, Allen Lane, 2015, p. 5.

3 Ibid., p. 29.

4 Streeck, Wolfgang: *How Will Capitalism End?*, Verso, 2016, p. 56.

5 The *Economic Times*: 'Raghuram Rajan Says Capitalism Is "Under Serious Threat"', 12th March 2019.

6   Jenkins, Patrick: 'City Fund Managers Call for Rethink of Capitalism', in the *Financial Times*, 15th November 2019.

7   Collier, Paul: *The Future of Capitalism: Facing the New Anxieties*, Allen Lane, 2018, pp. 3 and 4.

8   Milanovic, Branko: *Capitalism, Alone: The Future of the System That Rules the World*, Harvard University Press, 2019, p. 177.

9   Ibid., p. 178.

10 Ibid., p. 199.

11 Ibid., p. 200.

12 Ibid., pp. 215–18.

13 Collier, Paul: *The Future of Capitalism: Facing the New Anxieties*, op. cit., p. 19.

14 Ibid., p. 212.

15 As examples of corruption, Streeck mentions pay-offs from legal, semi-legal and illegal activities to politicians and public authorities; revolving doors between employment in the private and the public sectors; capture of regulatory agencies and of public administration itself by corporate interests; bailouts of private banks by public authorities as citizens endure deepening austerity; money laundering and offshore accounts being extensively used by elites in both the public and private sectors; widespread evasion of taxes by some of the largest global corporations; fraudulent activities by major banks and financial institutions; and the role played by rating agencies and auditors in hiding shady financial dealing from the public eye.

16 Streeck, Wolfgang: *How Will Capitalism End?*, op. cit., pp. 65–72.

17 Ibid., p. 72.

18 Di Muzio, Tim: *Carbon Capitalism: Energy, Social Reproduction and World Order*, Rowman & Littlefield, 2015.

19 The term 'peak oil' refers to the point where the maximum rate of extraction of oil is reached after which it begins to enter into terminal decline. While experts differ on when this will occur, with some estimating it was already passed in the early 2000s and others pushing it back to the 2020s, few deny that it is imminent.

20 IEA: *Global Energy and CO2 Status Report*, International Energy Agency, 2019.

21 Carrington, Damian, Jillian Ambrose and Matthew Taylor: 'Will the Coronavirus Kill the Oil Industry and Help Save the Climate?' in the *Guardian*, 1st April 2020.

22 Quoted in Fred Pearce: 'After the Coronavirus, Two Sharply Divergent Paths on Climate', in *Yale Environment 360*, 7th April 2020.

23 Pirani, Simon: *Burning Up: A Global History of Fossil Fuel Consumption*, Pluto Press, 2018, p. 187.

24 Ibid., pp. 189–90.

25 Streeck, Wolfgang: *How Will Capitalism End?*, op. cit., p. 64.

26 Fulcher, James: *Capitalism: A Very Short Introduction*, Oxford University Press, 2004, pp. 13–18.

27 Editorial Board of the Financial Times: 'Virus Lays Bare the Frailty of the Social Contract', in the *Financial Times*, 3rd April 2020.

28 Klein, Naomi: *This Changes Everything: Capitalism vs the Climate*, Allen Lane, 2014.

29 Ibid., p. 158.

30 Ibid., p. 255.

31 Emissions trading schemes allocate permits to emit greenhouse gases. These permits can be given free or auctioned. They can be allocated to countries (in international schemes) or companies: those whose emissions fall below their allowance generate credits which they can sell to those who exceed their allowance. The range of sectors covered varies greatly in different schemes as does the price of carbon per ton: in 2018 it varied from \$20 to less than \$5.

32 International Carbon Action Partnership: *Emissions Trading Worldwide: Status Report 2019*, ICAP, 2019.

33 See https://newclimateeconomy.net/content/about, accessed 3rd May 2019.

34 Newell, Peter and Matthew Paterson: *Climate Capitalism: Global Warming and the Transformation of the Global Economy*, Cambridge University Press, 2010.

35 See Climate Home News report from Madrid Climate Summit, 10th December 2019, www.climatechangenews.com, accessed 11th December 2019.

36 Elliott, Larry: 'Capitalism Can Crack Climate Change: But Only if It Takes Risks', in the *Guardian*, 16th August 2018.

37 Newell and Paterson, op. cit., p. 175.

38 Pearce, Fred: 'After the Coronavirus, Two Sharply Divergent Paths on Climate', op.cit.

39 Jackson, Tim and Peter. E. Victor: 'Unraveling the Claims for (and against) Green Growth', in *Science*, 22nd November 2019: 950–1.

40 Hckel, Jason and Giorgos Kallis: 'Is Green Growth Possible?', in *New Political Economy*, April 2019, https://doi.org/10.1080/13563467.2019.1598964, p. 12, accessed 19th April 2019.

41 Gough, Ian: *Heat, Greed and Human Need: Climate Change, Capitalism and Sustainable Wellbeing*, Edward Elgar, 2017, p. 83.

42 Ibid., pp. 78–9.

43 Green New Deal Group: *A Green New Deal*, New Economics Foundation, 2008, quote at p. 23.

44 Roberts, David: 'The Green New Deal Explained', *Vox*, March 2019: https://www.vox.com/energy-and-environment/2018/12/21/18144138/green-new-deal-alexandria-ocasio-cortez, accessed 3rd May 2019.

45 Dale, Gareth: *Reconstructing Karl Polanyi*, Pluto Press, 2016, p. 69.

46 See Fred Block and Margaret R. Somers: *The Power of Market Fundamentalism: Karl Polanyi's Critique*, op.cit.

47 Runciman, David: *How Democracy Ends*, op. cit., p. 71.

48 Shenker, Jack: *Now We Have Your Attention: The New Politics of the People*, The Bodley Head, 2019, p. 240.

49 Polanyi, Karl: *The Great Transformation*, op. cit., p. 120.

50 Ibid., p. 74.

51 Ibid., p. 60.

52 Monbiot, George: 'Future Lives Should Not Be Sacrificed to Fuel Our Greed', in the *Guardian Weekly*, 22nd March 2019, pp. 48–9.

53 Quoted in Gareth Dale: *Karl Polanyi*, op. cit., p. 199.

54 Holmes, Christopher: *Polanyi in Times of Populism: Vision and Contradiction in the History of Economic Ideas*, Routledge, 2018, p. 24.

55 Felber, Christian: *Change Everything: Creating an Economy for the Common Good*, Zed Books, 2015, p. 1.

56 Polanyi, op. cit., p. 258.

57 Polanyi Levitt, Kari: 'Tracing Polanyi's Institutional Political Economy to Its Central European Source', in Kenneth McRobbie and Kari Polani Levitt, eds: *Polanyi in Vienna: The Contemporary Significance of the Great Transformation*, Black Rose Books, 2006, pp. 378–91, quote on p. 388.

58 UNDP: *Human Development Report 2011: Sustainability and Equity*, Palgrave Macmillan, 2011, p. 15.

59 Roy, J., P. Tschakert, H. Waisman, W. Abdul Halim, P. Antwi-Agyei, P. Dasgupta, B. Hayward, M. Kanninen, C. Okereke, P.F. Pinho, K. Riahi and A.G. Suarez Rodriguez, 2018: Sustainable Development, Poverty Eradication and Reducing Inequalities. In: Global Warming of 1.5°C. An IPCC Special Report on the impacts of global warming of 1.5°C above pre-industrial levels and related global greenhouse gas emission pathways, in the context of strengthening the global response to the threat of climate change, sustainable development and efforts to eradicate poverty. Masson-Delmotte, V., P. Zhai, H.-O. Pörtner, D. Roberts, J. Skea, P.R. Shukla, A. Pirani, W. Moufouma-Okia, C. Péan, R. Pidcock, S. Connors, J.B.R. Matthews, Y. Chen,

X. Zhou, M.I. Gomis, E. Lonnoy, T. Maycock, M. Tignor and T. Waterfield (eds): IPCC, 2018, pp. 450, 458.

60 IPBES: 'Summary for Policymakers of the Global Assessment Report on Biodiversity and Ecosystem Services', 2019, https://www.ipbes.net/system/tdf/spm_global_unedited_advance.pdf?file=1&type=node&id=35245, pp. 29 and 31, accessed 8th May 2019.

61 European Environment Agency: *The European Environment: State and Outlook 2020*, EEA, 2019.

Chapter 4

1 Bregman, Rutger: *Utopia for Realists*, Bloomsbury, 2017, pp. 256, 258.

2 Jones, Owen: 'Corby and Sanders May Have Gone, but They Have Radically Altered Our Politics', in the *Guardian*, 16th April 2020.

3 Judt, Tony: *Ill Fares the Land*, Penguin, 2011, p. 236.

4 Honneth, Axel: *The Idea of Socialism*, Polity, 2017, pp. vii, 1.

5 Judt, Tony: *Ill Fares the Land*, op. cit., p. 236.

6 Fernández-Viagas, Javier Flores: *La Izquierda: Utopía, Praxis y Colapso: Historia y Evolución*, Almuzara, 2017, p. 105–6.

7 Fraser, Nancy: 'A Triple Movement? Parsing the Politics of Crisis after Polanyi', in Michael Brie, ed.: *Karl Polanyi in Dialogue: A Socialist Thinker for Our Times*, Black Rose Books, 2017: 65–78, quotes on pp. 73, 74.

8 See Chantal Mouffe: *For a Left Populism*, Verso, 2018, pp. 31–2.

9 Mair, Peter: *Ruling the Void: The Hollowing of Western Democracy*, Verso, 2013, pp. 17–44.

10 Judt, Tony: *Ill Fares the Land*, op. cit., p. 135.

11 See Gutierrez, Gustavo: *A Theology of Liberation*, SCM Press, 1974.

12 Bahro, Rudolf: *From Red to Green*, Verso, 1984.

13 Newman, Michael: *Socialism: A Very Short Introduction*, Oxford University Press, 2005, p. 136.

14 Giddens, Anthony: *The Third Way*, Polity, 1998.

15 Judt, Tony: *Ill Fares the Land*, op. cit., p. 150.

16 Ibid., pp. 142–3.

17 Honneth, Axel: *The Idea of Socialism*, op. cit., p. viii.

18 Polanyi, Karl: *The Great Transformation*, op. cit., p. 242.

19 Honneth, Axel: *The Idea of Socialism*, op. cit., p. 32.

Notes 193

20 Ibid., p. 47.

21 Frase, Peter: *Four Futures: Life after Capitalism*, Verso, 2016, p. 1.

22 Ibid., pp. 22, 23.

23 Ibid., pp. 29, 31.

24 Polanyi, Karl: 'On Freedom', in Michael Brie and Claus Thomasberger, eds: *Karl Polanyi's Vision of a Socialist Transformation*, Black Rose Books, 2018: 298–319, quote at p. 316.

25 Ibid., p. 300.

26 Ibid., p. 304.

27 Ibid., p. 308.

28 See Stephan Lessenich: *Living Well at Others' Expense: The Hidden Costs of Western Prosperity*, Polity, 2019 for a contemporary expression of Polanyi's point.

29 Dale, Gareth: *Polanyi*, op. cit., p. 118.

30 Polanyi, Karl: *The Great Transformation*, op. cit., p. 133.

31 Quoted in Gibin Hong: 'Young Marx's "Paris Writings" and Polanyi: Beyond the State and the Market' in Fikret Adaman and Pat Devine, eds: *Economy and Society: Money, Capitalism and Transition*, Black Rose Books, 2002: 355–81, quote at p. 374.

32 See Keith Taylor: *The Political Ideas of the Utopian Socialists*, Frank Cass, 1982.

33 Polanyi, Karl: *The Great Transformation* op. cit., p. 133.

34 Quoted in Kari Polanyi Levitt, 2013, p. 48.

35 See, for example, Bockman, Johanna, Ariane Fischer and David Woodruff: '"Socialist Accounting" by Karl Polanyi: With Preface "Socialism and the Embedded Economy"', in *Theor Soc*, 45, 2016: 385–427. This has only recently been translated into English.

36 The 'participatory economics' of Robin Hahnel bears a similarity to some of these ideas about organizing the economy. See Robin Hahnel: 'The Case for Participatory Economics', in Robin Hahnel and Erik Olin Wright: *Alternatives to Capitalism: Proposals for a Democratic Economy*, Verso, 2016: 7–16.

37 Polanyi, 'On Freedom', op. cit., p. 314.

38 See Chapter 8 for a further elaboration of the distinction.

39 Bockman, Johanna et al.: '"Socialist Accounting" by Karl Polanyi: With Preface "Socialism and the Embedded Economy"', op. cit., p. 393.

40 Polanyi, 'On Freedom', op. cit., pp. 315, 316.

41 Block, Fred and Margaret R. Somers: *The Power of Market Fundamentalism: Karl Polanyi's Critique*, Harvard University Press, 2014, p. 221

Notes

42 Bockman, Johanna: 'Not the New Deal and Not the Welfare State: Karl Polanyi's Vision of Socialism', in Michael Brie and Claus Thomasberger, eds: *Karl Polanyi's Vision of a Socialist Transformation*, Black Rose Books, 2018, pp. 200–8, quote at p. 204.

43 Honneth, Axel: *The Idea of Socialism*, op. cit., pp. 52–3.

44 Polanyi, 'On Freedom', op. cit., p. 306.

45 Kirby, Peadar and Tadhg O'Mahony: *The Political Economy of the Low-Carbon Transition: Pathways beyond Techno-Optimism*, Palgrave Macmillan, 2018.

46 Roy, J., P. Tschakert, H. Waisman, W. Abdul Halim, P. Antwi-Agyei, P. Dasgupta, B. Hayward, M. Kanninen, C. Okereke, P.F. Pinho, K. Riahi and A.G. Suarez Rodriguez: 'Sustainable Development, Poverty Eradication and Reducing Inequalities', in: *Global Warming of 1.5°C. An IPCC Special Report on the Impacts of Global Warming of 1.5°C above Pre-industrial Levels and Related Global Greenhouse Gas Emission Pathways, in the Context of Strengthening the Global Response to the Threat of Climate Change, Sustainable Development, and Efforts to Eradicate Poverty* Masson-Delmotte, V., P. Zhai, H.-O. Pörtner, D. Roberts, J. Skea, P.R. Shukla, A. Pirani, W. Moufouma-Okia, C. Péan, R. Pidcock, S. Connors, J.B.R. Matthews, Y. Chen, X. Zhou, M.I. Gomis, E. Lonnoy, T. Maycock, M. Tignor and T. Waterfield (eds), IPCC, 2018, p. 475.

47 Walker, Shaun: 'Migration v Climate: Europe's New Political Divide', in the *Guardian*, 2nd December 2019.

48 Shenker, Jack: *Now We Have Your Attention*, op. cit., p.174.

49 For a fuller discussion, see Peadar Kirby and Tadhg O'Mahony: *The Political Economy of the Low-Carbon Transition: Pathways beyond Techno-Optimism*, Palgrave Macmillan, 2018, Chapter 9: 'Identifying an Emerging Paradigm: Towards Ecosocialism?'.

50 See Baer, Hans A.: *Toward Democratic Eco-socialism as the New World System*, The Next System Project, April 2016; Löwy, Michael: *Ecosocialismo: La alternativa radical a la catástrofe ecológica capitalista*, Editorial El Colectivo, 2011.

51 Löwy, Michael: 'Red and Green: The Ecosocialist Perspective', in the *Bullet*, 4th February 2018.

52 Rutherford, Jonathan: 'Varieties of Eco-Socialism: Comparing the Thought of John Bellamy Foster and Saral Sarkar', *Simplicity Institute Report* 18a, 2018, 3, 4.

53 Burkett, Paul: 'Two Stages of Ecosocialism? Implications of Some Neglected Analyses of Ecological Conflict and Crisis', in *International Journal of Political Economy*, Vol. 35, No. 3, Fall 2006: 23–45.

54 Planetary boundaries or limits refer to the nine critical processes that threaten the conditions keeping the planet safe for humanity. These were identified by a team

at the Stockholm Resilience Institute which by 2015 had identified that we have severely overshot four of these limits. See Steffen, W., K. Richardson, J. Rockström, S.E. Cornell, I. Fetzer, E. M Bennett, R. Biggs et al.: 'Planetary Boundaries: Guiding Human Development on a Changing Planet', in *Science*, Vol. 347, No. 6223, 2015: 1259855. These are also central to Kate Raworth's concept of doughnut economics and are explained in her book on the subject: Kate Raworth: *Doughnut Economics*, Business Books, 2017, pp. 48–51 and Appendix.

55 Hogenboom, Barbara: 'The Return of the State and New Extractivism: What about Civil Society?', in Barry Cannon and Peadar Kirby, eds: *Civil Society and the State in Left-Led Latin America: Challenges and Limitations to Democratization*, Zed Books, 2012: 111–25.

56 Polanyi, *The Great Transformation*, op. cit., pp. 34–6.

57 Holmes, Christopher: *Polanyi in Times of Populism*, Routledge, 2018, p. 26.

58 Higgins, Michael D.: 'Rethinking Economics: The Role of the State', address to seminar in Áras an Uachtaráin, Dublin, 12th November 2019.

59 Meadows, Donella H., Dennis L. Meadows, Jørgen Randers and William W. Behrens III: *The Limits to Growth*, Universe Books, 1972.

60 Meadows, Donella H.: *Leverage Points: Places to Intervene in a System*, The Sustainability Institute, 1999, p. 18.

61 Polanyi, Karl: 'The Livelihood of Man: Introduction', in Michele Cangiani and Claus Thomasberger, eds: *Karl Polanyi: Economy and Society: Selected Writings*, Polity, 2018: 251–62, quote at p. 258.

62 Mason, Paul: *Clear Bright Future: A Radical Defence of the Human Being*, Allen Lane, 2019, p. xii.

63 Polanyi, Karl: 'Freedom in a Complex Society', in Michael Brie and Claus Thomasberger, eds: *Karl Polanyi's Vision of a Socialist Transformation*, Black Rose Books, 2018: 320–24, quotes at pp. 320, 322.

64 Hollo, Tim: 'With the Climate Crisis and Coronavirus Bearing Down on Us, the Age of Disconnection Is Over', in the *Guardian*, 27th March 2020.

Introduction to Part Three

1 Of course, just because these activities moved outside the family does not mean that they were necessarily commodified. Various forms of welfare state provided non-commodified alternatives such as institutional care funded from taxation or food subsidies. However, the growing influence of neoliberal thinking since the 1970s has spurred an immense wave of commodification of these activities.

2   The word 'subsistence' as commonly used today has undertones of having barely enough to survive but Polanyi may be using it in an earlier sense, as used for example in writings of Locke. This views a subsistence economy as one in which people use only enough to meet their needs, thereby keeping population, economy and material resources in greater balance than in a growth economy like ours (see Christopher Holmes: *Polanyi in Times of Populism*, Routledge, 2018, pp. 50–4). A similar understanding of the need for balance between the economy and finite resources is again receiving attention today. See Rob Dietz and Dan O'Neill: *Enough Is Enough: Building a Sustainable Economy in a World of Finite Resources*, Earthscan/Routledge, 2013.

3   Polanyi, Karl: *The Great Transformation*, op. cit., p. 44.

4   Fraser, Nancy: 'Why Two Karls Are Better than One: Integrating Polanyi and Marx in a Critical Theory of the Current Crisis', in Michael Brie and Claus Thomasberger, eds: *Karl Polanyi's Vision of a Socialist Transformation*, Black Rose Books, 2018: 67–76, quote at p. 69.

5   For Polanyi commodification arises from the attempt to make central features of our social and natural world into commodities to be bought and sold in the economy; for Marx on the other hand, the central contradiction within the capitalist system arises from the appropriation by those who own the means of production of the value created by the workers. See Gareth Dale: *Reconstructing Karl Polanyi*, Pluto Press, 2016, p. 49.

6   Block, Fred and Margaret R. Somers: *The Power of Market Fundamentalism*, op. cit., p. 112.

7   Polanyi Levitt, Kari: *From the Great Transformation to the Great Financialization*, Zed Books, 2013, pp. 97–8.

8   See Chapter 8 for further elaboration on Polanyi's alternative view of the economy.

9   All quotes in this section to this point are taken from chapter 6 of Karl Polanyi *The Great Transformation*, op. cit., pp. 71–80.

10   Quotes taken from ibid., chapter 11, pp. 136–40.

11   Burawoy, Michael: 'For a Sociological Marxism: The Complementary Convergence of Antonio Gramsci and Karl Polanyi' in *Politics and Society*, Vol. 31, No. 2, June 2003: 193–261, quote on p. 229.

12   Burawoy offers the following quote from Polanyi which makes this point forcefully: 'Never has there been such an absurd superstition as the belief that the history of man is governed by laws which are independent of his will and action. The concept of a future which awaits us somewhere is senseless because the future does not exist, not now or later. This future is constantly being remade by

those who live in the present. The present only is reality. There is no future that gives validity to our actions in the present.' See Michael Burawoy, op. cit., p. 203.

13 Fraser, Nancy, op. cit., p. 70.

14 Rodrik, Dani: *The Globalization Paradox*, Oxford University Press, 2012.

15 Dale, Gareth: *Karl Polanyi*, op. cit., pp. 62–3.

16 Dale, Gareth: *Reconstructing Karl Polanyi*, op. cit., p. 53.

17 Polanyi, Karl: *The Great Transformation*, op. cit., p. 223.

18 Ibid., p. 201.

19 Ibid., p. 204.

20 Quoted in Gareth Dale: *Karl Polanyi*, op. cit., p. 205.

21 Ruggie, John Gerard: 'International Regimes, Transactions, and Change: Embedded Liberalism in the Postwar Economic Order', in *International Organization*, Vol. 36, No. 2, 1982: 379–415.

22 Blyth, Mark: *Great Transformations: Economic Ideas and Institutional Change in the Twentieth Century*, Cambridge University Press, 2002, p. 6.

23 Polanyi, Karl, C.M. Arensberg and H.W. Pearson, eds: *Trade and Market in the Early Empires*, Free Press, 1957; Karl Polanyi: *Dahomey and the Slave Trade*, Washington University Press, 1966; Pearson, H.W., ed.: *The Livelihood of Man*, Academic Press, 1977.

24 Polanyi, Karl: 'The Economy as Instituted Process', in George Dalton, ed.: *Primitive, Archaic and Modern Economies: Essays of Karl Polanyi*, Anchor Books, 1968: 139–74, quote is at p. 149.

25 Ibid., p. 152.

26 Ibid., p. 155.

27 Dale, Gareth: *Karl Polanyi*, op. cit., p. 115.

28 Lomnitz, Larissa: 'Reciprocity, Redistribution and Market Exchange in the Informal Economy' in Fikret Adaman and Pat Devine, eds: *Economy and Society: Money, Capitalism and Transition*, Black Rose Books, 2002: 172–91, quote at p. 174.

29 Ibid., p. 178.

30 Ibid., p. 180.

31 Ibid., p. 183.

32 Dale's conclusion about a key debate on the economy in ancient Greece in which Polanyi was involved, in Gareth Dale, *Reconstructing Karl Polanyi*, op. cit., p. 201.

33 Glimpses of such socializing forces active in the economy were seen in many places throughout the world during the coronavirus pandemic as local groups came together to provide meals and other services for people in need, motivated not by any personal gain but rather 'to neutralise the disruptive effect of hunger' and loneliness.

34 Polanyi, Karl: 'The Economy Embedded in Society', in Michele Cangiani and
    Claus Thomasberger, eds: *Karl Polanyi: Economy and Society: Selected Writings*,
    Polity, 2018: 290–8, quote at p. 298. This is a reprint of a section from W.H.
    Pearson, ed.: *The Livelihood of Man*, Academic Press, 1977.

Chapter 5

1   Polanyi, Karl: *The Great Transformation*, op. cit., p. 187.
2   Monbiot, George: 'Covid-19 Is Nature's Wake-up Call to Complacent Civilisation',
    in the *Guardian*, 25th March 2020.
3   Intergovernmental Panel on Climate Change: *Climate Change and Land*, IPCC,
    2019.
4   Ibid., p. 2.
5   Salleh, Ariel: 'The Value of a Synergistic Economy', in Anitra Nelson and Frans
    Timmerman, eds: *Life without Money: Building Fair and Sustainable Economies*,
    Pluto Press, 2011: 94–110, quote at p. 96.
6   Ibid., pp. 96–7.
7   Rohr, Jason R. et al.: 'Emerging Human Infectious Diseases and the Links to
    Global Food Production', in *Nature Sustainability*, 11th June 2019, pp. 445–56,
    quote on p. 446.
8   Ibid., p. 449.
9   Ibid., p. 452, 453.
10 Quoted in Laura Spinnery: 'Is Factory Farming behind Covid-19?', in the
    Guardian Weekly, 3rd April 2020.
11 Shiva, Vandana: *Soil, Not Oil: Climate Change, Peak Oil and Food Insecurity*,
    Zed Books, 2016, quotes at p. 143 and p. 109.
12 Phillips, Tom: '"It Is Chaos" – Inside Bolsonaro's Amazon Inferno', in the
    Guardian Weekly, 20th September 2019, pp. 15–17.
13 Smyth, Patrick: 'MEPs Have Beef with Mercosur Climate Consequences', in the
    Irish Times, 21st September 2019, p. 12.
14 Crouch, Colin: *Post-Democracy*, Polity, 2004.
15 See Saskia Sassen: 'Who Owns Our Cities – and Why Yhis Urban Takeover
    Should Concern Us All', in the *Guardian*, 24th November 2015.
16 Chatterton, Paul: *Unlocking Sustainable Cities*, Pluto Press, 2019, p. 94.
17 Ibid., p. 91.
18 Pettifor, Ann: 'Irish House Prices Sky-high Due to Finance Not Scarcity', in the
    Irish Times, 22nd June 2018.

19 Daft.ie: *House Price Report*, 3rd quarter 2019: www.daft.ie, accessed 26th September 2019.

20 Reddan, Fiona: 'Housing Costs: How Dublin Compares with Other Global Cities', in the *Irish Times*, 5th February 2019.

21 Ó Broin, Eoin: *Home: Why Public Housing Is the Answer*, Merrion Press, 2019, p. 139.

22 Nelson, Anitra: *Small Is Necessary: Shared Living on a Shared Planet*, Pluto Press, 2018, pp. 4,5.

23 Pirani, Simon: *Burning Up: A Global History of Fossil Fuel Consumption*, Pluto Press, 2018, pp. 153–58.

24 See the special investigation published in the *Guardian* which shows that twenty large fossil fuel companies can be directly linked to more than one-third of all greenhouse gas emissions in the modern era: the *Guardian Weekly*, 18th October 2019: 10–16.

25 Carrington, Damian, Jillian Ambrose and Matthew Taylor: 'Will the Coronavirus Kill the Oil Industry and Help Save the Climate?', in the *Guardian*, 1st April 2020.

26 This has subsequently been denied by Exxon. See Ken Cohen: 'When It Comes to Climate Change, Read the Documents', ExxonMobil Perspectives Archive, 21st October 2015: www.exxonmobilperspectives.com, accessed 16th December 2019.

27 McKibbon, Bill: *Falter*, Wildfire, 2019, p. 73.

28 Yeomans, Matthew: *Oil: A Concise Guide to the Most Important Product on Earth*, The New Press, 2004, p. 216.

29 See www.waterhumanrighttreaty.org.

30 Polanyi, Karl: *The Great Transformation*, op. cit., p. 79.

31 Scheper-Hughes, Nancy: 'The Market for Human Organs Is Destroying Lives', in the *Washington Post*, 5th January 2016.

32 Sandel, Michael J.: *What Money Can't Buy: The Moral Limits of Markets*, Penguin, 2012, pp. 3, 4.

33 Ibid., p. 14.

34 Polanyi, Karl: *The Great Transformation*, op. cit., p. 187.

35 Roszak, Theodore, Mary E. Gomes and Allen D. Kanner, eds: *Ecopsychology: Restoring the Earth, Healing the Mind*, Counterpoint, 1995.

36 Quoted in Dale, Gareth: *Karl Polanyi*, op. cit., p. 203.

37 Holmes, Christopher: *Polanyi in Times of Populism*, op. cit., p. 26.

38 Polanyi, Karl: *The Great Transformation*, op. cit., p. 35.

39 Intergovernmental Panel on Climate Change: *Climate Change and Land*, op. cit., p. 31.

40 Ibid., p. 34.

41 Badgley, Catherine: 'Feeding the World', in *Nature*, Vol. 419, 24th October 2002, p. 777.

42 Moore, Oliver: 'Arguing a Case for Organic Farming, with an Emphasis on Biodiversity', unpublished paper, Centre for Cooperative Studies, University College Cork, 2012.

43 Badgley, Catherine, Jeremy Moghtader, Eileen Quintero, Emily Zakem, M. Jahi Chappell, Katia Avilés-Vázquez, Andrea Samulon and Ivette Perfecto: 'Organic Agriculture and the Global Food Supply', in *Renewable Agriculture and Food Systems*, Vol. 22, No. 2, 2007: 86–108, quote at p. 86.

44 Ibid., p. 94.

45 Penha-Lopes, Gil, and Tom Henfrey, eds: *Reshaping the Future: How Communities Are Catalysing Social, Economic and Ecological Transformation in Europe. The First Status Report on Community-led Action on Sustainability and Climate Change*, Ecolise, 2019.

46 North, Peter: 'Transitioning towards Low Carbon Solidarity Economies?', in Peter North and Molly Scott Cato, eds: *Towards Just and Sustainable Economies: The Social and Solidarity Economy North and South*, Policy Press, 2018: 73–95, quote on p. 75.

47 Akbulut, Bengi: 'Commons', in Clive L. Spash, ed.: *Routledge Handbook of Ecological Economics*, Routledge, 2018, p. 399.

48 See Guy Standing: *Plunder of the Commons: A Manifesto for Sharing Public Wealth*, Pelican, 2019.

49 Mendell, Marguerite: 'Commoning and the Commons: Alternatives to a Market Society', in Michael Brie and Claus Thomasberger, eds: *Karl Polanyi's Vision of a Socialist Transformation*, Black Rose Books, 2018: 221–40, quote at p. 223.

50 Ibid., p. 107–8.

51 Crabb, Grace and Adam Thorogood: 'Land Use Scenario 2050', in Horace Herring, ed.: *Living in a Low-carbon Society in 2050*, Palgrave Macmillan, 2012: 129–48, quote on p. 131.

52 Sustainable Food Trust: *The Hidden Cost of UK Food*, 2017.

53 Monbiot, George, Robin Grey, Tom Kenny, Laurie Macfarlane, Anna Powell-Smith, Guy Shrubsole and Beth Stratford: *Land for the Many*, a report commissioned by the Labour Party, Labour Party, 2019.

54 Nelson, Anitra: *Small Is Necessary: Shared Living on a Shared Planet*, op. cit., p. 218.

55 Chatterton, Paul: *Unlocking Sustainable Cities*, op. cit., p. 95.

56 Shenker, Jack: 'What Will Cities Look Like after Covid-19?', in the *Guardian Weekly*, 3rd April 2020.

Chapter 6

1   Polanyi, Karl: 'The Fascist Virus', in Michele Cangiani and Claus Thomasberger, eds: *Karl Polanyi: Economy and Society, Selected Writings*, Polity, 2018 [written in 1934–35]: 108–22, quote at p. 117.

2   Ibid., p. 118.

3   Polanyi, Karl: *The Great Transformation*, op. cit., p. 82. However, the historical accuracy of Polanyi's claim that the repeal of the Poor Laws was what ushered in a market society has been sharply criticized, with some historians arguing that it began to emerge centuries earlier. See Gareth Dale: *Polanyi*, op. cit., pp. 84–6.

4   Polanyi, Karl: 'The Fascist Virus', op. cit., pp. 118, 120.

5   Polanyi, Karl: *The Great Transformation*, op. cit., p. 89.

6   Ibid., p. 89.

7   See Lovett, Adrian: 'Make Poverty History? A Decade on from Gleneagles, It Is a Genuine Possibility', in the *Guardian*, 6th July 2015.

8   See, for example, the 2000/01 *World Development Report* of the World Bank entitled 'Attacking Poverty'.

9   See www.oxfam.org.uk, accessed 3rd October 2019.

10 Hickel, Jason: 'A Letter to Steven Pinker (and Bill Gates, for That Matter) about Global Poverty', blog 4th February 2019, accessed at www.jasonhickel.org/blog/2019/2/3/pinker-and-global-poverty, 4th October 2019.

11 See Deepa Narayan, Robert Chambers, Meera K. Shah and Patti Petesch: *Crying Out for Change*, Oxford University Press for the World Bank, 2000.

12 Kanbur, Ravi and Lyn Squire: 'The Evolution of Thinking about Poverty: Exploring the Interactions', The World Bank, 1999, p. 21.

13 Polanyi, Karl: *The Great Transformation*, op. cit., p. 164–5.

14 See Kirby, Peadar: 'The World Bank or Polanyi: Markets, Poverty and Social Well-being in Latin America', in *New Political Economy*, Vol. 7, No. 2, 2002: 199–219.

15 Sen, Amartya: *Development as Freedom*, Oxford University Press, 1999, p. 285.

16 See Kirby, Peadar: *Vulnerability and Violence: The Impact of Globalisation*, Pluto Press, 2006, pp. 143–4.

17 Mkandawire, Thandika: *Targeting and Universalism in Poverty Reduction*, UNRISD, December 2005.

18 Gough, Ian: *Heat, Greed and Human Need: Climate Change, Capitalism and Sustainable Wellbeing*, Edward Elgar, 2017, pp. 78, 79.

19 Litfin, Karen: *Ecovillages: Lessons for Sustainable Community*, Polity, 2014, p. 3.

20 Ibid., pp. 80, 81.

21 Ibid., p. 190.

22 Esping-Andersen, Gösta: *The Three Worlds of Welfare Capitalism*, Polity, 1990, p. 22.

23 Ibid., p. 26.

24 Gough, Ian: *Heat, Greed and Human Need*, op. cit., p. 115.

25 Greer, Ian: 'Welfare Reform, Precarity and the Re-commodification of Labour', in *Work, Employment and Society* Vol. 30 No. 1, 2016: 162–73.

26 OECD: *Social Expenditure Update 2019*, OECD, 2019. This shows public social expenditure below where it was in 1990 which marked a high point. However, the expansion of the OECD in the intervening period to include countries like Chile and Mexico weakens the basis for comparison.

27 Holmes, Christopher: *Polanyi in Times of Populism*, op. cit., p. 120.

28 See IMF: *World Economic Outlook*, April 2020.

29 Foundational Economy Collective: *What Comes after the Pandemic? A Ten-point Platform for Foundational Renewal*, March 2020, p. 6: www.foundationaleconomy.com, accessed 3rd April 2020.

30 Ibid., p. 12.

31 McGreal, Chris: 'The Inequality Virus: How the Pandemic Hit America's Poorest', in the *Guardian*, 9th April 2020.

32 Jones, Owen: 'Coronavirus Is Not Some Great Leveller: It Is Exacerbating Inequality Right Now', in the *Guardian*, 9th April 2020.

33 Rubery, Jill, Damian Grimshaw, Arjan Keizer and Mathew Johnson: 'Challenges and Contradictions in the "Normalising" of Precarious Work', in *Work, Employment and Society*, Vol. 32 No. 3, 2018: 509–27, quote at p. 524.

34 Holmes, Jack: 'As Coronavirus Disrupts … Everything, Both Parties Want to Send Every American a Check. What Does That Mean?' in *Esquire*, 18th March 2020.

35 Ruiz de Almirón, Victor and María Cuesta: 'Iglesias se impone y pacta con Sánchez el ingreso mínimo vital', in *ABC*, 16th April 2020.

36 Quoted in Anna Coote: 'Universal Basic Income Doesn't Work. Let's Boost the Public Realm Instead', in the *Guardian*, 6th May 2019.

37 Pavanelli, Rosa: 'Why Should Governments Give Cash-handouts before Providing Free, Quality Public Services to All?', in *Social Europe*, 6th June 2019.

38 Pettifor, Ann: *The Case for the Green New Deal*, Verso, 2019, p. 102.

39 Piketty, Thomas: *Capital in the Twenty-first Century*, Harvard University Press, 2014, pp. 294, 298.

40 Ibid., p. 319.

41 Oxfam: *Public Good or Private Wealth*, Oxfam Briefing Paper, January 2019, p. 12.

42 Leonhardt, David: 'The Rich Really Do Pay Lower Taxes than You', in the *New York Times*, 6th October 2019.

43 See John Baker, Kathleen Lynch, Sara Cantillon and Judy Walsh: *Equality: From Theory to Action*, Palgrave Macmillan, 2004.

44 UNDP: *Human Development Report 1995*, Oxford University Press, 1995, p. 29.

45 Yeates, Nicola: 'A Global Political Economy of Care', in *Social Policy and Society*, 4 (2), 2005: 227–34, quote on p. 228.

46 Cullen, Pauline: 'The Discursive Politics of Marketization in Home Care Policy Implementation in Ireland', in *Policy and Society*, 2019: https://doi.org/10.1080/14 494035.2019.1622274

47 Fine, Michael and Bob Davidson: 'The Marketization of Care: Global Challenges and National Responses in Australia', in *Current Sociology Monograph*, Vol. 66 No. 4, 2018: 503–16, p.512.

48 Emejulu, Akwugo and Leah Bassel: 'Austerity and the Politics of Becoming', in *Journal of Common Market Studies*, Vol. 56, 2018: 109–19.

49 Lewis, Hannah, Peter Dwyer, Stuart Hodkinson and Louise Waite: 'Hyper-precarious Lives: Migrants, Work and Forced Labour in the Global North', in *Progress in Human Geography*, Vol. 39 No. 5, 2015: 580–600, quote at p. 580.

50 Toivanen, Tero: 'Commons against Capitalism', in Borgnäs, Kajsa, Teppo Eskelinen, Johanna Perkiö and Rikard Warlenius, eds: *The Politics of Ecosocialism: Transforming welfare*, Routledge, 2015: 116–34, quote at p. 124.

51 Wilkinson, Richard and Kate Pickett: *The Spirit Level: Why More Equal Societies Almost Always Do Better*, Allen Lane, 2009.

52 O'Sullivan, Kevin: 'Richest 10 Per Cent Cause Half of Lifestyle Carbon Emissions – Climate Expert', in the *Irish Times*, 11th December 2018.

53 Polanyi, Karl: Karl: 'The Fascist Virus', op. cit., p. 122. While it was not published until 2018, the original dates from 1934–5 and is in the Karl Polanyi Archive in the Concordia University Library, Montreal.

54 Polanyi, Karl: 'Our Obsolete Market Mentality: Civilization Must Find a New Thought Pattern', in *Commentary*, Vol. 3 No. 2, 1947: 109–17, quote at p. 109.

55 Mason, Paul: *Clear Bright Future: A Radical Defence of the Human Being*, Allen Lane, 2019, pp. xi–xiii.

56 Polanyi, Karl: 'The Livelihood of Man', op. cit., p. 257.

57 Pope Francis: *Laudato Sí*, op. cit., par. 107.

58 Niño-Becerra, Santiago: *El Crash: Tercera Fase*, Roca Editorial, 2019.

59 Meyer, Henning: 'The Digital Revolution: How Should Governments Respond?', in Tony Dolphin, ed.: *Technology, Globalisation and the Future of Work in*

Europe: Essays on Employment in a Digitised Economy, Institute for Public Policy Research, 2015: 95–9, quote at p. 95.

60   Manning, Alan: 'Automation and Equality: The Challenge to Progressive Politics', in Tony Dolphin, ed.: *Technology, Globalisation and the Future of Work in Europe: Essays on Employment in a Digitised Economy*, Institute for Public Policy Research, 2015: 106–9, quote at p. 108.

61   Storrie, Donald: 'Manufacturing a Life of Leisure', in Tony Dolphin, ed.: *Technology, Globalisation and the Future of Work in Europe: Essays on Employment in a Digitised Economy*, Institute for Public Policy Research, 2015: 110–12, quote at p. 111.

62   Interview with Yuval Noah Harari in *Clarin*, 6th April 2020.

63   Meyer, Henning, op. cit., pp. 96, 98.

64   Mason, Paul: *Clear Bright Future*, op. cit., p. 148.

65   McEwan, Ian: *Machines Like Me*, Jonathan Cape, 2019.

66   Mason, Paul: *Clear Bright Future*, op. cit., p. 160.

67   Stiglitz, Joseph: 'Joseph Stiglitz on Artificial Intelligence: We're Going towards a More Divided Society', in the *Guardian*, 8th September 2018.

68   Mason, Paul: *Clear Bright Future*, op. cit., pp. 165–6.

69   Esping-Andersen, Gösta: *The Three Worlds of Welfare Capitalism*, op. cit., p. 46.

70   Stiglitz, Joseph: *The Price of Inequality*, Penguin Books, 2013, p. 353.

71   Atkinson, Anthony B.: *Inequality: What Can Be Done?*, Harvard University Press, 2015, pp. 128–32.

72   Jones, Owen: 'Young People Are Rewiring Capitalism with Their McStrike', in the *Guardian*, 4th October 2018.

73   Shenker, Jack: 'Rise App!', in the *Guardian Weekly*, 6th September 2019, pp. 40–4, quotes on pp. 42, 43.

74   Perkiö, Johanna: 'Universal Basic Income: A Cornerstone of the New Economic Order', in Borgnäs, Kajsa, Teppo Eskelinen, Johanna Perkiö and Rikard Warlenius, eds: *The Politics of Ecosocialism: Transforming Welfare*, op. cit.: 137–47, quote at p. 139.

Chapter 7

1   Wallerstein, Immanuel: *Historical Capitalism*, Verso, 1983, p. 16.

2   Ibid., p. 15.

3   Polanyi, Karl: 'Christianity and Economic Life', in Michele Cangiani and Claus Thomasberger, eds: *Karl Polanyi: Economy and Society, Selected Writings*, Polity, 2018 [written in 1937]: 154–64, quote at p. 159.

Notes

4 Ibid., p. 159.

5 Ibid., p. 161.

6 Ibid., p. 162.

7 Polanyi, Karl: *The Great Transformation*, op. cit., pp. 75, 76.

8 Quoted in Dale, Gareth: *Karl Polanyi*, op. cit., p. 186.

9 Holmes, Christopher: *Polanyi in Times of Populism*, op. cit., p. 88.

10 Polanyi, Karl: *The Great Transformation*, op. cit., p. 25, 26.

11 Block, Fred and Margaret R. Somers: *The Power of Market Fundamentalism*, op. cit., p. 15.

12 Polanyi, Karl: *The Great Transformation*, op. cit., p. 31.

13 Means of payment, unit of account and store of value are regarded as the main functions of money. Money as a means of payment or medium of exchange is simply a generally accepted means to allow the easy buying and selling of goods and services; money is also a common measure of value expressed in terms of prices; and as a store of value money is an easily exchanged medium to store wealth.

14 Polanyi, Karl: 'The Semantics of Money-uses', in George Dalton, ed.: *Primitive, Archaic and Modern Economies: Essays of Karl Polanyi*, Anchor Books, 1968: 175–203, quote on p. 202.

15 Fleming, David: *Lean Logic: A Dictionary for the Future and How to Survive It*, Chelsea Green Publishing, 2016, p. 312.

16 To give one practical example from a community-supported agriculture (CSA) project to which the author belongs: Cloughjordan Community Farm, situated within Cloughjordan Ecovillage, Co. Tipperary, Ireland, is a membership farm: a monthly payment of €64 per adult (children are free) gives access to the produce of the farm delivered twice a week to a central collection point. Members take as much produce as they need. In this project, the livelihoods of the farmers are guaranteed through the monthly payments while there is no direct correlation between the payment made and the produce received. The payment is more like an investment in the overall project which includes the systematic regeneration of the soil and experimentation with planting new fruits and vegetables. Thus the farm does not commodify money (indeed it is effectively a non-commercial enterprise), and money is a unit of account only for accounting purposes; it functions indirectly as a means of exchange, and the store of value is measured much more in environmental terms (extent of soil regeneration and quality/ quantity of produce) than in monetary terms.

17 Polanyi Levitt, Kari: 'Keynes and Polanyi: the 1920s and the 1990s', in *Review of International Political Economy*, Vol. 13, No. 1, 2006: 152–77, quote at p. 170.

18 Ibid., p. 153.

19 Ingham, Geoffrey: *Capitalism*, Polity, 2012, p. 169.

20 Mason, Paul: *Clear Bright Future: A Radical Defence of the Human Being*, Allen Lane, 2019, p. 54.

21 Tooze, Adam: 'How Coronavirus Almost Brought Down the Global Financial System', in the *Guardian*, 14th April 2020.

22 Crow, David, Stephen Morris and Laura Noonan: 'Will the Coronavirus Crisis Rehabilitate the Banks?' in the *Financial Times*, 1st April 2020.

23 Ingham, Geoffrey: *Capitalism*, op. cit., pp. 148, 233.

24 Ibid., p. 234.

25 Holmes, Christopher: *Polanyi in Times of Populism*, op. cit., p. 92.

26 Ibid., pp. 93–4.

27 Crow, David et al., op. cit.

28 Deakin, Simon and Scott Stern: 'Chapter 6: Markets, Finance and Corporations: Does Capitalism Have a Future?', in *Rethinking Society for the 21st Century*, International Panel on Social Progress, 2018, Cambridge University Press, 2018, pp. 30–3.

29 Ibid., p. 81.

30 Moore, Jason W.: 'World Accumulation and Planetary Life, or, Why Capitalism Will Not Survive until the "Last Tree Is Cut"', in *Progressive Review*, Vol. 24, No. 3, 2017: 175–202, quotes on pp. 199, 200

31 Rayner, Jay: 'Diet, Health, Inequality: Why Britain's Food Supply System Doesn't Work', in the *Guardian*, 22nd March 2020.

32 Cagle, Susie: '"A Disastrous Situation": Mountains of Food Wasted as Coronavirus Scrambles Supply Chain', in the *Guardian*, 9th April 2020.

33 Carney, Mark, François de Galhau and Frank Elderson: 'The Financial Sector Must Be at the Heart of Tackling Climate Change', in the *Guardian*, 17th April 2019.

34 Deakin, Simon and Scott Stern: 'Chapter 6: Markets, Finance and Corporations: Does Capitalism Have a Future?', in *Rethinking Society for the 21st Century*, op. cit., p. 39.

35 Quoted in Reardon, Jack, Maria Alejandra Madi and Molly Scott Cato: *Introducing a New Economics: Pluralist, Sustainable and Progressive*, Pluto Press, 2018, p. 221.

36 Di Muzio, Tim and Richard H. Robbins: *An Anthropology of Money: A Critical Introduction*, Routledge, 2017, p. 6.

37 Ibid., p. 28.

38 Needleman, Jacob: *Money and the Meaning of Life*, Doubleday, 1994, p. 112.

39 Boyle, Mark: *The Moneyless Man: A Year of Freeconomic Living*, Oneworld, 2011, p. 3.

40 Ibid., p. 186.

41 Ibid., p. 192.

42 Ibid., p. 5.

43 Ibid., p. 13.

44 Ibid., p. 196.

45 Polanyi, Karl: *The Great Transformation*, op. cit., p. 56.

46 Nelson, Anitra: 'Money versus Socialism', in Anitra Nelson and Frans Timmerman, eds: *Life without Money: Building Fair and Sustainable Economies*, Pluto Press, 2011: 23–46, reference to p. 39.

47 Quoted in Eric Clark and Håkan Johansson: 'Social Economy and Green Social Enterprises: Production for Sustainable Welfare?' in Max Koch and Oksana Mont, eds: *Sustainability and the Political Economy of Welfare*, Routledge, 2016: 158–70, quote at pp. 165–6.

48 Ibid., p. 166.

49 Sandel, Michael J.: *What Money Can't Buy: The Moral Limits of Markets*, Penguin, 2013, p. 14.

50 Ibid., p. 13.

51 Ibid., p. 188.

52 Ibid., p 15.

53 Polanyi, Karl: *The Great Transformation*, op. cit., p. 138.

54 See Gareth Dale: *Karl Polanyi*, op. cit., pp. 210–20.

55 Polanyi Levitt, Kari: *From the Great Transformation to the Great Financialization*, op. cit., p. 4.

56 Polanyi, Karl: 'The Mechanism of the World Economic Crisis', in Michele Cangiani and Claus Thomasberger, eds: *Karl Polanyi: Economy and Society, Selected Writings*, op. cit. [written in 1933]: 66–80, quote at p. 72.

57 Adrian, Tobias: 'The Financial System Is Stronger but New Vulnerabilities Have Emerged in the Decade since the Crisis', in *IMFBlog*, 9th October 2018, www.blogs.imf.org, accessed 29th October 2019.

58 Mbaye, Samba and Marialuz Moreno Badia: 'New Data on Global Debt', in *IMFBlog*, 2nd January 2019, www.blogs.imf.org, accessed 29th October 2019.

59 Di Muzio, Tim and Richard H. Robbins: *An Anthropology of Money: A Critical Introduction*, op. cit., p. 82.

60 Dietz, Rob and Dan O'Neill: *Enough Is Enough: Building a Sustainable Economy in a World of Finite Resources*, Routledge, 2013, p. 106–7.

61 Boyle, Mark: *The Moneyless Man*, op. cit., p. 189.

62 Di Muzio, Tim and Richard H. Robbins: *An Anthropology of Money*, op. cit., p. 106.

63 Scott, Brett: 'Can Cryptocurrency and Blockchain Technology Play a Role in Building Social and Solidarity Finance?', UNRISD Working Paper 2016: 1, p. 9.

64 Dini, Paolo and Alexandros Kioupkiolis: 'The Alter-politics of Complementary Currencies; The Case of Sardex', in *Cogent Social Sciences*, 5, 2019, quote at p. 12: https://doi.org/10.1080/23311886.2019.1646625

65 Felber, Christian: *Change Everything: Creating an Economy for the Common Good*, Zed Books, 2015, p. 64. Chapter 3 'The Democratic Bank' gives a comprehensive outline of Felber's banking proposals.

66 See Andrew Cumbers: *Reclaiming Public Ownership: Making Space for Economic Democracy*, Zed Books, 2012, especially Chapter 12 'Financial Crisis and the Rediscovery of the State in the Neo-liberal Heartland'.

67 Foundational Economy Collective: *What Comes after the Pandemic?*, p. 6, accessed at www.foundationaleconomy.com, 30th March 2020.

Conclusion to Part Three

1 Eisenstein, Charles: 'The Coronation', blog on www.charleseisenstein.org, accessed 2nd April 2020.

2 As a *Guardian* foreign affairs commentator wrote: 'A growing intolerance among ordinary citizens for corrupt, oppressive and incompetent rulers around the world was another encouraging feature of 2019.' See Simon Tisdall: '2019: Reasons to Be Fearful and … Reasons to Be Cheerful', in the *Guardian Weekly*, 20th December 2019, p. 25.

3 Eisenstein, Charles: 'The Coronation', op. cit.

4 See Burawoy, Michael: 'For a Sociological Marxism', op. cit., pp. 211–13.

5 Beckett, Andy: 'The Age of Perpetual Crisis: How the 2010s Disrupted Everything but Resolved Nothing', in the *Guardian*, 17th December 2019.

6 Burawoy, Michael: 'For a Sociological Marxism', op. cit., pp. 239–40.

7 Dale, Gareth: *Reconstructing Karl Polanyi*, op. cit., p. 24.

8 Eisenstein, Charles: *Sacred Economics: Money, Gift and Society in the Age of Transition*, North Atlantic Books, 2011, p. 328.

9 Arrighi, Giovanni: *The Long Twentieth Century*, Verso, 1994, p. 194.

Notes 209

Chapter 8

1 Harari Yuval, Noah: *21 Lessons for the 21st Century*, Jonathan Cape, 2018, p. xiii

2 Monbiot, George: *Out of the Wreckage: A New Politics for an Age of Crisis*, Verso, 2017, p. 1.

3 Higgins, Michael D.: 'The Role of the University at a Time of Intellectual Crisis', address by President Higgins on the occasion of his conferring with the Honorary Degree of Doctor of Laws of the National University of Ireland, 25th January 2012.

4 Higgins, Michael D.: 'Public Intellectuals and the Universities', address at the London School of Economics and Political Science, 21st February 2012, in Michael D. Higgins: *When Ideas Matter: Speeches for an Ethical Republic*, Head of Zeus, 2016, p. 264.

5 Higgins, Michael D.: 'The President of Ireland's Ethics Initiative National Seminar', address at Áras an Uachtaráin, 28th March 2015, in Michael D. Higgins: *When Ideas Matter: Speeches for an Ethical Republic*, Head of Zeus, 2016, p. 326.

6 Indeed, at the end of his best-known work, *The Road to Serfdom*, Hayek wrote: 'It is at least doubtful whether at this stage a detailed blueprint of a desirable internal order of society would be of much use – or whether anyone is competent to furnish it. The important thing now is that we shall come to agree on certain principles and free ourselves from some of the errors which have governed us in the recent past.' See F.A. Hayek: *The Road to Serfdom*, Routledge, 2001 [original 1944], p. 243.

7 Polanyi, Karl: *The Great Transformation*, op. cit., p. 166.

8 Polanyi, Karl: 'Our Obsolete Market Mentality', in George Dalton, ed.: *Primitive, Archaic and Modern Economies: Essays of Karl Polanyi*, Anchor Books, 1968: 59–77, quote on p. 60

9 Block, Fred and Margaret R. Somers: *The Power of Market Fundamentalism*, op. cit., p. 236.

10 The words of academic David Thunder on the impacts of the pandemic echo this: 'It casts a penetrating light over aspects of our shared humanity that had receded from view in recent decades, in particular our profound vulnerability to each others' behaviour and choices'. See Thunder, David: 'Pandemic May Shake Us From Individualist Slumber', in the *Irish Times*, 15th April 2020.

11 Polanyi, Karl: 'On Freedom', in Michael Brie and Claus Thomasberger, eds: *Karl Polanyi's Vision of a Socialist Transformation*, Black Rose Books, 2018, [written in 1927]: 298–319, quote on p. 311.

12 Karl Polanyi: 'The Economy as Instituted Process', in George Dalton, ed.: *Primitive, Archaic and Modern Economies: Essays of Karl Polanyi*, Anchor Books, 1968: 139–74, quote on p. 139.

13 Ibid., p. 140.

14 See Jonathan Aldred: *Licence to Be Bad: How Economics Corrupted Us*, Allen Lane, 2019.

15 Polanyi, Karl: 'The Economy as Instituted Process', op. cit. p. 148.

16 Polanyi, Karl: 'The Two Meanings of *Economic*', in Michele Cangiani and Claus Thomasberger, eds: *Karl Polanyi: Economy and Society, Selected Writings*, op. cit. [written in 1977]: 275–89, quote on p. 284.

17 Polanyi, Karl: 'Community and Society: The Christian Criticism of Our Social Order', in Michele Cangiani and Claus Thomasberger, eds: *Karl Polanyi: Economy and Society, Selected Writings*, op. cit. [written in 1937]: 144–53, quote on p. 147.

18 Gough, Ian: *Heat, Greed and Human Need: Climate Change, Capitalism and Sustainable Wellbeing*, Edward Elgar, 2017, especially Chapter 2.

19 Both base their distinction on Aristotle: Polanyi refers to his distinction between 'production for use as against production for gain', while Raworth distinguishes economics, 'the practice of household management as an art', from chrematistics, 'the art of acquiring wealth'. See Karl Polanyi: 'Societies and Economic Systems', in George Dalton, ed.: *Primitive, Archaic and Modern Economies: Essays of Karl Polanyi*, op. cit.: 3–25, quote on p. 17, and Kate Raworth: *Doughnut Economics*, Random House, 2017, p. 32.

20 Raworth, Kate: *Doughnut Economics,* op. cit., p. 23.

21 This is the subtitle of *Doughnut Economics.*

22 Raworth, Kate: *Doughnut Economics,* op. cit., pp. 286–7.

23 Duflo, Esther and Abhijit Banerejee: 'If We're Serious about Changing the World, We Need a Better Kind of Economics to Do It', in the *Guardian*, 30th October 2019.

24 Varoufakis, Vanis: 'Human Economics' in the *Guardian Weekly*, 22nd November 2019.

25 Kallis, Giorgos: *Degrowth*, Agenda Publishing, 2018, p. 73.

26 See Dale, Gareth: 'Economic Growth: A Short History of a Controversial Idea', in *Open Democracy*, 14th June 2019.

27 Kallis, Giorgos: *Degrowth,* op. cit., p. 73.

28 Ibid., p. vii.

29 Ibid., p. 9.

Notes

30 Degrowth.info editorial team: 'A Degrowth Perspective on the Coronavirus Crisis', 19th March 2020, https://www.degrowth.info/en/2020/03/a-degrowth-perspective-on-the-coronavirus-crisis/, 8th April 2020.

31 Kallis, Giorgos: *Degrowth*, op. cit., p. vii.

32 Wilkinson, Richard and Kate Pickett: *The Spirit Level*, op. cit., p. 5–6.

33 On degrowth, see Giacomo D'Alisa, Federico Demaria and Giorgos Kallis, eds: *Degrowth: A Vocabulary for a New Era*, Routledge, 2015; Tim Jackson: *Prosperity without Growth: Economics for a Finite Planet*, Earthscan, 2016; Serge Latouche: *Farewell to Growth*, Polity, 2009.

34 Hickel, Jason: 'Degrowth: A Theory of Radical Abundance', *Real-World Economics Review*, No. 87, 2019, pp. 54–68, quote at p. 57.

35 Ibid., p. 66.

36 Hickel, Jason: 'Why Growth Can't Be Green', in *Foreign Policy*, September 2018.

37 Kuper, Simon: 'The Myth of Green Growth', in the *Financial Times*, 24th October 2019.

38 Latouche, Serge: *La Sociedad de la abundancia frugal*, Icaria, 2012.

39 Polanyi, Karl: *The Great Transformation*, op. cit., p. 35.

40 Kallis, Giorgos: *Degrowth,* op. cit., p. 188.

41 Skidelsky, Robert and Edward Skidelsky: *How Much Is Enough? Money and the Good Life*, Penguin Books, 2013.

42 Ibid., p. xi.

43 Berry, Wendell: 'Faustian Economics: Hell Hath No limits', in *Harper's Magazine*, May 2008: 35–42, quote on p. 36.

44 Polanyi, Karl: *The Great Transformation,* op. cit., p. 265.

45 Kallis, Giorgos: *Limits: Why Malthus Was Wrong and Why Environmentalists Should Care*, Stanford University Press, 2019, p. 50.

46 Ibid., p. 57.

47 Bramall, Rebecca: 'Austerity Pasts, Austerity Futures?', in Ernest Garcia, Mercedes Martinez-Iglesias and Peadar Kirby, eds: *Transitioning to a Post-Carbon Society: Degrowth, Austerity and Wellbeing*, Palgrave Macmillan, 2016: 111–29.

48 Quoted in Bramall, op. cit., p. 124.

49 Freedland, Jonathan: 'Coronavirus Crisis Has Transformed Our View of What's Important', in the *Guardian*, 8th April 2020.

50 Kallis, Giorgos: *Limits,* op. cit., p. 128.

51 Pope Francis: *Laudato Sí,* op. cit., par. 116.

52 Shenker, Jack: *Now We Have Your Attention: The New Politics of the People*, The Bodley Head, 2019, p. 65.

53 Ibid., p. 74.

54 Polanyi, Karl: 'Community and Society: The Christian Criticism of Our Social Order', in Michele Cangiani and Claus Thomasberger, eds: *Karl Polanyi: Economy and Society, Selected Writings*, op. cit., p. 149. I wonder if the word 'unforced' in this text is a mistake either of Polanyi himself or of its transcription, and whether he meant to write 'enforced'.

55 McKnight, John and Peter Block: *The Abundant Community: Awakening the Power of Families and Neighbourhoods*, Berrett-Koehler Publishers, 2012, p. 100.

56 Ibid., p. 111.

57 Polanyi, Karl: 'Community and Society: The Christian Criticism of Our Social Order', in Michele Cangiani and Claus Thomasberger, eds: *Karl Polanyi: Economy and Society, Selected Writings*, op. cit., p. 149.

58 Ibid.

59 Shenker, Jack: *Now We Have Your Attention: The New Politics of the People*, op. cit., p. 12.

60 Kirby, Peadar: *Vulnerability and Violence: The Impact of Globalisation*, Pluto Books, 2006, p. 125.

61 See, for example, Smith, Nicola Jo-Anne: *Showcasing Globalisation? The Political Economy of the Irish Republic*, Manchester University Press, 2005.

62 Gillespie,Paul: 'How Will Crisis Affect International Order?', in the *Irish Times*, 11th April 2020.

63 Mason, Paul: 'How Coronavirus Could Destroy the Western Multilateral Order', in the *New Statesman*, 25th March 2020.

64 Burawoy, Michael: 'For a Sociological Marxism', op. cit., p., 240.

65 Polanyi, Karl: 'Universal Capitalism or Regional Planning?' in Michele Cangiani and Claus Thomasberger, eds: *Karl Polanyi: Economy and Society, Selected Writings*, op. cit.: 231–40, quote on p. 238 (originally published in *The London Quarterly of World Affairs*, 10 (3), 1945).

66 Ibid., p. 239.

67 See Gareth Dale: *Reconstructing Karl Polanyi*, op. cit., Chapter 6 'Regionalism and the European Union'.

68 Red-Green Alliance (RGA/EL): 'A Green Earth with Peace and Room for Us All', www.transform-network.net, accessed 11th November 2019. Transform! Europe is a network of thirty-four European organizations from twenty-two countries, active in the field of political education and critical scientific analysis, and is the recognized political foundation corresponding to the Party of the European Left (EL).

69 Stiglitz, Joseph: 'No More Half Measures on Corporate Taxes', in *Project Syndicate*, 7th October 2019.

70 Brand et al. distinguish three types of transformation: incremental adaptation, greening capitalism and a postcapitalist great transformation that imply a profound structural change of the mode of production and living. They draw on Polanyian perspectives and on regulation theory to argue for the last of these. See Ulrich Brand, Christoph Görg and Markus Wissen: 'Overcoming Neoliberal Globalization: Socio-ecological Transformation from a Polanyian Perspective and Beyond', in *Globalizations*, 17 (1), 2020: 161–76.

71 Polanyi, Karl: *The Great Transformation*, op. cit., p. 52.

72 Higgins, Michael D.: 'At Precipice of Global Ecological Collapse', in the *Irish Examiner*, 14th November 2019.

73 Reich, Robert: 'The Lack of a Real US Public Health System Is a Free Hit for Covid-19', in the *Guardian Weekly*, 20th March 2020.

74 Wong, Julia Carrie: 'Is Amazon Becoming the Future of US Government?' in the *Guardian Weekly*, 3rd April 2020.

75 Staff and agencies: 'Amazon Closes French Warehouses after Court Ruling on Coronavirus', in the *Guardian*, 16th April 2020.

76 Blyth, Mark: 'The US Economy Is Uniquely Vulnerable to the Coronavirus', in *Foreign Affairs*, March/April 2020.

77 The Foundational Economy Collective's 'Ten-Point Platform for Foundational Renewal' is one example of such practical policies for the post-pandemic economy outlining 'priorities of collective provision'. See *What Comes after the Pandemic?*, at www.foundationaleconomy.com.

78 Polanyi, Karl: *The Great* Transformation, op. cit., p. 162.

79 Shenker, Jack: *Now We Have Your Attention*, op. cit., pp. 143–4.

Chapter 9

1 Watts, Jonathan: 'Domino-effect of Climate Events Could Move Earth into a "Hothouse" State', in the *Guardian*, 7th August 2018.

2 Willis, Rebecca: *Too Hot to Handle? The Democratic Challenge of Climate Change*, Bristol University Press, 2020, p. 46.

3 Higgins, Michael D.: 'Rethinking Economics: The Role of the State', Áras an Uachtaráin, 12th November 2019.

4 Anderson, Kevin: 'Hope from Chaos: Could Political Upheaval Lead to a New Green Epoch?' in the *Conversation*, 15th March 2018.

5   Quoted in Aditya Chakrabortty: 'Can the New Left Win Power in Britain? The World Is Watching', in the *Guardian Weekly,* 6th December 2019.

6   Mason, Paul: *Postcapitalism,* op. cit., p. xxi.

7   Shenker, Jack: *New We Have Your Attention: The New Politics of the People,* op. cit., p. 220.

8   Olin Wright, Erik: 'Socialism and Real Utopias' in Robert Hahnel and Erik Olin Wright: *Alternatives to Capitalism: Proposals for a Democratic Economy,* Verso, 2016: 75–105, quotes from pp. 100–1.

9   Shenker, Jack: *New We Have Your Attention,* op. cit., p. 228.

10 Ibid., p. 240.

11 Chakrabortty, Aditya: 'The Other Ways', in the *Guardian Weekly,* 5th October 2018.

12 Sheffield, Hazel: 'The Preston Model: UK Takes Lessons in Recovery from Rustbelt Cleveland', in the *Guardian,* 11th April 2017.

13 Henley, Jon: 'Poll Reveals Majority of Eastern Europeans "Fearful for Democracy"', in the *Guardian,* 4th November 2019.

14 Harris, John: 'Politics May Feel Apocalyptic, but New Ideas Are Taking Root', in the *Guardian Weekly,* 4th October 2019.

15 Hutton, Will: 'The Left Is Fighting Back, even in Republican states, as It Attempts to Reshape Capitalism', in the *Guardian,* 23rd June 2019.

16 Warren, Elizabeth: 'Here's How We Can Break Up Big Tech', Team Warren, 8th March 2019, www.//medium.com/@teamwarren, accessed 21st November 2019. See also Mazeweski, Matt: 'Elizabeth Warren's Plan to Get Workers into the Boardroom', in *Commonweal,* 22nd March 2019: 17–21.

17 Quoted in Shenker, Jack: 'This Wave of Global Protest Is Being Led by the Children of the Financial Crash', in the *Guardian,* 29th October 2019.

18 Phillips, Tom and Charis McGowan: 'Santiago Convulses during a "Weekend of Rage"', in the *Guardian Weekly,* 25th October 2019.

19 Shenker, Jack: 'This Wave of Global Protest Is Being Led by the Children of the Financial Crash', in the *Guardian,* 29th October 2019.

20 Giuffrida, Angela: 'Sardines Squeeze into Italian Cities for Biggest Anti-Salvini Protests Yet', in the *Guardian,* 13th December 2019.

21 An initial response saw a major boost in opinion poll support for mainstream leaders such as Merkel in Germany, Macron in France, Johnson in the United Kingdom and Conti in Italy, though it also included Orban in Hungary and, to a lesser extent, Trump in the United States. See 'Coronavirus: European Leaders Enjoy Surging Approval Ratings amid Crisis', Europe Elects, 1st April 2020.

22 Harvey, Fiona, Jennifer Rankin and Daniel Boffey: 'European Green Deal Will Change Economy to Solve Climate Crisis, Says EU', in the *Guardian*, 11th December 2019.

23 See Rifkin, Jeremy: *The Green New Deal*, St Martin's Press, 2019, pp. 215–21.

24 Riofrancos, Thea: 'Plan, Mood, Battlefield – Reflections on the Green New Deal', in *Viewpoint Magazine*, 16th May 2019, p. 6.

25 Ibid., p. 10.

26 Pettifor, Ann: *The Case for the Green New Deal*, Verso, 2019, pp. 7, 8.

27 Ibid., p. 8.

28 Ibid., p. 91.

29 Global Commission on the Economy and Climate: *Unlocking the Inclusive Growth Story of the 21st Century*, www.newclimateeconomy.report/2018, p. 12, accessed 26th November 2019.

30 Rifkin, Jeremy: *The Green New Deal*, op. cit., pp. 140–65.

31 Ibid., p. 186–7.

32 Pettifor, Ann: *The Case for the Green New Deal*, op. cit., pp. 155, 161–2.

33 Carrington, Damian: 'Most Countries' Climate Plans "Totally Inadequate" – Experts', in the *Guardian*, 5th November 2019.

34 Milman, Oliver: '"Americans Are Waking Up": Two Thirds Say Climate Crisis Must Be Addressed', in the *Guardian*, 15th September 2019.

35 Rifkin, Jeremy: *The Green New Deal*, op. cit., p. 211.

36 Available on www.gndforeurope.com, accessed 18th December 2019.

37 Quoted in Shenker, Jack: *New We Have Your Attention: The New Politics of the People*, op. cit., p. 239.

38 Coughlin, Joseph: 'Having It All, but Owning None of It: Welcome to the Rentership Society', in *Forbes*, 12th August 2018.

39 McKibben, Bill: *Falter: Has the Human Game Begun to Play Itself Out?*, op. cit., p. 159.

40 Shenker, Jack: *New We Have Your Attention: The New Politics of the People*, op. cit., p. 239.

41 'Cosmo-local Work: Organisational Practices for Equitable and Sustainable Living', www.cosmolocalism.eu, accessed 26th November 2019.

42 Ibid.,

43 Mason, Paul: *Clear Bright Future*, op. cit., pp. 250–5.

44 Foroohar, Rana: 'Beware the Tech Bubble', in the *Guardian Weekly*, 15th November 2019: 40–4.

45 Mason, Paul: *Clear Bright Future*, op. cit., p. 253.

46 Foroohar, Rana: 'Beware the Tech Bubble', op. cit., p. 42.

47 Hayek, F.A.: *The Road to Serfdom*, Routledge, 2005, p. 96 [original published in 1944].

48 The features of a gift economy, as defined by Eisenstein, found rich expression during the pandemic. These are: (1) how to connect the provider of a gift with the person who needs that gift, (2) how to acknowledge and honour those who give generously of their gifts and (3) how to coordinate the gifts of many people across space and time in order to create things transcending the needs or gifts of any individual. 'Though it may not be obvious, these goals correspond roughly to the three cardinal functions of money: medium of exchange, unit of account, and store of value.' See Charles Eisenstein: *Sacred Economics: Money, Gift and Society in the Age of Transition*, North Atlantic Books, 2011, p. 320.

49 Akbulut, Bengi: 'Commons', in *Routledge Handbook of Ecological Economics*, op. cit., p. 398.

50 See www.carnegieuktrust.org.uk, accessed 18th December 2019.

51 Dale, Gareth: *Karl Polanyi*, Polity, 2010, pp. 42, 43.

52 On similarities between Pope Francis and Polanyi, see Gregory Baum: 'Tracing the Affinity between the Social Thought of Karl Polanyi and Pope Francis', paper presented at the 13th International Karl Polanyi Conference, Concordia University, 6th–8th November 2014.

53 See Kirby, Peadar: 'Pope Francis on Power, Politics and the Techno-Economic Paradigm', in Sean McDonagh, ed.: *Laudato Sí: An Irish Response*, Veritas, 2017: 125–36.

54 Pope Francis: *Laudato Sí*, op. cit., par. 107.

55 Ibid., par. 122.

56 Ghosh, Amitav: *The Great Derangement: Climate Change and the Unthinkable*, The University of Chicago Press, 2016, p. 159.

57 Polanyi Levitt, Kari: 'Karl Polanyi and Co-Existence', in Kari Polanyi Levitt, ed.: *The Life and Work of Karl Polanyi*, Black Rose Books, 1990: 253–63, quote on p. 262.

Appendix

1 Polanyi Levitt, Kari: 'Freedom of Action and Freedom of Thought', in Michael Brie and Claus Thomasberger, eds: *Karl Polanyi's Vison of a Socialist Transformation*, Black Rose Books, 2018: 18–50, quote at p. 22.

2   Congdon, Lee: 'The Sovereignty of Society: Polanyi in Vienna', in Kari Polanyi-Levitt, ed.: *The Life and Work of Karl Polanyi*, Black Rose Books, 1990: 78–84.

3   Ibid., p. 81.

4   Block, Fred and Margaret R. Somers: *The Power of Market Fundamentalism: Karl Polanyi's Critique*, Harvard University Press, 2014, p. 218.

5   Polanyi, Karl: 'Economic History and the Problem of Freedom', in Giorgio Resta and Mariavittoria Catanzariti, eds: *Karl Polanyi: For a New West: Essays, 1919–1958*, op. cit.: 39–46, quote on p. 40 [text of a 1949 lecture.].

6   Gareth Dale: *Reconstructing Karl Polanyi*, Pluto Press, 2016, p. 42.

7   Quoted in Kari Polanyi Levitt and Marguerite Mendell: 'Karl Polanyi: His Life and Times', in *Studies in Political Economy*, Vol. 22, 1987: 7–39, quote at p. 22.

8   Polanyi, Karl: 'Our Obsolete Market Mentality', in George Dalton, ed.: *Primitive, Archaic and Modern Economies: Essays of Karl Polanyi*, Doubleday Anchor, 1968: 59–77, quote at p. 59.

9   Ibid., p. 46.

10 Quoted in Dale, ibid., p. 46.

11 Polanyi Levitt, Kari: *From the Great Transformation to the Great Financialization*, Zed Books, 2013, p. 47.

12 Polanyi Levitt, Kari: 'Freedom of Action and Freedom of Thought', in Michael Brie and Claus Thomasberger, eds: *Karl Polanyi's Vision of a Socialist Transformation*, Black Rose Books, 2018: 18–50, quote at p. 29.

Bibliography

Adrian, Tobias: 'The Financial System Is Stronger but New Vulnerabilities Have Emerged in the Decade since the Crisis, in *IMFBlog*, 9th October 2018, www.blogs.imf.org.

Akbulut, Bengi: 'Commons', in Clive L. Spash, ed.: *Routledge Handbook of Ecological Economics*, Routledge, 2018.

Aldred, Jonathan: *Licence to Be Bad: How Economics Corrupted Us*, Allen Lane, 2019.

Anderson, Kevin: 'Hope from Chaos: Could Political Upheaval Lead to a New Green Epoch?' in the *Conversation*, 15th March 2018.

Arrighi, Giovanni: *The Long Twentieth Century*, Verso, 1994.

Atkinson, Anthony B.: *Inequality: What Can Be Done?*, Harvard University Press, 2015.

Badgley, Catherine: 'Feeding the World, in *Nature*, Vol. 419, 24th October 2002.

Badgley, Catherine, Jeremy Moghtader, Eileen Quintero, Emily Zakem, M. Jahi Chappell, Katia Avilés-Vázquez, Andrea Samulon and Ivette Perfecto: 'Organic Agriculture and the Global Food Supply', in *Renewable Agriculture and Food Systems*, Vol. 22, No. 2, 2007: 86–108.

Baer, Hans A.: *Toward Democratic Eco-socialism as the New World System*, The Next System Project, April 2016.

Bahro, Rudolf: *From Red to Green*, Verso, 1984.

Baker, John, Kathleen Lynch, Sara Cantillon and Judy Walsh: *Equality: From Theory to Action*, Palgrave Macmillan, 2004.

Baum, Gregory: 'Tracing the Affinity between the Social Thought of Karl Polanyi and Pope Francis', paper presented at the 13th International Karl Polanyi Conference, Concordia University, 6th–8th November 2014.

Bauman, Zygmunt: 'Symptoms in Search of an Object and a Name', in Heinrich Geiselberger, ed.: *The Great Regression*, Polity, 2017: 13–25.

Beckett, Andy: 'The Age of Perpetual Crisis: How the 2010s Disrupted Everything but Resolved Nothing', in the *Guardian*, 17th December 2019.

Berry, Wendell: 'Faustian Economics: Hell Hath No Limits', in *Harper's Magazine*, May 2008: 35–42.

Block, Fred and Margaret R. Somers: *The Power of Market Fundamentalism: Karl Polanyi's Critique*, Harvard University Press, 2014.

Blyth, Mark: 'The US Economy Is Uniquely Vulnerable to the Coronavirus', in *Foreign Affairs*, March/April 2020.

Bibliography

Blyth, Mark: *Great Transformations: Economic Ideas and Institutional Change in the Twentieth Century*, Cambridge University Press, 2002.

Bockman, Johanna, Ariane Fischer and David Woodruff: '"Socialist Accounting" by Karl Polanyi: With Preface "Socialism and the Embedded Economy"', in *Theor Soc*, Vol. 45, 2016: 385–427.

Bockman, Johanna: 'Not the New Deal and Not the Welfare State: Karl Polanyi's Vision of Socialism', in Michael Brie and Claus Thomasberger, eds: *Karl Polanyi's Vision of a Socialist Transformation*, Black Rose Books, 2018, pp. 200–08.

Boyle, Mark: *The Moneyless Man: A Year of Freeconomic Living*, Oneworld, 2011.

Bramall, Rebecca: 'Austerity Pasts, Austerity Futures?', in Ernest Garcia, Mercedes Martinez-Iglesias and Peadar Kirby eds: *Transitioning to a Post-Carbon Society: Degrowth, Austerity and Wellbeing*, Palgrave Macmillan, 2016: 111–29.

Brand, Ulrich, Christoph Görg and Markus Wissen: 'Overcoming Neoliberal Globalization: Socio-ecological Transformation from a Polanyian Perspective and Beyond', in *Globalizations*, Vol. 17, No. 1, 2020: 161–76.

Bregman, Rutger: *Utopia for Realists: And How We Can Get There*, Bloomsbury, 2017.

Bridle, James: *New Dark Age: Technology and the End of the Future*, Verso, 2018.

Burawoy, Michael: 'For a Sociological Marxism: The Complementary Convergence of Antonio Gramsci and Karl Polanyi' in *Politics and Society*, Vol. 31, No. 2, June 2003: 193–261.

Burkett, Paul: 'Two Stages of Ecosocialism? Implications of Some Neglected Analyses of Ecological Conflict and Crisis', in *International Journal of Political Economy*, Vol. 35, No. 3, Fall 2006: 23–45.

Cagle, Susie: '"A Disastrous Situation": Mountains of Food Wasted as Coronavirus Scrambles Supply Chain', in the *Guardian*, 9th April 2020.

Carney, Mark, François de Galhau and Frank Elderson: 'The Financial Sector Must Be at the Heart of Tackling Climate Change', in the *Guardian*, 17th April 2019.

Carrington, Damian, Jillian Ambrose and Matthew Taylor: 'Will the Coronavirus Kill the Oil Industry and Help Save the Climate?' in the *Guardian*, 1st April 2020.

Carrington, Damian: 'Most Countries' Climate Plans "Totally Inadequate" – Experts', in the *Guardian*, 5th November 2019.

Castells, Manuel: *Ruptura: La Crisis de la Democracia Liberal*, Alianza Editorial, 2017.

Chakrabortty, Aditya: 'Can the New Left Win Power in Britain? The World Is Watching', in the *Guardian Weekly*, 6th December 2019.

Chakrabortty, Aditya: 'The End Is Nigh for Davos Man and His Way of Doing Business', in the *Guardian Weekly*, 1st February 2019.

Chakrabortty, Aditya: 'The Other Ways', in the *Guardian Weekly*, 5th October 2018.

Chatterton, Paul: *Unlocking Sustainable Cities*, Pluto Press, 2019.

Clark, Eric and Håkan Johansson: 'Social Economy and Green Social Enterprises: Production for Sustainable Welfare?' in Max Koch and Oksana Mont, eds: *Sustainability and the Political Economy of Welfare*, Routledge, 2016: 158–70.

Cohen, Ken: 'When It Comes to Climate Change, Read the Documents', ExxonMobil Perspectives Archive, 21st October 2015: www.exxonmobilperspectives.com.

Collier, Paul: *The Future of Capitalism: Facing the New Anxieties*, Allen Lane, 2018.

Collins, Randall: 'The End of Middle-Class Work: No More Escapes', in Immanuel Wallerstein, Randall Collins, Michael Mann, Georgi Derluguian and Craig Calhoun: *Does Capitalism Have a Future?*, Oxford University Press, 2013: 37–69.

Coman, Julian: 'Law and Justice and the Fight for the Soul of Poland', in the *Guardian Weekly*, 11th October 2019.

Congdon, Lee: 'The Sovereignty of Society: Polanyi in Vienna', in Kari Polanyi-Levitt, ed.: *The Life and Work of Karl Polanyi*, Black Rose Books, 1990: 78–84.

Conroy, Catherine: 'This Is Not the Fall of the Roman Empire, This Is a Larger Scale', in the *Irish Times*, 17th October 2018.

Coote, Anna: 'Universal Basic Income Doesn't Work. Let's Boost the Public Realm Instead', in the *Guardian*, 6th May 2019.

Cosmo-Localism: 'Cosmo-local Work: Organisational Practices for Equitable and Sustainable Living', www.cosmolocalism.eu

Coughlin, Joseph: 'Having It All, but Owning None of It: Welcome to the Rentership Society', in *Forbes*, 12th August 2018.

Crabb, Grace and Adam Thorogood: 'Land Use Scenario 2050', in Horace Herring, ed.: *Living in a Low-Carbon Society in 2050*, Palgrave Macmillan, 2012: 129–48.

Crouch, Colin: *Post-Democracy*, Polity, 2004.

Crow, David, Stephen Morris and Laura Noonan: 'Will the Coronavirus Crisis Rehabilitate the Banks?' in the *Financial Times*, 1st April 2020.

Cullen, Pauline: 'The Discursive Politics of Marketization in Home Care Policy Implementation in Ireland', in *Policy and Society*, 2019: https://doi.org/10.1080/14 494035.2019.1622274

Cumbers, Andrew: *Reclaiming Public Ownership: Making Space for Economic Democracy*, Zed Books, 2012.

D'Alisa, Giacomo, Federico Demaria and Giorgos Kallis, eds: *Degrowth: A Vocabulary for a New Era*, Routledge, 2015.

Daft.ie: *House Price Report*, 3rd quarter 2019.

Dale, Gareth: 'Economic Growth: A Short History of a Controversial Idea', in *Open Democracy*, 14th June 2019.

Dale, Gareth: *Reconstructing Karl Polanyi*, Pluto Press, 2016.

Dale, Gareth: *Karl Polanyi*, Polity, 2010.

Deakin, Simon and Scott Stern: 'Chapter 6: Markets, Finance and Corporations: Does Capitalism Have a Future?', in *Rethinking Society for the 21st Century*, International Panel on Social Progress, 2018, Cambridge University Press, 2018.

Degrowth.info editorial team: 'A Degrowth Perspective on the Coronavirus Crisis', 19th March 2020: https://www.degrowth.info/en/2020/03/a-degrowth-perspective-on-the-coronavirus-crisis/

Di Muzio, Tim and Richard H. Robbins: *An Anthropology of Money: A Critical Introduction*, Routledge, 2017.

Di Muzio, Tim: *Carbon Capitalism: Energy, Social Reproduction and World Order*, Rowman & Littlefield, 2015.

Dietz, Rob and Dan O'Neill: *Enough Is Enough: Building a Sustainable Economy in a World of Finite Resources*, Earthscan/Routledge, 2013.

Dini, Paolo and Alexandros Kioupkiolis: 'The Alter-politics of Complementary Currencies; The Case of Sardex', in *Cogent Social Sciences*, Vol. 5, 2019: https://doi.org/10.1080/23311886.2019.1646625

Duflo, Esther and Abhijit Banerejee: 'If We're Serious about Changing the World, We Need a Better Kind of Economics to Do It', in the *Guardian*, 30th October 2019.

Eatwell, Roger and Matthew Goodwin: *National Populism: The Revolt against Liberal Democracy*, Pelican, 2018.

Economic Times: 'Raghuram Rajan Says Capitalism Is "under Serious Threat"', 12th March 2019.

Economist: 'In Europe, Right-wing Parties Are Offering Bigger Handouts than Traditional Ones', in the *Economist*, 25th January 2018.

Editorial Board of the Financial Times: 'Virus Lays Bare the Frailty of the Social Contract', in the *Financial Times*, 3rd April 2020.

Eisenstein, Charles: 'The Coronation', 2020, blog on www.charleseisenstein.org.

Eisenstein, Charles: *Sacred Economics: Money, Gift and Society in the Age of Transition*, North Atlantic Books, 2011.

Elliott, Larry: 'Capitalism Can Crack Climate Change: But Only if It Takes Risks', in the *Guardian*, 16th August 2018.

Emejulu, Akwugo and Leah Bassel: 'Austerity and the Politics of Becoming', in *Journal of Common Market Studies*, Vol. 56, 2018: 109–19.

Esping-Andersen, Gösta: *The Three Worlds of Welfare Capitalism*, Polity, 1990.

Europe Elects: 'Coronavirus: European Leaders Enjoy Surging Approval Ratings amid Crisis', *Europe Elects*, 1st April 2020.

European Environment Agency: *The European Environment: State and Outlook 2020*, EEA, 2019.

Felber, Christian: *Change Everything: Creating an Economy for the Common Good*, Zed Books, 2015.

Fernández-Viagas, Javier Flores: *La Izquierda: Utopía, Praxis y Colapso: Historia y Evolución*, Almuzara, 2017.

Fine, Michael and Bob Davidson: 'The Marketization of Care: Global Challenges and National Responses in Australia', in *Current Sociology Monograph*, Vol. 66, No. 4, 2018: 503–16.

Fleming, David: *Lean Logic: A Dictionary for the Future and How to Survive It*, Chelsea Green Publishing, 2016.

Ford, Martin: *The Rise of the Robots: Technology and the Threat of Mass Unemployment*, Oneworld Publications, 2016.

Foroohar, Rana: 'Beware the Tech Bubble', in the *Guardian Weekly*, 15th November 2019.

Foundational Economy Collective: *What Comes after the Pandemic? A Ten-point Platform for Foundational Renewal*, March 2020: www.foundationaleconomy.com.

Frase, Peter: *Four Futures: Life after Capitalism*, Verso, 2016.

Fraser, Nancy: 'Why Two Karls Are Better than One: Integrating Polanyi and Marx in a Critical Theory of the Current Crisis', in Michael Brie and Claus Thomasberger eds: *Karl Polanyi's Vision of a Socialist Transformation*, Black Rose Books, 2018: 67–76.

Fraser, Nancy: 'A Triple Movement? Parsing the Politics of Crisis after Polanyi', in Michael Brie, ed.: *Karl Polanyi in Dialogue: A Socialist Thinker for Our Times*, Black Rose Books, 2017: 65–78.

Freedland, Jonathan: 'Coronavirus Crisis Has Transformed Our View of What's Important', in the *Guardian*, 8th April 2020.

Fulcher, James: *Capitalism: A Very Short Introduction*, Oxford University Press, 2004.

Garcés, Marina: *Nueva ilustración radical*, Editorial Anagrama, 2017.

Ghosh, Amitav: *The Great Derangement: Climate Change and the Unthinkable*, The University of Chicago Press, 2016.

Giddens, Anthony: *The Third Way*, Polity, 1998.

Gillespie, Paul: 'How Will Crisis Affect International Order?', in the *Irish Times*, 11th April 2020.

Giuffrida, Angela: 'Sardines Squeeze into Italian Cities for Biggest Anti-Salvini Protests Yet', in the *Guardian*, 13th December 2019.

Global Commission on the Economy and Climate: *Unlocking the Inclusive Growth Story of the Twenty-first Century*, www.newclimateeconomy.report/2018.

Goodhart, David: *The Road to Somewhere: The Populist Revolt and the Future of Politics*, Hurst and Company, 2017.

Gough, Ian: *Heat, Greed and Human Need: Climate Change, Capitalism and Sustainable Wellbeing*, Edward Elgar, 2017.

Greer, Ian: 'Welfare Reform, Precarity and the Re-commodification of Labour, in *Work, Employment and Society*, Vol. 30, No. 1, 2016: 162–73.

Green New Deal Group: *A Green New Deal*, New Economics Foundation, 2008.

Gutierrez, Gustavo: *A Theology of Liberation*, SCM Press, 1974.

Hahnel, Robin: 'The Case for Participatory Economics', in Robin Hahnel and Erik Olin Wright: *Alternatives to Capitalism: Proposals for a Democratic Economy*, Verso, 2016: 7–16.

Harari, Yuval Noah: *21 Lessons for the 21st Century*, Jonathan Cape, 2018.

Harris, John: "Politics May Feel Apocalyptic, but New Ideas Are Taking Root', in the *Guardian Weekly*, 4th October 2019.

Harris, Nigel: *The End of the Third World*, Penguin, 1987.

Harvey, David: *A Brief History of Neoliberalism*, Oxford University Press, 2005.

Harvey, Fiona, Jennifer Rankin and Daniel Boffey: 'European Green Deal Will Change Economy to Solve Climate Crisis, Says EU', in the *Guardian*, 11th December 2019.

Hayek, F.A.: *The Road to Serfdom*, Routledge, 2001 [original 1944].

Henley, Jon: 'Poll Reveals Majority of Eastern Europeans "Fearful for Democracy"', in the *Guardian*, 4th November 2019.

Hickel, Jason and Giorgos Kallis: 'Is Green Growth Possible?', in *New Political Economy*, April 2019, https://doi.org/10.1080/13563467.2019.1598964

Hickel, Jason: 'Degrowth: A Theory of Radical Abundance', *Real-World Economics Review*, No. 87, 2019: 54–68.

Hickel, Jason: 'A Letter to Steven Pinker (and Bill Gates, for That Matter) about Global Poverty', blog 4th February 2019, www.jasonhickel.org/blog/2019/2/3/pinker-and-global-poverty.

Hickel, Jason: 'Why Growth Can't Be Green', in *Foreign Policy*, September 2018.

Higgins, Michael D.: 'At Precipice of Global Ecological Collapse', in the *Irish Examiner*, 14th November 2019.

Higgins, Michael D.: 'Rethinking Economics: The Role of the State', address to seminar in Áras an Uachtaráin, Dublin, 12th November 2019.

Higgins, Michael D.: 'The President of Ireland's Ethics Initiative National Seminar', address at Áras an Uachtaráin, 28th March 2015, in Michael D. Higgins: *When Ideas Matter: Speeches for an Ethical Republic*, Head of Zeus, 2016: 323–35.

Higgins, Michael D.: 'Public Intellectuals and the Universities', address at the London School of Economics and Political Science, 21st February 2012, in Michael D. Higgins: *When Ideas Matter: Speeches for an Ethical Republic*, Head of Zeus, 2016: 255–68.

Higgins, Michael D.: 'The Role of the University at a Time of Intellectual Crisis', address by President Higgins on the occasion of his conferring with the Honorary Degree of Doctor of Laws (LLD) of the National University of Ireland, 25th January 2012.

Hogenboom, Barbara: 'The Return of the State and New Extractivism: What about Civil Society?, in Barry Cannon and Peadar Kirby, eds: *Civil Society and the State in Left-Led Latin America: Challenges and Limitations to Democratization*, Zed Books, 2012: 111–25.

Holleran, Max: 'The Opportunistic Rise of Europe's Far Right', in *New Republic*, 16th February 2018.

Hollo, Tim: 'With the Climate Crisis and Coronavirus Bearing Down on Us, the Age of Disconnection Is Over', in the *Guardian*, 27th March 2020.

Holmes, Jack: 'As Coronavirus Disrupts … Everything, Both Parties Want to Send Every American a Check. What Does That Mean?' in *Esquire*, 18th March 2020.

Homes, Christopher: *Polanyi in Times of Populism: Vision and Contradiction in the History of Economic Ideas*, Routledge, 2018.

Hong, Gibin: 'Young Marx's "Paris Writings" and Polanyi: Beyond the State and the Market' in Fikret Adaman and Pat Devine, eds: *Economy and Society: Money, Capitalism and Transition*, Black Rose Books, 2002: 355–81.

Honneth, Axel: *The Idea of Socialism*, Polity, 2017.

Hutton, Will: 'The Left Is Fighting Back, Even in Republican States, as It Attempts to Reshape Capitalism', in the *Guardian*, 23rd June 2019.

IEA: *Global Energy and CO2 Status Report*, International Energy Agency, 2019.

Ignatieff, Michael: *The Ordinary Virtues: Moral Order in a Divided World*, Harvard University Press, 2017.

IMF: *World Economic Outlook*, IMF, April 2020.

Ingham, Geoffrey: *Capitalism*, Polity, 2012.

Intergovernmental Panel on Climate Change: *Climate Change and Land*, IPCC, 2019.

Intergovernmental Panel on Climate Change: *Special Report on Global Warming of 1.5°C*, IPCC, 2018.

International Carbon Action Partnership: *Emissions Trading Worldwide: Status Report 2019*, ICAP, 2019.

IPBES: 'Summary for Policymakers of the Global Assessment Report on Biodiversity and Ecosystem Services', 2019, https://www.ipbes.net/system/tdf/spm_global_unedited_advance.pdf?file=1&type=node&id=35245

IPPR: *This Is a Crisis: Facing Up to the Age of Environmental Breakdown*, IPPR, 2019.

Jackson, Tim and Peter. E. Victor: 'Unraveling the Claims for (and against) Green Growth', in *Science*, 22nd November 2019: 950–1.

Jackson, Tim: *Prosperity without Growth: Economics for a Finite Planet*, Earthscan, 2016.

Jenkins, Patrick: 'City Fund Managers Call for Rethink of Capitalism', in the *Financial Times*, 15th November 2019.

Jones, Owen: 'Corby and Sanders May Have Gone, but They Have Radically Altered Our Politics', in the *Guardian*, 16th April 2020.

Jones, Owen: 'Coronavirus Is Not Some Great Leveller: It Is Exacerbating Inequality Right Now', in the *Guardian*, 9th April 2020.

Jones, Owen: 'Young People Are Rewiring Capitalism with Their McStrike', in the *Guardian*, 4th October 2018.

Judis, John B.: *The Populist Explosion*, Columbia Global Reports, 2016.

Judt, Tony: *Ill Fares the Land*, Penguin, 2011.

Kallis, Giorgos: *Limits: Why Malthus Was Wrong and Why Environmentalists Should Care*, Stanford University Press, 2019.

Kallis, Giorgos: *Degrowth*, Agenda Publishing, 2018.

Kanbur, Ravi and Lyn Squire: 'The Evolution of Thinking about Poverty: Exploring the Interactions', The World Bank, 1999.

Kirby, Peadar and Tadhg O'Mahony: *The Political Economy of the Low-Carbon Transition: Pathways beyond Techno-Optimism*, Palgrave Macmillan, 2018.

Kirby, Peadar: 'Pope Francis on Power, Politics and the Techno-Economic Paradigm', in Sean McDonagh, ed.: *Laudato Sí: An Irish Response*, Veritas, 2017: 125–36.

Kirby, Peadar: *Vulnerability and Violence: The Impact of Globalisation*, Pluto Press, 2006.

Kirby, Peadar: 'The World Bank or Polanyi: Markets, Poverty and Social Well-being in Latin America', in *New Political Economy*, Vol. 7, No. 2, 2002: 199–219.

Klein, Naomi: *This Changes Everything: Capitalism vs the Climate*, Allen Lane, 2014.

Kuper, Simon: 'The Myth of Green Growth', in the *Financial Times*, 24th October 2019.

Latouche, Sergio: (with Susan George, Jean-Pierre Dupuy, and Yves Cochet): *Hacia Dónde Va el Mundo?*, Icaria, 2012.

Latouche, Serge: *La Sociedad de la abundancia frugal*, Icaria, 2012.

Latouche, Serge: *Farewell to Growth*, Polity, 2009.

Leonhardt, David: 'The Rich Really Do Pay Lower Taxes than You', in the *New York Times*, 6th October 2019.

Lessenich, Stephan: *Living Well at Others' Expense: The Hidden Costs of Western Prosperity*, Polity, 2019.

Levitsky, Steven and Daniel Ziblatt: *How Democracies Die: What History Reveals about Our Future*, Penguin, 2018.

Lewis, Hannah, Peter Dwyer, Stuart Hodkinson and Louise Waite: 'Hyper-precarious Lives: Migrants, Work and Forced Labour in the Global North', in *Progress in Human Geography*, Vol. 39, No. 5, 2015: 580–600.

Lewis, Paul, Seán Clarke and Caelainn Barr: 'People Power: Do populist Leaders Actually Reduce Inequality?' in the *Guardian Weekly*, 15th March 2019.

Litfin, Karen: *Ecovillages: Lessons for Sustainable Community*, Polity, 2014.

Lizoain Bennett: David *Fin del Primer Mundo*, Catarata, 2017.

Lomnitz, Larissa: 'Reciprocity, Redistribution and Market Exchange in the Informal Economy' in Fikret Adaman and Pat Devine, eds: *Economy and Society: Money, Capitalism and Transition*, Black Rose Books, 2002: 172–91.

Lovett, Adrian: 'Make Poverty History? A Decade on from Gleneagles, It Is a Genuine Possibility', in the *Guardian*, 6th July 2015.

Löwy, Michael: 'Red and Green: The Ecosocialist Perspective', in the *Bullet*, 4th February 2018.

Löwy, Michael: *Ecosocialismo: La alternativa radical a la catástrofe ecológica capitalista*, Editorial El Colectivo, 2011.

Luce, Edward: *The Retreat of Western Liberalism*, Little, Brown, 2017.

Mair, Peter: *Ruling the Void: The Hollowing-out of Western Democracy*, Verso, 2013.

Manning, Alan: 'Automation and Equality: The Challenge to Progressive Politics', in Tony Dolphin, ed.: *Technology, Globalisation and the Future of Work in Europe: Essays on Employment in a Digitised Economy*, Institute for Public Policy Research, 2015: 106–9.

Mason, Paul: 'How Coronavirus Could Destroy the Western Multilateral Order', in the *New Statesman*, 25th March 2020.

Mason, Paul: *Clear Bright Future: A Radical Defence of the Human Being*, Allen Lane, 2019.

Mason, Paul: *Postcapitalism: A Guide to Our Future*, Allen Lane, 2015.

Mazeweski, Matt: 'Elizabeth Warren's Plan to Get Workers into the Boardroom', in *Commonweal*, 22nd March 2019: 17–21.

Mbaye, Samba and Marialuz Moreno Badia: 'New Data on Global Debt', in *IMFBlog*, 2nd January 2019, www.blogs.imf.org.

McEwan, Ian: *Machines Like Me*, Jonathan Cape, 2019.

McGreal, Chris: 'The Inequality Virus: How the Pandemic Hit America's Poorest', in the *Guardian*, 9th April 2020.

McKibbon, Bill: *Falter: Has the Human Game Begun to Play Itself Out?*, Wildfire, 2019.

McKnight, John and Peter Block: *The Abundant Community: Awakening the Power of Families and Neighbourhoods*, Berrett-Koehler Publishers, 2012.

Meadows, Donella H., Dennis L. Meadows, Jørgen Randers and William W. Behrens III: *The Limits to Growth*, Universe Books, 1972.

Meadows, Donella, Jørgen Randers and Dennis Meadows: *Limits to Growth: The 30-year Update*, Chelsea Green Publishing Company, 2004.

Meadows, Donella H.: *Leverage Points: Places to Intervene in a System*, The Sustainability Institute, 1999.

Bibliography

Mendell, Marguerite: 'Commoning and the Commons: Alternatives to a Market Society', in Michael Brie and Claus Thomasberger, eds: *Karl Polanyi's Vision of a Socialist Transformation*, Black Rose Books, 2018: 221–40,

Meyer, Henning: 'The Digital Revolution: How Should Governments Respond?', in Tony Dolphin, ed.: *Technology, Globalisation and the Future of Work in Europe: Essays on Employment in a Digitised Economy*, Institute for Public Policy Research, 2015: 95–9.

Milanovic, Branko: *Capitalism, Alone: The Future of the System That Rules the World*, Harvard University Press, 2019.

Milman, Oliver: '"Americans Are Waking Up": Two Thirds Say Climate Crisis Must Be Addressed', in the *Guardian*, 15th September 2019.

Mishra, Pankaj: *Age of Anger: A History of the Present*, Penguin, 2017.

Mkandawire, Thandika: *Targeting and Universalism in Poverty Reduction*, UNRISD, December 2005.

Monbiot, George, Robin Grey, Tom Kenny, Laurie Macfarlane, Anna Powell-Smith, Guy Shrubsole, and Beth Stratford: *Land for the Many*, a report commissioned by the Labour Party, UK Labour Party, 2019.

Monbiot, George: 'Covid-19 Is Nature's Wake-up Call to Complacent Civilisation', in the *Guardian*, 25th March 2020.

Monbiot, George: 'Future Lives Should Not Be Sacrificed to Fuel Our Greed', in the *Guardian Weekly*, 22nd March 2019.

Monbiot, George: *Out of the Wreckage: A New Politics for an Age of Crisis*, Verso, 2017.

Monbiot, George: *How Did We Get into This Mess?*, Verso, 2016.

Moore, Jason W.: 'World Accumulation and Planetary Life, or, Why Capitalism Will Not Survive until the "Last Tree Is Cut"', in *Progressive Review*, Vol. 4, No. 3, 2017: 175–202.

Moore, Oliver: 'Arguing a Case for Organic Farming, with an Emphasis on Biodiversity', unpublished paper, Centre for Cooperative Studies, University College Cork, 2012.

Mouffe, Chantal: *For a Left Populism*, Verso, 2018.

Muddle, Cas and Cristóbal Rovira Kaltwasser: *Populism: A Very Short Introduction*, Oxford University Press, 2017.

Muller, Jan-Werner: *What Is Populism?*, Penguin, 2017.

Murray, Douglas: *The Strange Death of Europe: Immigration, Identity, Islam*, Bloomsbury, 2017.

Narayan, Deepa, Robert Chambers, Meera K. Shah and Patti Petesch: *Crying Out for Change*, Oxford University Press for the World Bank, 2000.

Needleman, Jacob: *Money and the Meaning of Life*, Doubleday, 1994.

Nelson, Anitra: *Small Is Necessary: Shared Living on a Shared Planet*, Pluto Press, 2018.

Nelson, Anitra: 'Money versus Socialism', in Anitra Nelson and Frans Timmerman, eds: *Life without Money: Building Fair and Sustainable Economies*, Pluto Press, 2011: 23–46.

New Economics Foundation: *The Great Transition*, NEF, 2009.

Newell, Peter and Matthew Paterson: *Climate Capitalism: Global Warming and the Transformation of the Global Economy*, Cambridge University Press, 2010.

Newman, Michael: *Socialism: A Very Short Introduction*, Oxford University Press, 2005.

Newport, Frank: 'Democrats More Positive about Socialism than Capitalism' in *Gallup News*, 13th August 2018.

Niño-Becerra, Santiago: *El Crash: Tercera Fase*, Roca Editorial, 2019.

North, Peter: 'Transitioning towards Low Carbon Solidarity Economies?', in Peter North and Molly Scott Cato, eds: *Towards Just and Sustainable Economies: The Social and Solidarity Economy North and South*, Policy Press, 2018: 73–95.

Ó Broin, Eoin: *Home: Why Public Housing Is the Answer*, Merrion Press, 2019.

O'Sullivan, Kevin: 'Richest 10 Per Cent Cause Half of Lifestyle Carbon Emissions – Climate Expert', in the *Irish Times*, 11th December 2018.

OECD: *Social Expenditure Update 2019*, OECD, 2019.

Olin Wright, Erik: 'Socialism and Real Utopias' in Robert Hahnel and Erik Olin Wright: *Alternatives to Capitalism: Proposals for a Democratic Economy*, Verso, 2016: 75–105.

Oreskes, Naomi and Erik M. Conway: *The Collapse of Western Civilization: A View from the Future*, Columbia University Press, 2014.

Oxfam: *Public Good or Private Wealth*, Oxfam Briefing Paper, January 2019.

Oxfam: *Extreme Carbon Inequality*, Oxfam, 2015.

Patel, Vikram et al.: 'The Lancet Commission on Global Mental Health and Sustainable Development', in *The Lancet*, Vol. 392, No. 10157: 1553–98.

Pavanelli, Rosa: 'Why Should Governments Give Cash-handouts before Providing Free, Quality Public Services to All?', in *Social Europe*, 6th June 2019.

Payne, Anthony: *The Global Politics of Unequal Development*, Palgrave Macmillan, 2005.

Pearce, Fred: 'After the Coronavirus, Two Sharply Divergent Paths on Climate', in *Yale Environment 360*, 7th April 2020.

Pearson, H. W., ed.: *The Livelihood of Man*, Academic Press, 1977.

Penha-Lopes, Gil, and Tom Henfrey, eds: *Reshaping the Future: How Communities Are Catalysing Social, Economic and Ecological Transformation in Europe. The First Status Report on Community-led Action on Sustainability and Climate Change*, Ecolise, 2019.

Perkiö, Johanna: 'Universal Basic Income: A Cornerstone of the New Economic Order', in Borgnäs, Kajsa, Teppo Eskelinen, Johanna Perkiö and Rikard Warlenius, eds: *The Politics of Ecosocialism: Transforming Welfare*, Routledge, 2015: 137–47.

Pettifor, Ann: *The Case for the Green New Deal*, Verso, 2019.

Pettifor, Ann: 'Irish House Prices Sky-high due to Finance Not Scarcity', in the *Irish Times*, 22nd June 2018.

Phillips, Tom and Charis McGowan: 'Santiago Convulses during a "Weekend of Rage"', in the *Guardian Weekly*, 25th October 2019.

Phillips, Tom: '"It Is Chaos" – Inside Bolsonaro's Amazon Inferno', in the *Guardian Weekly*, 20th September 2019.

Piketty, Thomas: *Capital in the Twenty-first Century*, Harvard University Press, 2014.

Pirani, Simon: *Burning Up: A Global History of Fossil Fuel Consumption*, Pluto Press, 2018.

Polanyi, Karl, C.M. Arensberg and H.W. Pearson, eds: *Trade and Market in the Early Empires*, Free Press, 1957.

Polanyi, Karl: 'Christianity and Economic Life', in Michele Cangiani and Claus Thomasberger, eds: *Karl Polanyi: Economy and Society, Selected Writings*, Polity, 2018 [written in 1937]: 154–64.

Polanyi, Karl: 'Community and Society: The Christian Criticism of Our Social Order', in Michele Cangiani and Claus Thomasberger, eds: *Karl Polanyi: Economy and Society, Selected Writings*, Polity, 2018 [written in 1937]: 144–53.

Polanyi, Karl: 'The Economy Embedded in Society', in Michele Cangiani and Claus Thomasberger, eds: *Karl Polanyi: Economy and Society: Selected Writings*, Polity, 2018 [posthumously published in 1977]: 290–8.

Polanyi, Karl: 'The Fascist Virus', in Michele Cangiani and Claus Thomasberger, eds: *Karl Polanyi: Economy and Society, Selected Writings*, Polity, 2018 [written in 1934–35]: 108–22.

Polanyi, Karl: 'On Freedom', in Michael Brie and Claus Thomasberger, eds: *Karl Polanyi's Vision of a Socialist Transformation*, Black Rose Books, 2018 [written in 1927]: 298–319.

Polanyi, Karl: 'Freedom in a Complex Society', in Michael Brie and Claus Thomasberger, eds: *Karl Polanyi's Vision of a Socialist Transformation*, Black Rose Books, 2018 [written in 1957]: 320–4.

Polanyi, Karl: 'The Livelihood of Man: Introduction', in Michele Cangiani and Claus Thomasberger, eds: *Karl Polanyi: Economy and Society: Selected Writings*, Polity, 2018 [posthumously published in 1977]: 251–62.

Polanyi, Karl: 'The Mechanism of the World Economic Crisis', in Michele Cangiani and Claus Thomasberger, eds: *Karl Polanyi: Economy and Society, Selected Writings*, Polity, 2018 [written in 1933]: 66–80.

Polanyi, Karl: 'The Two Meanings of *Economic*', in Michele Cangiani and Claus Thomasberger, eds: *Karl Polanyi: Economy and Society, Selected Writings*, Polity, 2018 [posthumously published in 1977]: 275–89.

Polanyi, Karl: 'Universal Capitalism or Regional Planning?' in Michele Cangiani and Claus Thomasberger, eds: *Karl Polanyi: Economy and Society, Selected Writings*, Polity 2018: 231–40 [originally published in *The London Quarterly of World Affairs*, 10 (3), 1945].

Polanyi, Karl: 'Economic History and the Problem of Freedom', in Giorgio Resta and Mariavittoria Catanzariti, eds: *Karl Polanyi: For a New West: Essays, 1919-1958*, Polity, 2014 [written in 1949]: 39–46.

Polanyi, Karl: 'General Economic History', in Giorgio Resta and Mariavittoria Catanzariti, eds: *Karl Polanyi: For a New West: Essays, 1919-1958*, Polity, 2014 [written between 1950-2]: 133–47.

Polanyi, Karl: *The Great Transformation: The Political and Economic Origins of Our Time*, Beacon Press, 2001 [original 1944].

Polanyi, Karl: 'The Economy as Instituted Process', in George Dalton, ed: *Primitive, Archaic and Modern Economies: Essays of Karl Polanyi*, Anchor Books, 1968: 139–74.

Polanyi, Karl: 'Our Obsolete Market Mentality' in George Dalton, ed.: *Primitive, Archaic and Modern Economies: Essays of Karl Polanyi*, Anchor Books, 1968: 59–77.

Polanyi, Karl: 'The Semantics of Money-uses', in George Dalton, ed.: *Primitive, Archaic and Modern Economies: Essays of Karl Polanyi*, Anchor Books, 1968: 175–203.

Polanyi, Karl: *Dahomey and the Slave Trade*, Washington UP, 1966.

Polanyi Levitt, Kari and Marguerite Mendell: 'Karl Polanyi: His Life and Times', in *Studies in Political Economy*, Vol. 22, 1987: 7–39.

Polanyi Levitt, Kari: 'Freedom of Action and Freedom of Thought', in Michael Brie and Claus Thomasberger, eds: *Karl Polanyi's Vison of a Socialist Transformation*, Black Rose Books, 2018: 18–50.

Polanyi Levitt, Kari: *From the Great Transformation to the Great Financialization*, Zed Books, 2013.

Polanyi Levitt, Kari: 'The Power of Ideas: Keynes, Hayek, and Polanyi', in *International Journal of Political Economy*, Vol. 41, No. 4, Winter 2012–13: 5–15.

Polanyi Levitt, Kari: 'Keynes and Polanyi: The 1920s and the 1990s', in *Review of International Political Economy*, Vol. 13, No. 1: 2006: 152–77.

Polanyi Levitt, Kari: 'Tracing Polanyi's Institutional Political Economy to Its Central European Source', in Kenneth McRobbie and Kari Polanyi Levitt, eds: *Polanyi in Vienna: the Contemporary Significance of the* Great Transformation, Black Rose Books, 2006: 378–91.

Polanyi Levitt, Kari: 'Karl Polanyi and Co-Existence', in Kari Polanyi Levitt, ed.: *The Life and Work of Karl Polanyi*, Black Rose Books, 1990: 253–63.

Pope Francis: *Laudato Sí: On Care for Our Common Home*, Vatican Press, 2015.

Rajan, Raghuram: *The Third Pillar: The Revival of Community in a Polarised World*, William Collins, 2019.

Raskin, Paul: *Journey to Earthland: The Great Transition to Planetary Civilization*, Tellus Institute, 2016.

Raworth, Kate: *Doughnut Economics*, Random House, 2017.

Rayner, Jay: 'Diet, Health, Inequality: Why Britain's Food Supply System Doesn't Work', in the *Guardian*, 22nd March 2020.

Reardon, Jack, Maria Alejandra Madi and Molly Scott Cato: *Introducing a New Economics: Pluralist, Sustainable and Progressive*, Pluto Press, 2018.

Red-Green Alliance (RGA/EL): 'A Green Earth with Peace and Room for Us All', www.transform-network.net.

Reddan, Fiona: 'Housing Costs: How Dublin Compares with Other Global Cities', in the *Irish Times*, 5th February 2019.

Reich, Robert: 'The Lack of a Real US Public Health System Is a Free Hit for Covid-19', in the *Guardian Weekly*, 20th March 2020.

Rendueles, César: 'From Global Regression to Post-capitalist Counter-movements', in Heinrich Geiselberger, ed.: *The Great Regression*, Polity, 2017: 142–56.

Rifkin, Jeremy: *The Green New Deal*, St Martin's Press, 2019.

Riofrancos, Thea: 'Plan, Mood, Battlefield – Reflections on the Green New Deal', in *Viewpoint Magazine*, 16th May 2019.

Roberts, David: 'The Green New Deal Explained', *Vox*, March 2019: https://www.vox.com/energy-and-environment/2018/12/21/18144138/green-new-deal-alexandria-ocasio-cortez

Rodrik, Dani: *The Globalization Paradox*, Oxford University Press, 2012.

Rohr, Jason R. et al.: 'Emerging Human Infectious Diseases and the Links to Global Food Production', in *Nature Sustainability*, 11th June 2019: 445–56.

Roszak, Theodore, Mary E. Gomes and Allen D. Kanner, eds: *Ecopsychology: Restoring the Earth, Healing the Mind*, Counterpoint, 1995.

Roy, J., P. Tschakert, H. Waisman, W. Abdul Halim, P. Antwi-Agyei, P. Dasgupta, B. Hayward, M. Kanninen, C. Okereke, P.F. Pinho, K. Riahi and A.G. Suarez Rodriguez, 2018: 'Sustainable Development, Poverty Eradication and Reducing Inequalities', in *Global Warming of 1.5°C. An IPCC Special Report on the Impacts of Global Warming of 1.5°C above Pre-industrial Levels and Related Global Greenhouse Gas Emission Pathways, in the Context of Strengthening the Global Response to the Threat of Climate Change, Sustainable Development, and Efforts to Eradicate Poverty* (Masson-Delmotte, V., P. Zhai, H.-O. Pörtner, D. Roberts, J. Skea, P.R. Shukla, A. Pirani, W. Moufouma-Okia, C. Péan, R. Pidcock, S. Connors, J.B.R. Matthews, Y. Chen, X. Zhou, M.I. Gomis, E. Lonnoy, T. Maycock, M. Tignor and T. Waterfield (eds)), IPCC, 2018.

Rubery, Jill, Damian Grimshaw, Arjan Keizer and Mathew Johnson: 'Challenges and Contradictions in the "Normalising" of Precarious Work', in *Work, Employment and Society*, Vol. 32, No. 3, 2018: 509–27.

Ruggie, John Gerard: 'International Regimes, Transactions, and Change: Embedded Liberalism in the Postwar Economic Order', in *International Organization*, Vol. 36, No. 2, 1982: 379–415.

Ruiz de Almirón, Victor and María Cuesta: 'Iglesias se impone y pacta con Sánchez el ingreso mínimo vital', in *ABC*, 16th April 2020.

Runciman, David: 'Coronavirus Is Revealing the True Nature of Political Power', in the *Guardian*, 27th March 2020.

Runciman, David: *How Democracy Ends*, Profile Books, 2018.

Rutherford, Jonathan: 'Varieties of Eco-Socialism: Comparing the Thought of John Bellamy Foster and Saral Sarkar', *Simplicity Institute Report*, Vol. 18a, 2018.

Salleh, Ariel: 'The Value of a Synergistic Economy', in Anitra Nelson and Frans Timmerman, eds: *Life Without Money: Building Fair and Sustainable Economies*, Pluto Press, 2011: 94–110.

Sandel, Michael J.: *What Money Can't Buy: The Moral Limits of Markets*, Penguin, 2012.

Sassen, Saskia: 'Who Owns Our Cities – and Why This Urban Takeover Should Concern Us All', in the *Guardian*, 24th November 2015.

Scheper-Hughes, Nancy: 'The Market for Human Organs Is Destroying Lives', in the *Washington Post*, 5th January 2016.

Schultheis, Emily: 'How Italy's Fire-star Movement Is Winning the Youth Vote', in the *Atlantic*, 2nd March 2018.

Scott, Brett: 'Can Cryptocurrency and Blockchain Technology Play a Role in Building Social and Solidarity Finance?', UNRISD Working Paper 2016: 1.

Sen, Amartya: *Development as Freedom*, Oxford University Press, 1999.

Sheffield, Hazel: 'The Preston Model: UK Takes Lessons in Recovery from Rust-belt Cleveland', in the *Guardian*, 11th April 2017.

Shenker, Jack: 'What Will Cities Look Like after Covid-19?', in the *Guardian Weekly*, 3rd April 2020.

Shenker, Jack: 'This Wave of Global Protest Is Being Led by the Children of the Financial Crash', in the *Guardian*, 29th October 2019.

Shenker, Jack: 'Rise App!', in the *Guardian Weekly*, 6th September 2019.

Shenker, Jack: *Now We Have Your Attention: The New Politics of the People*, The Bodley Head, 2019.

Shiva, Vandana: *Soil, Not Oil: Climate Change, Peak Oil and Food Insecurity*, Zed Books, 2016.

Skidelsky, Robert and Edward Skidelsky: *How Much Is Enough? Money and the Good Life*, Penguin Books, 2013.

Smith, Nicola: Jo-Anne: *Showcasing Globalisation? The Political Economy of the Irish Republic*, Manchester University Press, 2005.

Smyth, Patrick: 'MEPs Have Beef with Mercosur Climate Consequences', in the *Irish Times*, 21st September 2019.

Snyder, Timothy: *On Tyranny: Twenty Lessons from the Twentieth Century*, Bodley Head, 2017.

Spinnery, Laura: 'Is Factory Farming behind Covid-19?', in the *Guardian Weekly*, 3rd April 2020.

Staff and agencies: 'Amazon Closes French Warehouses after Court Ruling on Coronavirus', in the *Guardian*, 16th April 2020.

Standing, Guy: *Plunder of the Commons: A Manifesto for Sharing Public Wealth*, Pelican, 2019.

Steffen, W., K. Richardson, J. Rockström, S.E. Cornell, I. Fetzer, E.M. Bennett, R. Biggs et al. :'Planetary Boundaries: Guiding Human Development on a Changing Planet', in *Science*, Vol. 347, No. 6223, 2015: 1259855.

Steger, Manfred B. and Ravi K. Roy: *Neoliberalism: A Very Short Introduction*, Oxford University Press, 2010.

Stiglitz, Joseph: 'No More Half Measures on Corporate Taxes', in *Project Syndicate*, 7th October 2019.

Stiglitz, Joseph: 'Joseph Stiglitz on Artificial Intelligence: We're Going towards a More Divided Society', in the *Guardian*, 8th September 2018.

Stiglitz, Joseph: *The Price of Inequality*, Penguin Books, 2013.

Storrie, Donald: 'Manufacturing a Life of Leisure', in Tony Dolphin, ed.: *Technology, Globalisation and the Future of Work in Europe: Essays on Employment in a Digitised Economy*, Institute for Public Policy Research, 2015: 110–12.

Streeck, Wolfgang: 'The Return of the Repressed as the Beginning of the End of Neoliberal Capitalism', in Heinrich Geiselberger, ed.: *The Great Regression*, Polity, 2017: 157–72.

Streeck, Wolfgang: *How Will Capitalism End?*, Verso, 2016.

Sustainable Food Trust: *The Hidden Cost of UK Food*, 2017.

Taylor, Keith: *The Political Ideas of the Utopian Socialists*, Frank Cass, 1982.

Taylor, Steven: 'For the Generation Shaped by Coronavirus, Life May Never Fully Return to "Normal"', in the *Guardian*, 7th April 2020.

Ther, Philipp: *The Outsiders: Refugees in Europe since 1492*, Princeton University Press, 2016.

Thunder, David: 'Pandemic May Shake Us from Individualist Slumber', in the *Irish Times*, 15th April 2020.

Tisdall, Simon: '2019: Reasons to Be Fearful and … Reasons to Be Cheerful', in the *Guardian Weekly*, 20th December 2019.

234   *Bibliography*

Toivanen, Tero: 'Commons against Capitalism', in Borgnäs, Kajsa, Teppo Eskelinen, Johanna Perkiö and Rikard Warlenius, eds: *The Politics of Ecosocialism: Transforming welfare*, Routledge, 2015: 116–34.

Tooze, Adam: 'How Coronavirus Almost Brought Down the Global Financial System', in the *Guardian*, 14th April 2020.

Trisos, Christopher H., Cory Merow and Alex L. Pigot: 'The Projected Timing of Abrupt Ecological Disruption from Climate Change' in *Nature*, April 2020, https://doi.org/10.1038/s41586-020-2189-9.

UNDP: *Human Development Report 2011: Sustainability and Equity*, Palgrave Macmillan, 2011.

UNDP: *Human Development Report 1995*, Oxford University Press, 1995.

Varoufakis, Vanis: 'Human Economics' in the *Guardian Weekly*, 22nd November 2019.

Walker, Shaun: 'Migration v Climate: Europe's New Political Divide', in the *Guardian*, 2nd December 2019.

Wallerstein, Immanuel: *Historical Capitalism*, Verso, 1983.

Warren, Elizabeth: 'Here's How We Can Break Up Big Tech', Team Warren, 8th March 2019, www.//medium.com/@teamwarren.

Watts, Jonathan: 'Domino-effect of Climate Events Could Move Earth into a "Hothouse" State', in *The Guardian*, 7th August 2018.

WBGU: *World in Transition: A Social Contract for Sustainability*, Berlin, 2011.

White, Benjamin Thomas: 'Talk of an "Unprecedented" Number of Refugees Is Wrong – and Dangerous', in the *New Humanitarian*, 3rd October 2019.

Wilkinson, Richard and Kate Pickett: *The Spirit Level: Why More Equal Societies Almost Always Do Better*, Allen Lane, 2009.

Willis, Rebecca: *Too Hot to Handle? The Democratic Challenge of Climate Change*, Bristol University Press, 2020.

Wong, Julia Carrie: 'Is Amazon Becoming the Future of US Government?', in the *Guardian Weekly*, 3rd April 2020.

World Bank: *World Development Report 2000/01: Attacking Poverty*, the World Bank, 2001.

WWF: *Living Planet Report 2018: Aiming Higher*, WWF, 2018.

Yeates, Nicola: 'A Global Political Economy of Care', in *Social Policy and Society*, Vol. 4, No. 2, 2005: 227–34.

Yeomans, Matthew: *Oil: A Concise Guide to the Most Important Product on Earth*, The New Press, 2004.

Zielonka, Jan: *Counter-Revolution: Liberal Europe in Retreat*, Oxford University Press, 2018.

Index

adaptation 56, 97, 168, 213 n. 70
Afghanistan 8
Africa 23, 25, 82, 99
agriculture 128
    community supported 124, 205 n. 16
    conventional 88, 98, 100, 137
    industrial model 15, 89
    organic 97, 98, 99–100, 172
algorithms 9–10, 116
Alternativ fur Deutschland 8, 24
Amazon 90
Amazon (company) 157, 158, 166, 173
Anderson, Kevin 115, 162
Aristotle 131, 178, 210 n. 19
artificial intelligence 9, 118
Asia 22, 23, 92, 99, 184 n. 29
Atkinson, Anthony 119
Attenborough, David 3, 44
Austria 24, 27, 107, 108, 134, 135, 165, 179
automation ix, 9–10, 19, 20, 42, 65, 111,
    116–18, 120, 137, 156, 162, 170–4
Ayn Rand Institute 49

Bahro, Rudolf 62
Banerjee, Abhijit 147
Bank for International Settlements 133
Bauman, Zygmunt 8
Berlin
    ufaFabrik 101
Berlin Wall 6
Berry, Wendell 151
biodiversity x, 5, 10–11, 16, 67, 70, 74,
    87–9, 97, 100, 184 n. 29
bioengineering 9
Blair, Tony 63
Blyth, Mark 82, 158
Bolivia 27
Bolsonaro, Jair 90, 161
Bosnia 25
Boyle, Mark 130, 134
Brazil 8, 25, 89–90, 94

breakdown 3, 15, 31, 33, 34, 59, 117, 129,
    159, 161
    environmental, climate breakdown 11,
        50, 155
    systems breakdown 5–13, 18–19, 21–2,
        133, 143
Bregman, Rutger 5, 59
Bretton Woods 124
Brexit 8, 28, 37, 161, 165
Bridle, James 9
Bundesbank 133

capitalism 8, 18, 23, 41–57, 59–64, 68–9,
    118, 121, 137–38, 147, 151, 152,
    156
    Anglo-Saxon variety 49
    carbon capitalism 46–7
    Chinese model 45, 50
    climate capitalism 49–51, 72
    crisis of 15, 19, 38, 43, 63, 74, 78
    financialisation 19, 121–9
    and freedom 66–7
    future of 10, 12, 42–5, 57, 71
    radical reforms 45, 162
    stakeholder 44
    and technology 171–3
    three contradictions 81
    transforming 163
    welfare capitalism 107–8
carbon
    decarbonising 49–52, 149, 167
    emissions 47, 49, 91, 100, 115, 190 n.
        31
    low-carbon society 19, 42, 48, 63, 120,
        129, 152, 165, 168–9, 177
    price 150
Carnegie, Andrew 25
Carnegie Trust 175
Castells, Manuel 29
Cato Institute 49
Chakrabortty, Aditya 5, 164

236   *Index*

Chavez, Hugo 27
Che Guevara 131
Chile 84, 92, 159, 166
China 7, 22, 23, 50, 66, 89, 92, 124, 128,
 169, 183 n. 8
Christianity 62, 176, 180
cities 19, 31, 42, 45, 83, 87, 98, 164
 corporate takeover 90–1
civilization 9, 42, 64, 85, 123, 167, 179
 collapse 13–16, 22, 59
 technological 9, 73, 116
class structure 6, 30, 80
 middle class 10, 17, 45, 62, 71, 117
 working class 28, 61, 70, 71, 115, 125,
  153, 175, 180, 181
climate change 5, 9, 10–11, 13, 21, 31, 46,
 48–52, 65, 97, 115, 128
 breakdown 13–16, 71, 78, 129
 climate Keynesianism 50
 Paris Agreement 50, 51, 170
 warming 9–10, 51, 56, 92–3, 146
Clinton, Bill 29, 63
Clinton, Hilary 28
cooperatives 68, 162, 176
collectivism 64
Collier, Paul 44, 45, 47
Collins, Randall 10
commodities 77
 fictitious commodities, *see under*
  Polanyi
commons 93, 96, 99, 149, 172, 175
communism 47, 61, 63, 68, 178
 Eurocommunism 62
consumerism 12, 14, 106, 109
Conway, Erik M. 13, 16
Corbyn, Jeremy 59
coronavirus 3, 8, 13, 23, 47, 48, 50, 87, 89,
 102, 109, 110, 111, 117, 125, 127,
 128, 135, 138, 139, 152, 155, 158,
 159, 163, 167, 177
 Covid-19 6, 26, 74, 89, 93, 101, 110,
  128, 137, 138, 144, 148, 153, 155,
  156, 157, 162, 171, 175
Correa, Rafael 27
corruption 26, 46, 132, 136, 189 n. 15
currencies 123–4, 135, 156
 Bitcoin 134
 cryptocurrencies 134
 local 134, 138
 Sardex 134, 171

Dale, Gareth 3, 34, 67, 81, 84, 139, 176
Davos 5, 10, 115
debt 84, 92, 109, 125–6, 128, 133–4, 151,
 173
degrowth ix, 56, 144, 147–51
democracy 7, 12, 21, 41, 52–3, 153, 165,
 176
 deliberative 70
 illiberal 24
 liberal 22–6, 59
 social 19, 45, 48, 60–2, 118, 167, 179
Design Global – Manufacture Local 172
Duflo, Esther 147

East Germany 63
eco-psychology 95
Ecolise 98, 100
economics x, 36–7, 88, 139, 144–7, 150,
 151, 157, 177, 180
 economic anthropology 82, 123, 181
 doughnut economics 146
economy ix–xi, 4, 15, 17–20, 37, 43, 50,
 52–5, 68–70, 78–82, 85, 144–6, 180
 decentralised democratic economy 164
 gift economy 175, 216 n. 48
 Social and Solidarity Economy 99
ecovillages 98–9, 106
 Cloughjordan 205 n. 16
Ecuador 27
Eisenstein, Charles 137, 138, 139
emissions trading systems 49, 190 n. 31
employment 4, 9, 52, 109–11, 117, 125
energy 15, 46–7, 92
 community energy 99, 168
 fossil fuels 46–7, 92–3, 162, 169
 Low Energy Demand (LED) 150
environmental breakdown. *See*
 breakdown
Esping-Andersen, Gøsta 107–8, 118
Europe 7–9, 22–4, 27, 31, 91, 98–100, 112,
 117, 150, 158
 European Commission 167, 170
 European Environmental Agency 56
 European Monetary System 133
 Eurozone 133
Extinction Rebellion 44, 163, 166, 170
Exxon 93, 199 n. 26

Facebook 166, 173
fascism 18, 27, 31, 41, 53, 123, 178

Index

Felber, Christian 55, 135
finance 35, 49, 122–5, 169
Financial Times 44, 48, 150
First World 6
food 15, 56, 88, 156
    biodiverse and ecological 89, 97–9
    cheap nature model 128–9
    industrial model 15, 89, 100
Food and Agriculture Organisation 104
Ford 109
Frase, Peter 65, 170
Fraser, Nancy 62, 78, 81
French Revolution 71
Friedman, Milton xi, 13, 44

Garcés, Marina 12
General Motors 109
Germany 8, 24, 53, 107, 110, 119, 135, 165
Ghosh, Amitav 176
Gillespie, Paul 155
Global Ecovillage Network (GEN) 98
globalization x, 15, 16, 17, 42, 81, 109, 154–7
    glocalization 144, 154, 156
gold standard 123–4, 127, 133
Goodhart, David 30
    Anywheres 30
    Somewheres 30
Google 157, 166, 173–4
Gough, Ian ix, 51, 106, 108, 146
Gramsci, Antonio 138, 159
Great Depression 109, 127, 133
Greece 27, 82, 92
Green New Deal ix, 20, 51, 52, 162, 165,
    167–70
Gross Domestic Product (GDP) 44, 51,
    106, 146–8, 150
growth 6, 7, 12, 15, 36–7, 42, 43–4, 45, 71,
    146
    corporate growth model 72, 90, 139,
    158
    decoupling 50–1, 150
    green growth 49–50, 150
Gulf 93
Guterres, António 10, 184 n. 29

Haider, Jorg 27
Harari, Yuval Noah 4, 9, 117, 143
Hayek, Friedrich x, 4, 13, 62, 69, 71, 74,
    137, 139, 143, 144, 147, 174, 176,
    179, 181

hedge funds 127
Heritage Foundation 49
Hickel, Jason 51, 104, 149, 150
Higgins, President Michael D. ix, 73, 143,
    157, 161
Hollo, Tim 74
Holmes, Christopher 36–7, 73, 109
Honneth, Axel 61, 63–5, 69–70
housing 91–2
    public 101, 114, 176
human rights 25–6, 94, 128, 144

Ignatieff, Michael 25–6
India 7, 8, 94, 111, 128
individualism xi, 30, 31, 64, 109, 134, 137,
    143, 154
inequality x, 6, 12, 15, 22, 26, 31, 42, 46,
    51, 52, 65, 111, 118–19, 128, 132,
    156, 165, 170, 175
    and climate change 115
    gendered 112–14
    within cities 90–2
Institute for Public Policy Research 11
Intergovernmental Panel on Biodiversity
    and Ecosystem Services (IPBES) 56
Intergovernmental Panel on Climate
    Change (IPCC) 71, 150
    2019 report on land 87, 97
International Labour Office 111
International Monetary Fund 34, 124
Iraq 8
Ireland 91, 98

JD Wetherspoon 119
Judt, Tony 60, 60–3

Kallis, Giorgos 51, 147–8, 152
Keynes, John Maynard 4, 45, 69, 125, 144,
    147, 158
    Keynesianism x, 50, 60, 143
Kingsolver, Barbara 13
Klein, Naomi 48
Kyoto Protocol 93

Labour Party (UK) 52, 63, 165, 181
    2019 report on land 101
Lancet 12
    Lancet Commission 12
Lang, Tim 128
Latin America 23, 27, 72, 99

Index

Latouche, Serge 14, 150
Le Pen, Marine 8, 27
liberal
  embedded liberalism 82
  liberalization 7, 17, 34, 62, 81, 88,
    105–6, 127
  order 3, 4, 7–8, 18, 21–6, 33, 41–2, 45,
    122–3, 178
liberation theology 62
limits 15, 16, 44, 56, 71, 120, 128, 132, 146,
  151–2, 155, 158, 167
Limits to Growth 14, 73
localization 96, 134, 138, 154
Luce, Edward 22, 30
Luxemburg, Rosa 65

Mair, Peter 31–3
Make Poverty History 104
market x–xi, 4, 13–14, 16–17, 30, 34–6, 43,
  47–9, 53–7, 62–4, 69, 91–2, 97–102,
  107–9, 118, 121, 126, 128–9, 135,
  137, 145–6, 153, 154, 163–4, 172,
  173–5
  efficient markets hypothesis (EMH)
    126–7
  market mechanism 104–5, 114, 116,
    118, 123, 174–5
  market society ix, 18
  and morality 94, 132
Marx, Karl 60, 65–6, 67, 72, 78, 80, 131,
  179–81
Marxism 60, 70, 72, 80, 175, 179–81
Mason, Paul 42, 48, 73, 116, 117, 118, 125,
  155, 162, 173
McDonalds 119
McEwan, Ian 117
McStrike 119
Meadows, Donella H. 73
Mercosur 90
Mexico 84
migration 5, 8–9, 21, 29, 46, 71
Milanovic, Branko 44–5, 47
mitigation 97, 168
Monbiot, George 12, 54, 87, 143
money 25, 44, 47–8, 54, 64, 65, 67, 77–85,
  89, 91, 96, 109, 111, 121–36, 150,
  151, 166, 189 n. 15
Morales, Evo 27
Myanmar 25

nationalism 9, 41, 155
nature x, 11, 15, 17–18, 55, 72, 78–9, 85,
  102, 137–8, 145
  body parts 94
  cheap nature model 128
  commodification 38, 47, 87–8, 94–6,
    130
Nelson, Anitra 92, 101
neoliberalism 7, 16, 23, 42, 60, 63, 74, 85,
  104, 114, 125, 128, 137, 139, 143,
  179
  collapse 4
Network for Greening the Financial
  System (NGFS) 129
New Climate Economy 49
New Deal 52, 69, 82
New Economic Foundation 52, 186 n. 56
New Lanark 67
new left 27, 47, 53, 62–3, 72, 163
new right 7, 27, 59, 159, 167
Nike 90

Ó Broin, Eoin 92
Ocasio-Cortez, Alexandria 52
Olin Wright, Erik 163, 165
Orban, Victor 8
Oreskes, Naomi 13, 16
Organisation for Economic Cooperation
  and Development (OECD) 92, 108,
  109, 157
  projections for 2060 42
Ostrom, Elinor 93
Owen, Robert 66–7, 139
Oxfam 104–5

paradigm x–xi, 20, 36, 99, 116, 157, 161–2,
  170, 176
  eco-social ix, 19, 60, 70, 73
permaculture 98
Pettifor, Ann 91, 111, 168, 169
Philippines 8, 94
Piketty, Thomas 112
planetary boundaries 60, 72, 97, 151, 159,
  194 n. 54
Podemos 27
Poland 3, 33, 165
Polanyi Levitt, Kari 5, 133, 180
Polanyi, Karl ix–x, 4–5, 178–82
  Capital and capital 121–2

Index 239

central banking 81, 133
class 80, 115, 175
commodification 35, 77–82
Commune 68
community 34–5, 153–4
democracy 52–5, 99
double movement 17, 18, 54–6, 69, 156
economics 144–6
embeddedness 17, 54, 99
exchange 18, 83–5, 138
fictitious commodities 17, 47, 79–82, 137
forms of integration 18, 82–5
freedom 54, 60, 65–9, 71, 151, 180
The Great Transformation xi–x, 17, 34, 41, 54, 82, 87, 151, 181, 186 n. 56
habitation vs improvement 36–7, 72–3, 96, 127, 138–9
Vienna 68, 178–9
Industrial Revolution 17, 105
labour 17, 94, 103–20
land 17, 87–102
machine age 73–4, 74, 116, 180
market 34–5, 41, 54, 68, 175
market mechanism 17, 36
market society 17
money 17, 104–5, 121–39
protectionist institutions 80–1, 145
public philosophy 20, 143–4
reciprocity 18, 83–5, 138
redistribution 18, 83–5, 138
right to live 103, 120
social destruction 17, 35–6
socialism 19, 38, 56, 60, 64, 68, 70, 72, 81–2, 176, 180
society 17, 41, 66–9, 80, 95, 177
state 53, 55, 67–9, 74, 123, 138–9, 144, 175, 180
subsistence 77, 102, 196 n. 2
three sources of instability 81, 139
utopian experiment 55, 123, 174
youth in Budapest 178
political economy 19, 37, 43, 56, 69, 72
politics 7, 28–36, 59, 63, 65, 71–2, 128, 143, 157–8
identity 19, 22, 29–33, 112
in the gaps 163–7
Poor Laws 103, 201 n. 3
Pope Francis 116, 152, 176

populism 31, 53
conspiracy theories 29–32
new populism 4, 15, 19, 22, 27–9, 41, 55
poverty 5, 36, 51, 56, 98, 104–6, 111
Preston 164
Public Services International 111

Rajan, Raghuram 34–5, 43
Raskin, Paul 14, 16
scenarios 14–15
Raworth, Kate 146
Reagan, Ronald 61–2, 108, 109, 159
Reaganism 34
Red-Green Alliance 156
regionalism 156
Rendueles, César 16
rentership 170
Réseau Intercontinental de Promotion de l'Economie Sociale Solidaire (RIPESS) 99
Rifkin, Jeremy 169–70
robots 9–10, 65, 117
Rodrik, Dani 81
Roman empire 13
Roosevelt, Franklin D. 52
Russia 29

Salvini, Matteo 8, 28, 167
Sandel, Michael J. 94, 132
Sanders, Bernie 59, 165
Sardines movement 167
Schroeder, Gerhard 63
Second World 6, 178
Sen, Amartya 105
Shell 93
Shenker, Jack 53, 71, 101, 153, 159, 163, 171
Shiva, Vandana 89, 97
Skidelsky, Robert and Edward 151
social model x, 23, 56, 61, 164, 172, 180
unravelling 5–6, 13
socialism 38, 41, 56, 59–65, 68–70, 81–2, 176, 179–81
co-operative socialism 67
eco-socialism 72
guild socialism 19, 178
post-Marxist 70
utopian socialism 67, 162

South Africa 25, 98
Soviet Union 6, 60, 68, 84, 180
species extinction 21, 57
Starbucks 90, 157
state 4, 23, 35, 37, 45, 47, 53, 55, 61–2, 67–9, 84, 127, 137–9, 168, 175, 180
  enabling 175
  welfare 6, 31, 33, 46, 69, 107–11, 114, 120, 158, 163
Stiglitz, Joseph 16, 117, 119, 157, 186 n. 49
Streeck, Wolfgang 43, 45, 47
Sustainable Food Trust 100
Syria 8, 94, 183 n. 8
Syriza 27

Taylor, Steven 13
techno-optimism 5, 9
technology 22, 44, 50, 65, 73–4, 118, 119, 162, 170–3, 180
  dark sides 5, 9–10
  techno-economic paradigm 116, 176
Texaco 93
Thatcher, Margaret 61–2, 108, 109, 159
  Thatcherism 34
Third Way 63
Third World 6, 62
Thunberg, Greta 44, 166
Tilbury 153
Timmermans, Frans 167
trade unions 32, 55, 68, 109, 119
transformation 16, 52, 71, 77, 79, 91, 100, 118, 137, 148, 154, 159, 162, 168, 174–7
  strategic logics 56, 163–6, 173
Transition Towns 98
Trump, Donald 8, 27–9, 37, 109, 152, 155, 161
Turkey 8

United Kingdom x, 27, 34, 50, 59, 61, 63, 92, 100–1, 110, 112, 126–7, 159, 165, 168
United Nations 56, 94
  climate summit 3, 166
United States x, 8, 25, 28, 31, 34, 52, 59, 61–2, 82, 92, 94, 101, 110–11, 112, 118–19, 126–9, 132, 152, 156, 168–9, 172, 181
Universal Basic Income 36, 111, 149, 173

values 8, 16, 23, 33, 34, 53, 60, 68, 71, 82, 85, 96, 130–2, 176, 179
  exchange value vs use value 122, 131–2
  human or economic 54–5
  local 25–6
Van der Leyen, Ursula 167
Varoufakis, Yanis 147
Venezuela 27
virtue 25–6, 118
vulnerability 6, 101, 105, 109, 128, 135, 175

Wallerstein, Immanuel 121
Warren, Elizabeth 165–6
Washington Consensus 34
water 10, 12, 14, 52, 88, 93–4, 97–8, 100, 131, 149
wellbeing 10, 11, 12, 35, 51, 55, 66, 67, 95–6, 103, 116, 146, 147, 148–9, 153, 155, 173, 174
Wikipedia 172
Wilders, Geert 8, 27
Willis, Rebecca 161
Wörgl 134
World Bank 93, 104–5
World Wildlife Fund 10–11
  Living Planet Report 10

Zielonka, Jan 7, 23

CPSIA information can be obtained
at www.ICGtesting.com
Printed in the USA
LVHW082301050822
725273LV00013B/613